GW00992332

WELCOME

The climax to the Premier League's 20th season was the most nail-biting, the most dramatic and the most downright exciting since it began in 1992. When Sergio Aguero scored the winner for Man City in the dying seconds at the Etihad Stadium, he sealed the first ever Premier League title to be decided on goal difference. This staggering denouement makes a fitting introduction to this celebratory tome.

We've looked at the Premier League lives of all the 45 clubs that have played in the top flight since 1992/93, from Man Utd down to Swindon Town via Portsmouth and Oldham Athletic. We've looked at every season: the stories, the scandals, the stars and the sensations – and printed the all-time Premier League table in full. We've compiled top tens on everything from Magic Men to Memorable Moments. We've put together an A to Z covering everything from Roman Abramovich to Gianfranco Zola via Jean-Marc Bosman and the Prawn-Sandwich Brigade. Oh, and round the back we've listed all the most diverting facts and stats.

If you want to know anything about the last 20 years of the Greatest League in the World, this is not a bad place to start.

Now get stuck in! [*Blows whistle.*]

Stuart Messham, Editor

CONTENTS

II

A Z

OF THE
PREMIER
LEAGUE

An alphabet of the first 20 years, from a Russian multi-millionaire to an Italian footballing maestro

IIIIIIIIIIIIIIIIIIIIIIIIIIIIIIIIIIIIIIIIIIIIIIIIIIIIIIIIIIIIIIIIIIIIIIIIIIIIIIIIIIIIIIIIIIIIIIIIIIIIIIIIIIIIIIIIIIIIIIIIIII

Sulaiman al-Fahim (pictured on this fake note) was Sheikh Mansour's spokesperson during the Manchester City takeover bid

A IS FOR...

Abramovich, Roman

One of the richest people on the planet and owner of Chelsea FC, Roman Abramovich is notorious for his ruthless hiring-and-firing policy and for an alleged overbearing influence in the dressing room. The seemingly unnecessary £30m purchase of Andriy Shevchenko in 2006 increased frictions between Abramovich and his most successful manager, José Mourinho, resulting in the latter's departure despite winning two consecutive Premier League titles for the club. A hard taskmaster indeed.

Administration

After a sustained period of success – including an FA Cup win under Harry Redknapp and a vertigo-inducing eighth-place finish in the Premier League – Portsmouth's financial indiscretions and mismanagement cost them a place at the top table in 2010 and very nearly put an end to the club as a footballing entity. Despite various candidates apparently willing to bail the club out and passing the Premier League's "fit and proper persons" test, including Alexandre Gaydamak, Sulaiman al-Fahim (the "Donald Trump of Abu Dhabi"), Ali al-Faraj and Balram Chainrai, Her Majesty's Revenue and Customs

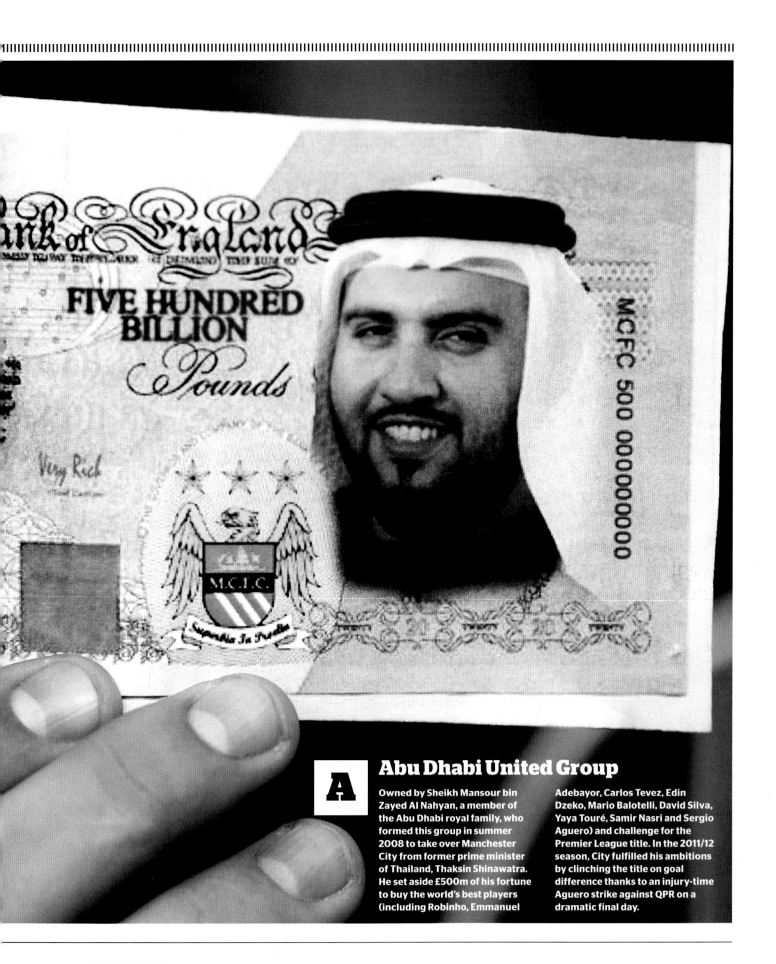

FIVE HUNDRED BILLION Pounds

MCFC 500 000000000

A Abu Dhabi United Group

Owned by Sheikh Mansour bin Zayed Al Nahyan, a member of the Abu Dhabi royal family, who formed this group in summer 2008 to take over Manchester City from former prime minister of Thailand, Thaksin Shinawatra. He set aside £500m of his fortune to buy the world's best players (including Robinho, Emmanuel Adebayor, Carlos Tevez, Edin Dzeko, Mario Balotelli, David Silva, Yaya Touré, Samir Nasri and Sergio Aguero) and challenge for the Premier League title. In the 2011/12 season, City fulfilled his ambitions by clinching the title on goal difference thanks to an injury-time Aguero strike against QPR on a dramatic final day.

issued a winding-up order and the club announced it had gone into administration on 26 February 2010, the first Premier League side to do so. (At the end of the 2011/12 season, Portsmouth entered administration for a second time in three seasons. They were docked 10 points by the FA and relegated to the third tier of English football. Let's hope they return soon).

Arsenal

Finished first in the Premier League three times and second five times in Arsène Wenger's first 11 seasons in charge, including an undefeated season in 2003/04 that earned them the nickname "The Invincibles".

B IS FOR...

Blackburn Rovers

Promoted to the top flight the year the Premier League began, and a year after Jack Walker became owner, the steel magnate's millions would propel Blackburn to the title in 1995. But that team would quickly disintegrate and Rovers have not seriously challenged for honours again. Briefly broke the early dominance of Alex Ferguson and Manchester United, though.

Bosman, Jean-Marc

In 1995, little-known Belgian footballer Jean-Marc Bosman single-handedly swung football's pendulum of power

from the clubs to the players by challenging transfer rules in the European courts. Their subsequent ruling allowed players in the European Union to move freely to another club when their contract was up. Previously, clubs in parts of Europe had the power to prevent players from leaving. In the UK, Transfer Tribunals had been used to resolve disputes since 1981.

C IS FOR...

Cantona, Eric

Acquired from title-winning adversaries Leeds United by an über-canny Alex Ferguson in 1992, Eric Cantona is widely regarded as the catalyst for Manchester United's ongoing Premier League success (p50-59). Unfortunately for Ferguson, the enigmatic Frenchman had the ability to publicly self-destruct, a trait no better displayed than during the Selhurst Park kung-fu kick episode of 25 January 1995 (p92).

Champions League

Europe's premier club competition shares its 20th birthday with the Premier League. Its enormous revenue has successfully created a league within a league and a place in the top four of the Premier League is now considered more of a coup for most sides than a Wembley appearance in the biggest domestic cup competition in the world, the FA Cup.

Chelsea

A sporting mirror of west London's more lavish tendencies, when Chelsea were taken over by Russian oligarch Roman Abramovich in 2003 their flirtations with honours became a cast-iron challenge – not only for the Premier League crown, but for dominance of English football. They won consecutive titles under José Mourinho – in 2004/05 and 2005/06 – but the Portuguese manager was sacked the next season. Carlo Ancelotti led Chelsea to the title again in 2009/10, as well as the FA Cup, and his side were the first to score more than 100 goals in the top flight since 1963. In 2011, though, Ancelotti was also sacked.

D IS FOR...

Dein, David

A principal architect in the development of the Premier League, Dein – alongside ITV's head of sport Greg Dyke and club chairmen Martin Edwards (Manchester United), Irving Scholar (Tottenham), Noel White (Liverpool) and Philip Carter (Everton) – saw the top flight's multimillion-pound potential, despite a difficult decade that had included the Bradford (1985), Heysel (1985) and Hillsborough (1989) disasters. "After seeing how the Americans operated their sport, particularly American football, baseball and basketball, I felt we were light years behind. We had so much more to give as an attraction," Dein said. "We had had enough and we knew what we were doing was right."

Derbies

There's nothing quite like a derby to get the blood racing in Europe's most passionate division, and the Premier League has seen a few during its 20-year existence: the East Anglian, east Lancashire, north London, south London, west London, Merseyside, Manchester, north-west, Roses, Second City, south-coast, Tees-Wear, Tyne-Wear and West Midlands.

Drama

Former Liverpool and Aston Villa manager Gérard Houllier wrote in his foreword to Joe Lovejoy's brilliant book *Glory, Goals And Greed: 20 Years Of The Premier League* that the "drama reaches a higher peak in the Premier League than anywhere else in the world. The competitiveness of the league is greater, too. Ask any manager – the bottom team can beat the leaders on their day. That doesn't happen in Spain or Italy or Germany. Here, though, you never take any result for granted." Hear, hear, Gérard.

Dalglish, Kenny

An Anfield legend, "King Kenny" brought the top-flight trophy back to Blackburn in the 1994/95 season for the first time since 1914, his expensively assembled side winning the title by one point from Manchester United. Dalglish's subsequent managerial stints at Newcastle United and, more recently, his beloved Liverpool, for a second time, have not been nearly as successful.

E IS FOR...

Euro '96

The first time a major tournament had been staged in the "home of football" since England won the World Cup on home soil in 1966. "Thirty years of hurt," to paraphrase the popular Frank Skinner and David Baddiel song, were not entirely put to rest, but the country's footballing reputation certainly did not suffer from its time under the spotlight. The so-called English disease (hooliganism) of the 1980s was beginning to heal – but Germany were once again England's nemesis from the penalty spot.

F IS FOR...

FA Cup

The self-appointed "greatest cup competition in the world" now plays second fiddle to qualification for the Champions League (at least for the country's biggest clubs) thanks to the latter competition's sheer earning potential. The FA Cup final is normally held on the weekend after the end of the Premier League, but in 2010/11 it was brought forward by a week so Wembley could be prepared for the Champions League final. Manchester United caused outcry in 1999/00 when they pulled out of the tournament to play in the FIFA World Club Championship instead.

Fans

The backbone, cornerstone, mainstay and fulcrum of the Premier League. It is no longer a rare sight to see supporters of colour, women and families inside major stadiums, a testament to better policing, clever marketing and the sport's broadening universal appeal.

Ferguson, Sir Alex

The longest-serving manager in Manchester United's history has won more Manager of the Year awards than anyone else and most of the mind games with opposing gaffers along the way. He has also led United to the league and Cup double on three occasions, an incredible league, Cup and Champions League treble in 1999, and two hat-tricks of Premier League titles, from 1998-2001 and 2006-2009. Not only the greatest Premier League manager ever, but also a crucial part of its drama.

Financial Fair Play Regulations

Devised by Michel Platini to stop professional football clubs spending more than they earn in the pursuit of success and to prevent cash-rich clubs with hugely wealthy owners from gaining an unfair advantage over clubs run on a more sustainable business model. The ultimate penalty for not adhering to the regulations is disqualification from European competitions and, at the time of writing, Premier League clubs will have had one season to begin balancing their "football-related expenditure" (their outgoings in terms of transfers and wages) in view of the 2014/15 UEFA assessment.

Football Association

Formed in 1863 in the Freemasons' Tavern on Long Acre in London, the FA does not run the day-to-day business of the Premier League, but governs all league rules. Its main commercial operations concern the English national team and the FA Cup.

Football Task Force

Set up in 1997 by sports minister Tony Banks, and chaired by former Conservative politician and Chelsea fan David Mellor, to investigate racism, ticket pricing, merchandising, community involvement, disabled access and commercialisation. A big step in building the Premier League's universal appeal.

G IS FOR...

Giggs, Ryan

The most decorated player in English football history, Giggs holds Manchester United's record for competitive appearances and is the only player to have played and scored in every season of the

Premier League. He also tops the competition's assists table (271), won the BBC Sports Personality of the Year in 2009 and was recently named Best Player at the Premier League 20 Seasons Awards.

Goals

Strikers invariably get paid the most money for a reason. Goals win games, wins mean points – and the more points you accumulate the more money the club earns and the more prestige it acquires. During its first 20 years, the Premier League has welcomed goalscorers from all over the world: consistent goalscorers, sporadic goalscorers and scorers of special, unforgettable goals. We've documented all 20 Goals of the Season in our Premier League Years section, which begins on p48.

Goal celebrations

From Temuri Ketsbaia kicking the advertising hoardings and Gary Neville taunting Liverpool supporters, to Robbie Fowler simulating snorting cocaine and Jimmy Bullard mocking manager Phil Brown, the Premier League has seen its fair share of controversial, passionate and just plain funny goal celebrations. Wonder what Peter Crouch has in store for 2012/13?

Goal-line technology

Still not introduced at the time of writing, despite Tottenham's goal-that-wasn't against Chelsea in the 2012 FA Cup semi-final and John Terry's "clearance" against Ukraine in Euro 2012. But why do we need specific technology when Sky's cameras are already at every ground? Consult them after game-changing incidents

and put an end to this unnecessary controversy for good. Simple.

H IS FOR...

Hodgson, Roy

Hodgson's managed teams in eight different countries and speaks five languages: he's the most European of any English manager ever. After another disappointing showing at a major tournament – in which Cristiano Ronaldo had more shots in his first four games than our whole team and Andrea Pirlo played more passes on his own during *that* quarter-final than our entire midfield – it's patently obvious that even a man of Hodgson's talent is going to need a lot longer than one month to eradicate the other English disease: being scared of possession.

I IS FOR...

Injuries

The bane of any Premier League side – and seemingly the middle name of players such as Kieron Dyer, Ledley King, Owen Hargreaves and Michael Owen – a crocked player can be anything from an irritant to a catastrophe, as illustrated by Dalian Atkinson's injury in 1992/93, which Ron Atkinson still believes cost Aston Villa the inaugural Premier League title.

Invincibles, The

In 2003/04, Arsenal's Jens Lehmann, Lauren, Sol Campbell, Kolo Touré, Ashley Cole, Freddie Ljungberg, Patrick Vieira, Gilberto, Robert Pires, Dennis Bergkamp and Thierry Henry went a whole Premier League season without losing a game – and were eventually unbeaten in 49 games, a new top-flight record.

J IS FOR...

January transfer window

That pivotal point, halfway through a season, when clubs can delve into the transfer market – sometimes calamitously, sometimes craftily – to make the purchase that they hope will kick their season on. One big transfer can cause a knock-on effect similar to that of a housing chain – which causes a great deal of excitement, especially on transfer deadline day, when Sky Sports cameras and correspondents are positioned outside all of the major clubs. The best example of this was during the 2011 January transfer window, when two of English football's biggest ever transfers were completed: Fernando Torres to Chelsea from Liverpool for £50m and Andy Carroll to Liverpool from Newcastle United for £35m.

K IS FOR...

Keegan, Kevin

The former Newcastle United manager won the Premier League 20 Seasons Award for Most Memorable Quote. In the 1995/96 season, Keegan – visibly buckling under the pressure being exerted by Manchester United manager Alex Ferguson and his re-invigorated side – declared live on Sky Sports that: "I would love it if we beat them. Love it!" (p92).

L IS FOR...

Lineker, Gary

One of England's greatest goal poachers (he scored 48 times in 80 international appearances), Gary Lineker joined *Match of the Day* as a pundit in 1995 and took over as the show's presenter after Des Lynam's departure in 1999.

M IS FOR...

Manchester City

City won their first title since 1968 in 2011/12, which was voted Best Season in the Premier League 20 Seasons Awards. They beat Manchester United 1-6 at Old Trafford and secured the title in the last seconds of the season.

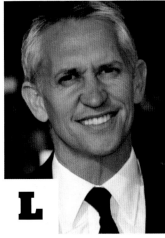

Manchester United

What is left to say about the Old Trafford legacy Sir Alex Ferguson set in motion when the Premier League started in 1992? You only need to flick through this book to understand the enormity of Manchester United's influence on the world's most popular football league. Who, if anyone, can knock them off *their* perch?

Massey, Sian

The most famous of a handful of female officials, a huge sexism scandal erupted at Sky Sports after her second EPL game on 22 January 2011, which resulted in pundit Andy Gray being sacked and Sky Sports' most senior analyst and presenter, Richard Keys, resigning.

Match of the Day

Once the country's big player when it came to live football broadcasting, *Match of the Day* is now firmly

regarded as a highlights programme of multiple matches (despite its title), with live rights limited to the national team and the FA Cup. Current presenter Gary Lineker is usually joined by two pundits – either Alan Shearer, Alan Hansen, Lee Dixon or Mark Lawrenson. Colin Murray presents *Match of the Day 2* on Sundays, with Hansen, Dixon, Martin Keown and Les Ferdinand the most regular pundits.

Money

In 1991, the Football League's accounts showed a net profit of £4,850 from a turnover of £29.46m. Twenty years on and the EPL is the most-watched football league in the world, broadcast in 212 territories to an audience of 643 million viewers, and the league's annual turnover exceeds £1.2bn, with clubs taking £2.1bn between them (after adding their own revenue streams). In short, the Premier League is Big Business.

Mourinho, José

The most sought-after coach in world football took the Premier League by storm as manager of Chelsea from 2004-07, setting a string of records, including the most points (95) achieved in a season and the fewest

N

can appeal if they feel the player is a "special talent" and "able to contribute significantly to development of the game at the top level in the UK".

P **IS FOR...**

Parachute payments

Before 1992, TV revenues from top-flight matches were shared between all 92 Football League clubs. They are now exclusively shared between the 20 clubs in the top flight. In 2011/12, all of the promoted teams – Swansea City, Norwich City and QPR – stayed up, suggesting the gulf in class is not as chasmic as some might think. But parachute payments are still given to relegated teams, in the form of £48m over four years, to help cushion the blow of missing out on crucial TV payments.

P

Prawn-sandwich brigade

A term coined by Manchester United's combative former captain Roy Keane. It refers to fans whose enthusiasm is more for the club's corporate hospitality than the game. "Away from home our fans are fantastic – I'd call them the hardcore fans," said Keane after a Champions League tie with Dynamo Kiev in 2000. "But at home they have a few drinks and probably the prawn sandwiches, and don't realise what's going on on the pitch."

Pundits

The proliferation of football on TV has created plenty of scope for ex-pros to earn a crust providing insight of varying quality, during, between and after matches. Andy Townsend's *Tactics Truck* on ITV was generally viewed as a fail, but Gary Neville's recent appointment as chief analyst on Sky Sports has been a widespread success.

goals (15) conceded in a season. He wasn't shy coming forward during his tenure at Stamford Bridge and lived up to the self-hype: "Please don't call me arrogant because what I am saying is true. I am European champion... I think I am the special one."

N **IS FOR...**

National team

Has the proliferation of foreign players affected the quality of the national team? That's a question often asked after another abysmal England performance at a major tournament. Do Englishmen suffer by not getting enough game time in the top flight because of foreigners taking their place? Or do they benefit from training alongside overseas talent and learning from them? England's Euro 2012 performance would suggest that it's a bit of both. While we need to watch and develop like our European brethren, there's nothing that beats a bit of the ol' Bulldog spirit.

O **IS FOR...**

Overseas players

When the Premier League began in 1992, there were only 11 players from outside of the UK or the Republic of Ireland in starting line-ups across the entire division. In 1999, Chelsea became the first Premier League team to field an entirely foreign starting XI

and, in 2005, Arsenal named a wholly foreign 16-man squad. A non-EU player applying for a work permit must have played for his country in at least 75% of its competitive A internationals and his country must have averaged at least 70th in the world over the previous 24-month period. Clubs

O

P

Q **IS FOR...**

Quotes

The stature of the Premier League befits men with big egos and big personalities, and this was recognised with the 20 Seasons Most Memorable Quote Award. Kevin Keegan won from a shortlist of big mouths that included Eric Cantona, Sir Alex Ferguson and José Mourinho. There was also this 1995 classic from super-pundit Alan Hansen: "The trick is always buy when you're strong, so he [Ferguson] needs to buy players. You can't win anything with kids." United won the double.

R IS FOR...

Referees

Oft-despised card-issuers, who make crucial calls week in, week out and who gently swallow the bile that emanates from the terraces and the dugouts. Though most managers believe they all get posh red wine from Sir Alex Ferguson at the end of every season, this has never been proven. Isn't that right, Mr Poll?

Rivalries

Life is sometimes more easily defined if you have an object on which to focus your antipathy – and the Premier League is no different. Sir Alex Ferguson had the BBC; Roy Keane had Alf-Inge Haaland, Patrick Vieira and the prawn-sandwich brigade; David Batty had Graeme Le Saux; Lee Bowyer had Kieron Dyer; and Martin Keown had Ruud van Nistelrooy. Don't the memories just bring joy to your heart?

S IS FOR...

Shearer, Alan

The Premier League's record goalscorer (260 for Blackburn Rovers and Newcastle United), Alan Shearer is an Officer of the Order of the British Empire (OBE), a Deputy Lieutenant of Northumberland, a Freeman of Newcastle upon Tyne and an honorary Doctor of Civil Law of Northumbria and Newcastle Universities. Oh, and a leading pundit on *Match of the Day*.

Shirt sponsors

According to *Sportingintelligence*, only one Premier League club – Blackburn Rovers – experienced a decline in revenue from shirt sponsorship in 2011/12. The overall total revenue of the league increased by almost 20% to £117.5m. Manchester United, Liverpool and Manchester City topped the revenue charts, earning around £20m each per year from their respective shirt sponsors, Aon, Standard Chartered and Etihad.

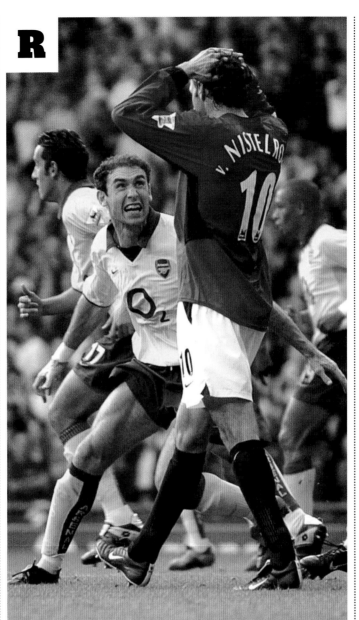

Shreeves, Geoff

Joined Sky Sports in the first season of the Premier League and now gets his kicks patrolling the touchline during big-match encounters and feeding the viewers the news from the dugouts, as it happens. The redoubtable stalwart of the weekend broadcasting effort.

Sky TV

The relationship between Sky TV and English football transformed the Premier League into the most prestigious division in the world. It began in 1992, with a £304m deal for exclusive live coverage of the new FA Premiership. Televised matches were the cornerstone of the satellite broadcaster's business model: by transferring live, top-flight football from terrestrial to paid-for channels, they could pump money back into the game, expand their coverage and improve their overall package. In 1999, Sky offered a free dish and box to accelerate the launch of Sky Digital and, by 2010, the company had reached its target of 10 million customers, making it the choice of 36% of UK and Ireland households.

Speed

No other league is played at the breakneck speed than the Premier League is. "They need to explain to their players that to reduce the tempo of the game would help their technique," Michel Platini once said. But that would also reduce the 100mph action that the division is globally renowned for. It's the guaranteed 90 minutes of explosive, end-to-end excitement that has sold the Premier League to every big market in the world. Why change that, Michel?

Sponsors

Beer company Carling were the Premier League's first title sponsors in 1993 (when it became known as the FA Carling Premiership), but they relinquished this status in 2001 and Barclaycard took up the mantle. Until 2004, the top flight of English football was known as the Barclays Premiership and, from 2007 to the present day, it has been known as the Barclays Premier League. Mitre were the official ball supplier until 2000/01, when Nike took over.

Stelling, Jeff

Staunch Hartlepool fan and the world's best anchorman for a TV programme that successfully broadcasts pictures of men watching televisions (which you cannot see) and thrives on their reactions. God bless the silly notion of *Soccer Saturday* – and god bless Jeff Stelling.

T **IS FOR...**

Trophy

Made by royal jewellers Asprey of London, the sterling silver Premier League trophy has a malachite base (its green colour indicative of football's fields of play) and a golden crown. It weighs 10kg, is 76cm tall and is designed around the English Three Lions. There is a lion positioned above each of the handles and the third one is represented by the victorious captain who lifts the trophy at the end of the season. In 2004, a unique, all-gold version of the trophy was commissioned to celebrate Arsenal's undefeated Invincibles season.

Tyler, Martin

In 2003, Martin Tyler was voted Premier League Commentator of the Decade by football fans. He is, quite simply, *the* voice of the Premier League: the man who provides the memorable words for the big occasions and the clever soundbites for those crucial moments. He's also first-team coach at non-league Kingstonian.

U **IS FOR...**

UEFA

With football legend Michel Platini as its top dog, UEFA has solidified its position as the guardian of European club football over the past two decades. It has grown the Champions League into the world's most-watched annual sporting event, garnering more than 300m viewers. The competition's influence on the transfer market and on the Premier League is undeniable.

V **IS FOR...**

Venky's

The Indian company took over Blackburn Rovers for £23m and,

despite being quick to give job assurances, promptly sacked manager Sam Allardyce. The club was lucky to avoid relegation on the last day of the 2010/11 Premier League season, but lessons were not learned. They went down

the very next year after losing to Wigan in their penultimate game of the campaign, to become the first Premier League title winners to be relegated from the division.

W **IS FOR...**

Wages

In 2011/12, the wages-to-revenue ratio of the Premier League was 70% and the amount clubs spend on wages is generally found to be commensurate with their league position at the end of a season. Barcelona's Lionel Messi is the world's most highly paid footballer and earned £27.5m in 2012. Wayne Rooney is the Premier League's highest earner (fifth in the world), raking in a measly £17.2m in 2012.

Walker, Jack

The Blackburn-born entrepreneur secured the title for his home-town club in 1995 by breaking the English transfer record twice – for Alan Shearer (£3.3m) and Chris Sutton (£5m) – and ploughing £20m into the reconstruction of Ewood Park. After his death in 2000, local MP Jack Straw said: "Jack Walker did more than any other individual in the last century to enhance the self-confidence and prosperity of his home town." And he was right.

Wenger, Arsène

Arsenal's most successful and longest-serving manager, Arsène Wenger has provided a stern test for Sir Alex

Ferguson since his arrival in 1996 and revolutionised English football, from diet and training to transfer policy and playing philosophy. Only the most learned fans had heard of him when he arrived at Highbury; now he could get a job at any club in the world.

Winter break

Michel Platini decided against transferring to play in England in the 1980s because of the hectic Christmas schedule – and it has long been a bone of contention for foreign managers that players be allowed to take a winter break to revitalise themselves. All European leagues except England and Portugal have a winter break, but it is unlikely to be seriously contemplated for the Premier League. After all, it adds to the competition's intensity and makes the league what it is – doesn't it? And what would we do over the festive season without Boxing Day matches? An unwanted proposal.

X IS FOR...

Xenophobia

In the 1980s, racism in English football was widespread and unrestrained. Today, images of major players back-heeling bananas from pitches is unheard of and drastic measures would be taken against the perpetrators if caught. England weren't as well supported at Euro 2012 because of the suspected racial animosity prevalent in the host nations: English football has changed.

Y IS FOR...

Yanks

The American influence on the Premier League is now vast and their manoeuvrings within the game have ranged from encouraging to calamitous. The Glazer family's arrival at Manchester United precipitated a minor revolt and the creation of FC United of Manchester, while the brief reign of Tom Hicks and George Gillett at Liverpool almost proved ruinous for the club. But Stan Kroenke's takeover of Arsenal, Ellis Short's of Sunderland and Randy Lerner's of Aston Villa have been more muted. Over the next few seasons, however, curious eyes will be on the Fenway Sports Group, parent company of the rejuvenated Boston Red Sox and Liverpool FC. Can their long-term strategy, with Brendan Rogers recently appointed as manager, return the Reds to their former glory? Time will tell.

Z IS FOR...

Zola, Gianfranco

One of the most admired players in the history of this famous league (see p99), Gianfranco Zola played with a smile on his face and the ball seemingly glued to his boots during his time at Chelsea. A great character and a great ambassador for the Premier League.

THE TEAMS

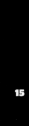

|||||||||||||||||||||||||||||||||||||||||||||||||||||||||||||||||||||||||||||||||||||||||||||||||||||||||||||||||||||||

Full name **Manchester United Football Club** | Nickname **The Red Devils** | Founded **1878** | Ground **Old Trafford** (Capacity, 75,811)

MAN UTD

If the Premier League trophy had to find a permanent home, it would be Old Trafford

PREMIER FACTFILE

Club homepage
manutd.com

Rivals Manchester City, Liverpool, Leeds

Premier League Seasons 20

Highest position
1st (x12)

Lowest position
3rd (x3)

Biggest victory in PL
9-0 v Ipswich Town
(4 March 1995)

Biggest defeat in PL
0-5 v Newcastle Utd
(20 Oct 1996)*

Biggest transfer paid
£30.75m for Dimitar Berbatov from Tottenham Hotspur

Biggest transfer received
£80m for Cristiano Ronaldo from Real Madrid

*ONLY EARLIEST RESULT STATED

Seasons played	20
Played	772
Won	500
Drawn	163
Lost	109
Goals for	1,376
Goals against	660
Goal difference	716
Points	1,663
Relegations	None
Average points	83.15

20 YEARS OF JOY

Overwhelmingly the most successful team in Premier League history, Manchester United have won the title 12 times, on two occasions winning it three times in a row. Sir Alex Ferguson, named Best Manager at the Premier League 20 Season Awards, has won 24 honours since he took charge at Old Trafford in 1986 and, in 1993, brought the club its first League title since 1963. In 1998/99, United achieved the treble of Premier League, FA Cup and Champions League, and they hold the record for highest number of top-flight league titles – 19.

NEWTON HEATH

Founded in 1878 as Newton Heath LYR (Lancashire and Yorkshire Railway), the club changed its name to Manchester United in 1902, moving to Old Trafford in 1910. Under the stewardship of Matt Busby, United recorded their first success in Europe, becoming the first English club to win the European Cup, in 1968. They have lifted it twice more since. Busby was acclaimed for the way he dealt with the consequences of the Munich air disaster in 1958, and the team he built in its aftermath – including Bobby Charlton, George Best and Denis Law – produced some of the most appealing football of a generation. The club has also won the Cup Winners' Cup, Super Cup, Intercontinental Cup, World Club Cup, 11 FA Cups, four League Cups and 19 Community Shields. Unsurprisingly, their success has made them one of the best-supported sports teams on the planet and, consequently, also one of the richest.

DID YOU KNOW?
In 1934, Utd changed to cherry and white hoops but finished in its lowest league position, so quickly reverted back

NEW CHALLENGE

Talking of vast wealth, the time has come for Sir Alex Ferguson to take up a new challenge: silencing the increasing din from his "noisy neighbours", Manchester City. He has transformed and re-energised many teams during his spell at Old Trafford, contended with the advances of north and west London, and now faces a serious battle for dominance with the blue half of Manchester. If he can overcome the spending power of Sheikh Mansour and his City rivals, it will be one of his most remarkable achievements yet.

★ **PREMIER STAR** ■ Eric Cantona ■ Appearances: 144 ■ 1992-1997

Quite simply, the man who brought the "winning" back to Old Trafford. Beautifully stolen from Leeds, he galvanized an underachieving bunch and turned them into the Red Devils we know today. Heroic stuff.

Full name **Arsenal Football Club** | Nickname **The Gunners** | Founded **1886** | Ground **Emirates Stadium** (60,361)

ARSENAL

Fluent, capable and always a threat but, as yet, not able to retain a Premier League title

PREMIER FACTFILE

Club homepage
arsenal.com

Rivals Spurs, Man Utd

Premier League Seasons 20

Highest position
1st (1997/98, 2001/02, 2003/04)

Lowest position
10th (1992/93)

Biggest victory in Premier League
7-0 v Everton
(11 May 2005)

Biggest defeat in Premier League
2-8 v Man Utd
(28 August 2011)

Biggest transfer paid
£15.8m for Samir Nasri from Marseille

Biggest transfer received
£35m for Cesc Fábregas from Barcelona

Seasons played	20
Played	772
Won	415
Drawn	204
Lost	153
Goals for	1,219
Goals against	717
Goal difference	502
Points	1,449
Relegations	None
Average points	72.45

DIAL SQUARE

Arsenal suffered something of an identity crisis early in their existence, changing their name from Dial Square (1886) to Royal Arsenal, Woolwich Arsenal (1891) and then just Arsenal (1913). They also switched the location of their stadium from south-east London to Highbury (1913), after low attendances bankrupted the club in 1910 and businessmen Henry Norris and William Hall took over. Thereafter, they enjoyed more success and, in 1919, by allegedly suspicious circumstances and at the expense of Tottenham Hotspur, were asked to join the First Division – so began a fierce north London rivalry.

THE HERBERT CHAPMAN ERA

Under Herbert Chapman, who had already won the league twice with Huddersfield Town, Arsenal became the dominant force in domestic football in the 1930s, winning the league in 1930-31 and 1932-33. After Chapman's sudden death from pneumonia in January 1934, they continued his legacy, winning the title in 1933-34, 1934-35 and 1937-38. They also won the FA Cup twice, in 1930 and 1936. After sporadic success in the 1940s, the 50s and 60s were largely silverware-free, the club unable to attract the players to compete at the highest level.

> **DID YOU KNOW?**
> Chapman pushed for Gillespie Road tube station to be renamed Arsenal – the only stop named after a football club

THE THIRD AND FOURTH ERAS

After his appointment in 1986, George Graham brought the title to north London in 1988-89 (thanks to Michael Thomas's last-minute goal in the final game of the season against title rivals Liverpool, at Anfield) and again in 1991/92. But, from 1996, the club's success has been down to one man, Arsène Wenger. The relatively unknown Frenchman brought in new tactics and an array of foreign talent that would turn Arsenal into purveyors of passing football and genuine title contenders. The Gunners are the Premier League's most successful London club and hold the record for the longest period in the English top flight in the 20th century. They have won 13 titles, including three Premier League titles, and expect to challenge for every title in the forseeable future.

★ PREMIER STAR ■ Thierry Henry ■ Appearances: 254 ■ 1999-2007

A frightfully quick gust of French majesty, Thierry Henry, transformed from a winger into the world's best striker, helped turn the Gunners from mortals to Invincibles, and heaped glory on north London.

Full name **Chelsea Football Club** | Nickname(s) **The Pensioners / The Blues** | Founded **1905** | Ground **Stamford Bridge** (42,449)

CHELSEA

From having the Blues to painting the entire continent the colours of west London

PREMIER FACTFILE

Club homepage
chelseafc.com

Rivals QPR, Fulham, Arsenal, Spurs

Premier League Seasons 20

Highest position
1st (2004/05, 2005/06, 2009/10)

Lowest position
14th (1993/94)

Biggest victory in Premier League
8-0 v Wigan
(9 May 2010)

Biggest defeat in PL
1-5 v Liverpool
(21 Sep 1996)

Biggest transfer paid
£50m for Fernando Torres from Liverpool

Biggest transfer received
£25m for Arjen Robben from Real Madrid

Seasons played	20
Played	772
Won	401
Drawn	199
Lost	172
Goals for	1,157
Goals against	741
Goal difference	416
Points	1,402
Relegations	None
Average points	70.10

CREATED OUT OF NECESSITY

Businessman Gus Mears acquired Stamford Bridge athletics stadium in 1904 and offered to lease it to Fulham because he wanted to turn it into a football ground. They turned him down, so he created a team of his own – and Chelsea was born.

SLOW STARTERS

The club's early years yielded an FA Cup final appearance in 1915 and third place in the league in 1920. It wasn't until manager Ted Drake began to modernise the club in 1952 that the Blues began to realise their true potential. Out went the Pensioner crest, to be replaced by a lion, and in came exciting new players from the lower divisions to revitalise the team and bring home the league title in 1954-55. Tommy Docherty followed Drake and in the 1964-65 season the club fought for honours on three fronts: the League, FA Cup and League Cup, only triumphing in the latter, 3-2 against Leicester. However, Docherty did deliver the club's first European silverware: the Cup Winners' Cup in 1971, beating Real Madrid 2-1 in a replay in Athens.

DID YOU KNOW?

Ron "Chopper" Harris holds the record for appearances for Chelsea. He made 795 between 1961 and 1980

GULLIT GETS THEM GOING

With the advent of the Premier League came some big changes at The Bridge. Erratic in the early days of the competition, the club appointed Ruud Gullit as manager in 1996 and he brought in some exceptional foreign talent, such as Gianfranco Zola. Chelsea moved up the table and ended a 26-year wait for a trophy by winning the FA Cup in 1997. Their reputation was also being enhanced in Europe – enter stage left, Roman Abramovich.

CHELSKI FOR THE TITLE

Abramovich wanted Chelsea to challenge on all fronts every season – and he wasn't afraid to dig deep into his pockets to make this happen. José Mourinho delivered the Russian oligarch's first Premier League success in 2004-05 and, the next season, Chelsea became only the fifth English team to win back-to-back titles since the Second World War. Carlo Ancelotti also took the Blues to the title in 2009-10, his team scoring more than 100 goals in the process.

★ **PREMIER STAR** ▪ Gianfranco Zola ▪ Appearances: 312 ▪ 1996-2003

Before arriving at Chelsea, Gianfranco Zola had trained and played alongside Careca and Maradona at Napoli, and it showed. To describe his impact on the team as immense and his performances as dazzling would be to do him an injustice.

Full name **Liverpool Football Club** | Nickname **The Reds** | Founded **1892** | Ground **Anfield** (45,276)

LIVERPOOL

Conquerors of Europe and the FA Cup, the Reds have yet to lift the Premier League title

PREMIER FACTFILE

Club homepage
liverpoolfc.tv

Rivals Everton, Manchester Utd

Premier League Seasons 20

Highest position
2nd (2001/02, 2008-09)

Lowest position
8th (1993/94, 2011/12)

Biggest victory in Premier League
7-1 v Southampton
(16 January 1999)

Biggest defeat in PL
1-5 v Coventry
(19 December 1992)

Biggest transfer paid
£35m for Andy Carroll from Newcastle

Biggest transfer received
£50m for Fernando Torres from Chelsea

Seasons played	20
Played	772
Won	380
Drawn	194
Lost	198
Goals for	1,122
Goals against	753
Goal difference	369
Points	1,334
Relegations	None
Average points	66.7

BOOT ROOM BOYS

Liverpool are one of the most decorated clubs in the UK, having won the league title 18 times, the FA Cup seven times and the League Cup a record eight times. They are also the most successful British club in Europe, having won the European Cup five times, the UEFA Cup three times and the UEFA Super Cup three times. Liverpool fans often refer to themselves as Kopites, in reference to the Kop terrace at Anfield, their home since 1892. Outside the ground is a statue of their legendary former manager Bill Shankly, who was appointed in 1959. He converted a boot-storage area into a place where he and coaches Joe Fagan, Reuben Bennett and Bob Paisley could discuss strategy. The Anfield "boot room" was born and the legacy began.

LEADERS OF THE PACK TO FADING STARS

Liverpool were the first English club to agree to have sponsors logos on their playing strip; they appeared on the first edition of *Match Of The Day* in 1964, beating Arsenal 3-2; and their 1969 2-0 home win over West Ham was the first game to be broadcast in colour. Liverpool's major successes came in the 1970s and 80s, but they surrendered their domination of English football to Manchester United in the 1990s, intensifying the rivalry – no player has been transferred directly between the clubs since Phil Chisnall in 1964. Liverpool have yet to win the Premier League.

A NEW PHILOSOPHY

The Taylor Report of 1990 slashed Anfield's capacity from 55,000 to 45,276 and, despite redevelopments, the club has fallen behind Manchester United in terms of attendance and gate receipts. This, plus poor signings, has seen the club drift down the domestic pecking order, but fans are hoping this will change under the recently appointed Brendan Rodgers. Despite winning the League Cup under "King" Kenny Dalglish in 2012, Liverpool ended the season in eighth place, with 52 points, their lowest finish since the 1993/94 season and their lowest ever points tally in the Premier League.

> **DID YOU KNOW?**
> Bill Shankly changed Liverpool's kit to all-red (from white socks/shorts) to make the players look more imposing

★ **PREMIER STAR** ■ Steven Gerrard ■ Appearances: 405 ■ 1998-present

Liverpool's engine room and talisman, when the big occasion comes, the skipper often makes the most telling contribution. With better players around him, he could have spearheaded a glorious Liverpool era. Craves the league title.

||||||||||||||||||||||||||||||||||||||||||||||||||||||||||||||||||||||||||||||||||||||||||||||||||||||||

Full name **Aston Villa Football Club** | Nickname(s) **Villa / Villains / Lions / The Claret and Blue** | Founded **1874** | Ground **Villa Park** (42,785)

ASTON VILLA

Founding member of the Football and Premier Leagues in search of new glory days

PREMIER FACTFILE

Club homepage
avfc.co.uk

Rivals Birmingham, Wolves, Coventry City

Premier League Seasons 20

Highest position
2nd (1992/93)

Lowest position
16th (2005/06, 11/12)

Biggest victory in Premier League
7-1 v Wimbledon
(11 February 1995)

Biggest defeat in Premier League
1-7 v Chelsea
(27 March 2010)

Biggest transfer paid
£24m to Sunderland for Darren Bent

Biggest transfer received
£26m for James Milner from Manchester City

Seasons played	20
Played	772
Won	283
Drawn	240
Lost	249
Goals for	879
Goals against	923
Goal difference	-44
Points	1,089
Relegations	None
Average points	54.45

MIDLANDS HEROES

Aston Villa were founded in 1874 by four members of the Villa Cross Wesleyan Chapel in Handsworth and their first match was truly a game of two halves: one playing rugby and one playing football! It didn't take them long to get the hang of the latter though, winning the Birmingham Senior Cup in 1880 and their first FA Cup in 1887. The Football League began the next year and Villa were among the initial 12 teams to contest it. They were the most successful English team during the reign of Queen Victoria, winning five titles and three FA Cups before 1901. A barren period followed and then more honours, when Villa became the first team to win English League Cup in 1960/61. In 1974, after another period of decline and renewal, manager Ron Saunders reinvigorated the club with his upfront style. He won the league title in 1980/81, then surprisingly quit under a cloud the season after, just before his team was about to contest the European Cup quarter-final. They went on to beat Bayern Munich 1-0 in the final in Rotterdam, thanks to a goal from Peter Withe, and defeated Barcelona in the European Super Cup the following year.

DID YOU KNOW?

Only Everton (109 seasons) have spent longer in the English league's top flight than Aston Villa (100)

RON-DERFUL STUFF!

Villa were one of the founder members of the Premier League and were very unlucky not to hold the trophy aloft in its inaugural year. They were top of the table with six games to go, but were eclipsed by Manchester United after what manager Ron Atkinson described as a pivotal injury to combative, livewire striker Dalian Atkinson. It hasn't really been the same at Villa Park since. Chairman Doug Ellis sold his shares to American tycoon Randy Lerner after a 23-year association with the club and, despite Martin O'Neill's reign signalling new optimism – plus two trips to Wembley in 2010 – a rapid decline occurred after the Northern Irishman quit. In 2011/12, Alex McLeish, the first manager to make a direct move between Birmingham and Villa, only narrowly avoided the Villains' first relegation from the PL. Can his replacement, Paul Lambert, reverse their fortunes?

*ONLY EARLIEST RESULT STATED

★ PREMIER STAR ■ Paul McGrath ■ Appearances: 252 ■ 1992-1996

One of Ireland's greatest ever players and the rock at the heart of Aston Villa's defence during the 1992/93 title challenge. Muscular, tenacious and inspiring despite dodgy knees in the latter part of his career.

|||||||||||||||||||||||||||||||||||||||||||||||||||||||||||||||||||||||||||||||||||||||||||||||||||||||||||||||||||||||||||||||||||||||||||||||||||||||||||||||||||||||||||||||||||||||||

Full name **Tottenham Hotspur Football Club** | Nickname(s) **Spurs / Lilywhites** | Founded **1882** | Ground **White Hart Lane** (36,230)

TOTTENHAM

Can you hear the Cockerel crow? After successive top-five finishes, Spurs need to push on

PREMIER FACTFILE

Club homepage
tottenhamhotspur.com

Rivals Arsenal, Chelsea, West Ham

Premier League Seasons 20

Highest position
4th (2009/10, 2011/12)

Lowest position
15th (1993/94)

Biggest victory in Premier League
9-1 v Wigan
(22 November 2009)

Biggest defeat in Premier League
1-7 v Newcastle
(28 Dec 1996)

Biggest transfer paid
£16.5m to Charlton
for Darren Bent

Biggest transfer received
£30.75m from Man Utd
for Dimitar Berbatov

Seasons played	20
Played	772
Won	294
Drawn	204
Lost	274
Goals for	988
Goals against	1,020
Goal difference	-32
Points	1,086
Relegations	None
Average points	54.30

EARNING THEIR SPURS

Tottenham's Latin motto may translate as 'To dare is to do', but only in the past few years have Spurs' fans dared to dream again. A real footballing force in the 1960s and 70s under the stewardship of club legend Bill Nicholson, their progress in the Premier League has been somewhat pedestrian. In recent years, however, Spurs have shrugged off the shackles of mediocrity, with consistent mid-table positions giving way to consecutive top-five finishes under the management of Harry Redknapp.

HISTORY BOYS

Founded in 1882, Tottenham Hotspur (formerly the Hotspur Football Club) made history in 1901 by becoming the only non-league side to win the FA Cup since the formation of the Football League in 1888. But further major honours eluded them until 1951, when Tottenham lifted the Division One title. This milestone would not be built upon for a few years however. Indeed, the club came precariously close to relegation before entering its rampant era of the 1960s. Nicholson etched Tottenham's name into football's annals in 1961, when they became the first English club in the 20th century to win the League and FA Cup double. Two years later, they became the first British team to win a European trophy (the Cup Winners' Cup). In Nicholson's 16-year tenure, Tottenham added two more FA Cups, the UEFA Cup and two League Cups to their cabinet. Although Spurs would enjoy various Cup successes after this period – with the White Hart Lane faithful privy to some dazzling displays by the likes of Paul Gascoigne, Ossie Ardiles and Glenn Hoddle – the heights they achieved under Nicholson have yet to be repeated.

DID YOU KNOW?
Spurs were the first club in the 20th century to win the FA Cup and league title double (1960–61)

THE FUTURE'S WHITE?

With a wealth of talent at their disposal – and having secured a top-five finish in the Premier League for three seasons in a row – Tottenham will be eager to push on from here, although they must do so without Redknapp, who was sacked in June. Holding on to their players will be essential if they are to break into the top three and finish above fierce rivals Arsenal.

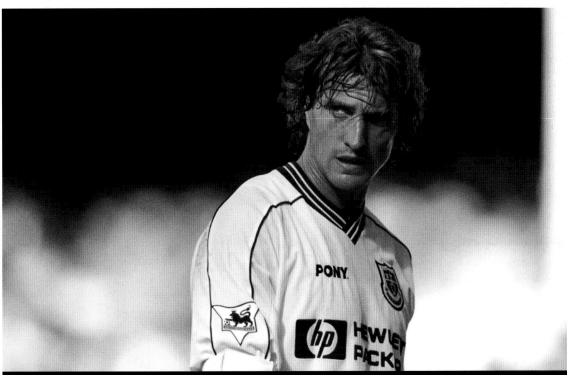

★ **PREMIER STAR** ■ David Ginola ■ Appearances: 100 ■ 1997-2000

Generously follicled Gallic maestro, who not only turned heads with flair and verve, but also found plenty of end product in his most productive phases. A magician with an eye for the flamboyant who was adored at the Lane.

Full name **Everton Football Club** | Nickname(s) **The Toffees / The Blues** | Founded **1878** | Ground **Goodison Park** (40,157)

EVERTON

Consistent overachievers could benefit from a cash injection to really compete

PREMIER FACTFILE

Club homepage
evertonfc.com

Rivals Liverpool

Premier League Seasons 20

Highest position
4th (2004/05)

Lowest position
17th (1993/94, 1997/98, 2003/04)

Biggest victory in PL
7-1 v Southampton
(16 November 1996)*

Biggest defeat in PL
0-7 v Arsenal
(11 May 2005)

Biggest transfer paid
£15m to Standard Liege for Marouane Fellaini

Biggest transfer received
£27m from Manchester United for Wayne Rooney

Seasons played	20
Played	772
Won	272
Drawn	218
Lost	282
Goals for	891
Goals against	979
Goal difference	-88
Points	1,034
Relegated	None
Average points	51.70

THE BLUE SIDE OF LIVERPOOL

Sharing Merseyside with the most successful side in English football history is far from ideal, but Everton have always ensured they stand apart from the shadow cast by their bitter rivals Liverpool. The Toffees have more top-flight appearances than any other club (109 seasons), won the league nine times and the FA Cup on five occasions, and have remained in the Premier League since its inception. At the helm is David Moyes, who last year celebrated a decade in charge of the club, a tenure that makes him the Premier League's third-longest-serving manager, behind Sir Alex Ferguson and Arsène Wenger.

EVERTON PAST

Founded in 1878 as St Domingo's (after a local Methodist church), the club was renamed Everton a year later. One of the founding members of the Football League in 1888/89, sustained success eluded Everton until the 1927/28 season, when an astonishing 60 goals from club legend Dixie Dean helped them to a third league title. Later decades were peppered with domestic triumphs for the club – with the 1960s a period to remember – but it was Howard Kendall's reign in the 1980s that signified Everton's most successful era to date. Two league titles, the FA Cup and the European Cup Winners' Cup made their way to the blue half of Liverpool between 1984 and 1987. Faced with big-spending Premier League clubs, there has been little silverware for Everton in recent seasons and their most notable achievement has been Champions League qualification thanks to a fantastic top-four finish in 2005.

DID YOU KNOW?

Everton's Goodison Park was the first ground in the league to have dugouts (1930s) and under-soil heating (58)

KEEPING UP WITH THE BIG BOYS

Everton's lack of financial clout could be a cause for concern, but Moyes has proved he can stretch a budget brilliantly. His history of overachieving with limited means has earned him a legion of admirers as he has built sides that consistently finish higher in the table than expected. With a bit more cash, the Toffees can continue to vie for European spot in the years to come.

*ONLY EARLIEST RESULT STATED

★ PREMIER STAR ■ Duncan Ferguson ■ Appearances: 230 ■ 1994-1998 & 2000-2006

Robust, determined and just a little bit mental, football's most famous pigeon-fancier Duncan Ferguson was the ultimate target man, unsettling even the hardest of centre-backs with his incessant aggression and bold, direct play.

||||||||||||||||||||||||||||||||||||||||||||||||||||||||||||||||||||||||||||||||||||||||||||||||||||||||||

Full name **Newcastle United Football Club** | Nickname(s) **The Magpies / The Toon** | Founded **1892** | Ground **Sports Direct Arena** (52,409)

NEWCASTLE

A proud history, but no Premier League silverware - can Pardew pave the way to success?

PREMIER FACTFILE

Club homepage
nufc.co.uk

Rivals Sunderland, Middlesbrough

Premier League Seasons 18

Highest position
2nd (1995/96, 1996/97)

Lowest position
18th (2008/09)

Biggest victory in Premier League
8-0 v Sheffield Weds
19 September 1999

Biggest defeat in Premier League
0-6 v Manchester Utd
12 January 2008

Biggest transfer paid
£16.8m to Real Madrid
for Michael Owen

Biggest transfer received
£35m from Liverpool
for Andy Carroll

Seasons played	18
Played	692
Won	277
Drawn	186
Lost	229
Goals for	891
Goals against	885
Goal difference	6
Points	1,017
Relegations	1
Average points	56.50

THE 'ENTERTAINERS'

Oh, how they blew it... and how it must still smart. Kevin Keegan's brilliantly assembled Newcastle team of 1995/96 - teeming with flair and arrogance - became full of nausea and nerves, and bottled it in the title race against Alex Ferguson's hardy men of Old Trafford.

They had been 12 points clear after beating Bolton 2-1 at St James' Park, at which point Keegan introduced Faustino Asprilla. Peter Beardsley was pushed to the right, the free-scoring Les Ferdinand stopped finding the net and the rot started to set in. The rest is history. It's a shame now to contemplate the capitulation, but Robert Lee said Newcastle lost it as much as United won it, although the Red Devils did win 13 of their final 15 games of the season.

PROUD HISTORY

Developed into an all-seater stadium in the mid-1990s, St James' Park has been Newcastle United's home since they formed in 1892. Things were slow to take off though, and the club were incensed by the local community's lack of support: "The Newcastle public do not deserve to be catered for as far as professional football is concerned," read a statement from them. But the fans soon began to flock to the ground and the Magpies dominated the top flight in the early 1900s, winning the title in 1904/05, 1906/07 and 1908/09 with football that was easy on the eye.

KEEP YOUR ALANS ON

Back to modern times and Newcastle's footballing attitude and philosophy of sharp-passing fluency has been instilled into manager Alan Pardew's current side, which finished a creditable fifth in 2011/12.

After Keegan's heroic failures and departure, the club suffered a dip in fortunes, but was reborn between 2001 and 2004 under the leadership of Sir Bobby Robson, enjoying Champions League football and the goals of Alan Shearer.

Now it appears the Geordie faithful have the manager and players to dream again. Come on - 2011/12 wasn't just a fluke, was it?

DID YOU KNOW?
When Sir Bobby Robson was hired as Porto boss in 1992, his interpreter was a certain José Mourinho

★ **PREMIER STAR** ■ Alan Shearer ■ Appearances: 303 ■ 1996-2006

Without doubt the greatest striker the Premier League has ever seen. Consistent wasn't the word for Alan Shearer: relentless, dogged and unflappable suit his scoring habits much better. Quite simply, a goal machine.

|||||||||||||||||||||||||||||||||||||||||||||||||||||||||||||||||||||||||||||||||||||||||||||||||||||||||||||||||||||||||||||||||||||||

Full name **Blackburn Rovers Football Club** | Nickname(s) **Rovers / Blue and Whites** | Founded **1875** | Ground **Ewood Park** (31,367)

BLACKBURN

Welcome to the house that Jack built. Not so sturdy these days, but solid foundations

PREMIER FACTFILE

Club homepage
rovers.co.uk

Rivals Burnley, Bolton, Man Utd

Premier League Seasons 18

Highest position
1st (1994/95)

Lowest position
19th (1998/99, 2011/12)

Biggest victory in Premier League
7-0 v Notts Forest
18 November 1995

Biggest defeat in Premier League
1-7 v Man Utd
27 November 2010

Biggest transfer paid
£8m to Manchester United for Andy Cole

Biggest transfer received
£17.5m from Man City for Roque Santa Cruz

Seasons played	18
Played	696
Won	262
Drawn	184
Lost	250
Goals for	927
Goals against	907
Goal difference	20
Points	970
Relegated	2
Average points	53.89

'BURN BABY, 'BURN!

One of the nominees for Best Team at the recent 20 Seasons Awards, Blackburn were in prime position to take advantage of the new Premier League when it began in 1992/93. They had recently been taken over by Blackburn fan-turned-steel baron Jack Walker, who was prepared to stake some of his £600m fortune to bring success to his home town.

Before this, Blackburn's most notable successes had been pre-1930, when English league titles and FA Cup winner's medals were in plentiful supply.

A SOLID SPINE

Signalling his intent from the off, Walker installed Kenny Dalglish as manager in October 1991 and that season the club ended a 26-year top-flight absence via the Division Two play-offs. Premier League status was just the start though, and more money was made available: Tim Flowers became the country's most expensive keeper (£2.4m) and Alan Shearer its most expensive player (£3.6m).

Finishing fourth in 1993 was no disgrace, nor was second in 1994, but Dalglish got the balance right in 1995. With buccaneering midfielder Tim Sherwood, and Chris Sutton partnering Shearer up front, Rovers took the title on the final day of the season, despite losing 2-1 away to Liverpool. The club's motto is *Arte et labore* – 'by skill and labour' they had become the best team in England.

> ### DID YOU KNOW?
> Jack Walker left school at 13 and began life as a sheet-metal worker. By 1990, he employed more than 3,000 people

DECLINE

Of course, continued hard work, mega investment and sheer grit are required to carry on being top dog – just ask Sir Alex Ferguson. Blackburn, unfortunately, didn't have this. Dalglish moved 'upstairs' as director of football, Manchester United won the title back in 1995/96 and Rovers have yet to make the top three again. As their defender Colin Hendry said: "It's difficult to win the league, but the hardest thing is trying to win it again. When only two or three teams can win the title every season, it makes it even harder. I never thought we could win the Premier League until the last minute of the season." A brilliant underdog story and a gratifying ode to a great supporter, Mr Jack Walker.

★ **PREMIER STAR** ■ Alan Shearer ■ Appearances: 138 ■ 1992-1996

His goals transformed Rovers from nearly men into title winners. Capable of scoring tap-ins, belters, headers and curlers, Blackburn-era Shearer was a formidable force, especially when partnered with an on-song Chris Sutton.

||||||||||||||||||||||||||||||||||||||||||||||||||||||||||||||||||||||||||||||||||||||||||||||||||||||||||||||||||||||||||

Full name **Manchester City Football Club** | Nickname(s) **City / The Sky Blues / Citizens** | Founded **1880** | Ground **Etihad Stadium** (47,405)

MAN CITY

The richest football club in the world has landed...

PREMIER FACTFILE

Club homepage
mcfc.co.uk

Rivals Manchester Utd

Premier League Seasons 15

Highest position
1st (2011/12)

Lowest position
18th (1995/96, 2000/01)

Biggest victory in Premier League
6-0 v Portsmouth
21 September 2008

Biggest defeat in Premier League
8-1 v Middlesbrough
11 May 2008

Biggest transfer paid
£35m to Atlético Madrid
for Sergio Agüero

Biggest transfer received
£21m from Chelsea for
Shaun Wright-Phillips

Seasons played	15
Played	582
Won	211
Drawn	151
Lost	220
Goals for	706
Goals against	736
Goal difference	-30
Points	784
Relegated	2
Average points	52.27

YIPPEE YIPPEE SHEIKH!

When Abu Dhabi United Group took over Manchester City in 2008, the rest of the footballing world turned their heads. With a £20bn fortune, the group's leader, Sheikh Mansour, had a bank balance double that of Chelsea's benefactor, Roman Abramovich, and rumour had it he was prepared to spend big to get success. The rumours were right: three years into his reign he had spent £1bn – £210m to acquire Thaksin Shinawatra's stake in the club and £433m on transfers, as well as accumulating a wage bill of £360m. Some investment, and one that resulted in City lifting the Premier League trophy for the first time in 2011/12, after one of the most dramatic and tense finales to any season, anywhere in the world. It was voted the Premier League's Best Season in the recent 20 Seasons Awards.

LONG TIME COMING

Before the Sheikh, Manchester City's most successful period had been in the late 1960s and early 70s, when they won the league title, the FA Cup, the League Cup and the Cup Winners' Cup under Joe Mercer and Malcolm Allison. In 1973/74, former Manchester United striker Denis Law even reluctantly consigned the Red Devils to relegation on the final day of the season with a cheeky backheel. But the 1976 League Cup trophy signalled the end of this golden era and the start of a rather dismal decline. In 1998, City became the first former winners of a European trophy to be relegated to the third tier of their domestic league.

DID YOU KNOW?
The oldest player to appear in the Premier League is Manchester City keeper John Burridge, who was 43 in 1995

NEW CITY!

After being at their lowest ebb, things got better, with chairman David Bernstein and managers Kevin Keegan, Sven-Göran Eriksson and Mark Hughes all playing their part in the club's rise back through the divisions. Then the Sheikh made his move. In came players such as Kolo Touré, Carlos Tevez, Joleon Lescott, David Silva, Mario Balotelli, Sergio Agüero and Samir Nasri, plus manager Roberto Mancini – and the Premier League title followed. Job done.

★**PREMIER STAR** ■ **Vincent Kompany** ■ **Appearances: 127** ■ **2008-present**

A leader of men, Vincent Kompany not only scored the decisive goal against Manchester United during the season's run-in, but he was the Belgian rock at the heart of every City performance. Lionhearted stuff from a brave captain.

|||||||||||||||||||||||||||||||||||||||||||||||||||||||||||||||||||||||||||||||||||||||||||||||||||||||||

Full name **West Ham United Football Club** | Nickname(s) **The Hammers / The Irons** | Founded **1895** | Ground **Upton Park** (35,303)

WEST HAM UTD

The Hammers are back in the big time and have an added incentive for sticking around

PREMIER FACTFILE

Club homepage
whufc.com

Rivals Millwall, Tottenham Hotspur

Premier League Seasons 16

Highest position
5th (1998/99)

Lowest position
20th (2010/11)

Biggest victory in Premier League
6-0 v Barnsley
10 January 1998

Biggest defeat in Premier League
1-7 v Man Utd
1 April 2004*

Biggest transfer paid
£9m to Brescia for
Savio Nsereko

Biggest transfer received
£18m from Leeds for
Rio Ferdinand

*ONLY EARLIEST RESULT STATED

Seasons played	16
Played	616
Won	202
Drawn	158
Lost	256
Goals for	650
Goals against	880
Goal difference	-230
Points	764
Relegated	2
Average points	47.75

BUBBLING UP!

After securing promotion last season with a dramatic 2-1 play-offs final win over Blackpool, 2012/13 represents West Ham's third return to the Premier League. Their major silverware extends to three FA Cups and one European Cup Winners' Cup, but Hammers fans are quick to point out the club's role in England's 1966 World Cup win, with heroes Bobby Moore, Geoff Hurst and Martin Peters the spine of the West Ham team that season.

HAMMERS' PAST

Founded in 1895 as Thames Ironworks FC before reforming five years later as West Ham United, it wasn't until 1919 that the club joined the Football League. Arguably their biggest milestone in these opening decades was taking part in the first FA Cup final at the new Empire Stadium – aka Wembley – in 1923, which they lost 2-0 to Bolton Wanderers. It was Ron Greenwood who eventually guided the Hammers to their first major trophies in the shape of the FA Cup in 1964 and the European Cup Winners' Cup a year later. But if the club is a little low on silverware, it has continued its tradition of nurturing formidable English playing talent, with Frank Lampard, Rio Ferdinand, and Jermain Defoe all graduates of its youth system. West Ham have also signed crowd-pleasing favourites such as Paolo Di Canio. In 2006, the club was in the headlines for off-the-pitch matters: firstly the controversial acquisition of Argentinian pair Carlos Tevez and Javier Mascherano; and then for the takeover of West Ham by Icelandic businessman Eggert Magnusson. In 2010, David Sullivan and David Gold bought a controlling stake in the club, giving the pair operational and commercial control.

DID YOU KNOW?

World Cup-winning captain Bobby Moore earned 108 England caps and played every minute of each one

SAM'S HAM

With old hand Sam Allardyce in the Upton Park hotseat, West Ham will be keen to make this latest sojourn into the Premier League a lengthy one. There are still issues around their proposed move to the Olympic Stadium, but the club will recognise that ensuring top-flight football for the foreseeable future is its best chance of guaranteeing this sought-after relocation.

★**PREMIER STAR** ■ Paolo Di Canio ■ Appearances: 118 ■ 1999-2003

Impassioned to the point of plain wild, Paolo Di Canio soared between the romantic and the ridiculous, and West Ham fans loved him for it. A hospitality suite at Upton Park is named after the Italian in homage to his achievements.

Full name **Leeds United Association Football Club** | Nickname(s) **The Whites / The Peacocks** | Founded **1919** | Ground **Elland Road** (39,460)

LEEDS UTD

Their decline was dramatic, but the once mighty Whites are bouncing back

PREMIER FACTFILE

Club homepage
leedsunited.com

Rivals Manchester Utd, Chelsea

Premier League Seasons 12

Highest position
3rd (1999-2000)

Lowest position
19th (2003-2004)

Biggest victory in Premier League
6-1 v Bradford
13 May 2001*

Biggest defeat in Premier League
1-6 v Portsmouth
8 Nov 2003

Biggest transfer paid
£18m to West Ham for Rio Ferdinand

Biggest transfer received
£30.8m from Man Utd for Rio Ferdinand

Seasons played	12
Played	468
Won	189
Drawn	125
Lost	154
Goals for	641
Goals against	573
Goal difference	68
Points	692
Relegated	1
Average points	57.66

THE FALL

Once comfortable in the upper tier of English football, Leeds' fall from grace is one of *the* cautionary tales of the beautiful game. Winners of three Division One titles, the FA Cup, League Cup and the European Fairs Cup (twice), the club's fortunes changed with their relegation from the Premier League in 2004, after 14 years in the top flight. Although now in the Championship, the halcyon days of the 1960s and 70s are but a distant memory.

LEEDS' PAST

After the disbandment of Leeds City in 1919, a new club was formed under the name of Leeds United and entered the Football League a year later. There followed something of yo-yo period for United, with years spent fluctuating between Divisions One and Two. This all changed in 1961, when manager Don Revie took a team on the brink of relegation to Division Three and led them to two Division One titles, and victory in the FA Cup and League Cup. For almost a decade, this iconic Leeds side never finished outside the top four. The closest the club has come to emulating this period of dominance was during their heady Premiership campaigns of the late 1990s and early 2000s. Marshalled by players such as Rio Ferdinand, they regularly achieved top-five finishes and reached two European Cup semi-finals in the process. But overspending and failure to qualify for the Champions League in 2002 led to massive financial problems and Leeds were forced to sell their best talent to repay their loans. What followed was an unchecked freefall, starting with relegation from the Premiership and then administration, and subsequent demotion to the third tier of English football, League One, for the first time in their history.

DID YOU KNOW?
Frankfurt fans who saw Leeds legend Tony Yeboah's volleys refer to themselves as "Yeboah's Witnesses"

LEED-ING THE CHARGE BACK

After a torrid 10 years, it seems the rot has finally been stopped. Chairman Ken Bates has helped to steady a once sinking ship, Leeds United are back in the Championship and – with talks of future investment – the Elland Road fans may be confident of a return to top-flight football sooner than they had thought possible.

*ONLY EARLIEST RESULT STATED

★ **PREMIER STAR** ■ Gary McAllister ■ Appearances: 231 ■ 1990-1996

Alongside Gordon Strachan, Gary Speed and David Batty, Gary McAllister made up a formidable midfield quartet. A creator and leader of some repute, he was awarded an MBE for services to football in the 2001 New Year Honours.

|||||||||||||||||||||||||||||||||||||||||||||||||||||||||||||||||||||||||||||||||||||||||||||||||||||||||||||||||||||||||||||||||

Full name **Middlesbrough Football Club** | Nickname **The Boro** | Founded **1876** | Ground **Riverside Stadium** (34,988)

MIDDLESBROUGH

Ups and downs aplenty at the Riverside, but with their fair share of star names

PREMIER FACTFILE

Club homepage
mfc.co.uk

Rivals Sunderland, Newcastle, Leeds

Premier League Seasons 14

Highest position
7th (2004/05)

Lowest position
21st (1992/93)

Biggest victory in Premier League
8-1 v Manchester City
11 May 2008*

Biggest defeat in Premier League
0-7 v Arsenal
14 January 2006

Biggest transfer paid
£12m to SC Heerenveen for Afonso Alves

Biggest transfer received
£12m from Atlético Madrid for Juninho

Seasons played	14
Played	536
Won	160
Drawn	156
Lost	220
Goals for	621
Goals against	741
Goal difference	-120
Points	636
Relegated	3
Average points	45.20

*ONLY FIRST RESULT STATED

IN AND OUT AT THE START

Middlesbrough, founding members of the Premier League, were relegated after the first season, but bounced straight back after the arrival of England and Manchester United legend Bryan Robson as manager. They moved to a new home, the Riverside Stadium, but could not avoid relegation again in 1996/97. However, the signing of Paul Merson from Arsenal was cause for celebration – as was promotion the next season. In 2001, Robson made way for Steve McClaren and, in 2004, Boro won their first silverware: the Carling Cup. The next season they secured their highest league finish (seventh) and a second trip into Europe, but McClaren then left to take the England job and captain Gareth Southgate took charge. He smashed the club transfer record for Brazilian Afonso Alves (£12m), but Boro were relegated on the last day of the 2008/09 season.

SLOW BURNERS

Middlesbrough FC was founded in 1876 and switched between amateur and professional status, before going pro permanently in 1899. They secured promotion to Division One in 1901/02, having conceded only 24 goals all season, and, in 1905, the club spent the first four-figure sum (£1,000) on a player, forward Alf Common. They were not relegated again for 54 years. In the mid-1950s, a certain Brian Clough rose to prominence at the club, scoring 204 goals in 222 appearances, and England legend Jack Charlton managed Middlesbrough from 1973-77, securing promotion back to Division One. Boro had to be rescued from going into liquidation in 1986, but by 1992/93 were able to secure a place in the Premier League.

THE WILDERNESS YEARS

Southgate was replaced by Gordon Strachan in October 2009, but the club sank to 20th in the Championship in the 2010/11 season. Strachan resigned and Tony Mowbray came in to guide the club to safety. Despite an electric start to the 2011/12 season, Boro only finished seventh, ensuring another year of Championship football.

DID YOU KNOW?

Boro were the first club to broadcast full, time-delayed match highlights on their own channel, Boro TV

★**PREMIER STAR** ◼ **Juninho** ◼ **Appearances: 126** ◼ **1995-1997, (1999-2000 on loan), 2002-2004**

One of the most sought-after players in the world produced some his best stuff at the Riverside and was a joy for all who saw. He lay sobbing on the pitch after Boro's relegation from the Premiership in 1997, endearing himself to fans forever.

|||||||||||||||||||||||||||||||||||||||||||||||||||||||||||||||||||||||||||||||||||||||||||||||||||||||||||||||||||||

Full name **Southampton Football Club** | Nickname **The Saints** | Founded **1885** | Ground **St Mary's** (32,689)

SOUTHAMPTON

The Saints have their marching boots on again and are determined to set up camp

PREMIER FACTFILE

Club homepage
saintsfc.co.uk

Rivals Portsmouth

Premier League Seasons 13

Highest position
8th (2002/03)

Lowest position
20th (2004/05)

Biggest victory in Premier League
5-1 v Swindon
25 August 1993

Biggest defeat in Premier League
7-1 v Everton
16 November 1996*

Biggest transfer paid
£7m to Burnley for
Jay Rodriguez

Biggest transfer received
£12m from Arsenal
for Alex Oxlade-Chamberlain

Seasons played	13
Played	506
Won	150
Drawn	137
Lost	219
Goals for	535
Goals against	738
Goal difference	-203
Points	587
Relegated	1
Average points	45.15

BACK IN THE GAME

Southampton celebrated promotion back to the Premier League in 2011/12 after seven years in the Championship and League One. When the club was relegated in 2005, it signified the end of 27 successive seasons of top-flight football.

SAINTS' PAST

Formed in 1885 by members of St Mary's Church Young Men's Association (hence the nickname "Saints"), Southampton joined the newly formed Football League Division Three in 1920. Promotion followed two years later and marked the start of a 31-year stay in Division Two. In 1966, the club secured a long-awaited promotion to Division One and would stay there for eight years before falling victim to a new "bottom-three-down" relegation ruling. Promotion wouldn't be achieved again for four years, but during this hiatus Southampton produced perhaps their greatest achievement to date – an against-all-odds FA Cup final victory over Division One's Manchester United in 1976. Once back in the top flight, the south-coast club would stay there for almost 30 years, attaining a hugely impressive runners-up spot in 1984 and introducing the genius of Matthew Le Tissier to the English game in the early 1990s. The first midfielder to score 100 goals, Le Tissier's performances can be credited with greatly helping the Saints to maintain their top-tier status. However, their run ended in 2004/05, when even the headline-grabbing appointment of former Portsmouth boss Harry Redknapp couldn't save them from relegation and they bid a temporary farewell to the upper echelons of the English game.

THE SAINTS GO MARCHING ON?

Restored to the Premier League after finishing as runners-up in the Championship last season, survival will be Southampton's main concern in 2012/13. Retaining last year's Championship top scorer Rickie Lambert is essential, as is shoring up their defence. But buoyed by their lengthy stay at the top last time, the Saints will want to set up camp for good.

DID YOU KNOW?
Striker Rickie Lambert has won a divisional Golden Boot in three of his past four seasons (2008/09, 09/10 and 11/12)

*ONLY EARLIEST RESULT STATED

★**PREMIER STAR** ■ Matt Le Tissier ■ Appearances: 443 ■ 1986-2002

One of the greatest ever penalty takers (he converted 47 of 48 attempts) and a scorer of magical, incredulous goals. Le Tissier spent his entire professional career with Saints, whose fans nicknamed him "Le God".

||||||||||||||||||||||||||||||||||||||||||||||||||||||||||||||||||||||||||||||||||||||||||||||||||||||||||||||||||

Full name **Bolton Wanderers Football Club** | Nickname(s) **The Trotters / The Wanderers** | Founded **1874** | Ground **Reebok Stadium** (28,101)

BOLTON

They've wandered out of the top flight but the Trotters hope for a speedy return

PREMIER FACTFILE

Club homepage
bwfc.co.uk

Rivals Blackburn
Rovers, Bury

**Premier League
Seasons** 13

Highest position
6th (2004/05)

Lowest position
20th (1995/96)

**Biggest victory in
Premier League**
0-5 v Leicester
18 August 2001*

Biggest defeat in PL
0-6 v Manchester Utd
25 February 1996*

Biggest transfer paid
£8.2m to Toulouse for
Johan Elmander

**Biggest transfer
received**
£15m from Chelsea for
Nicolas Anelka

*ONLY FIRST RESULT STATED

Seasons played	13
Played	494
Won	149
Drawn	128
Lost	217
Goals for	575
Goals against	745
Goal difference	-170
Points	575
Relegations	3
Average points	44.23

BYE BYE BOLTON

The Premier League's 20th season was not one to celebrate for Bolton, marking as it did their exit from the top flight after an 11-year stay. Their campaigns have been tumultuous to say the least, in some seasons clinging on for survival by the narrowest of margins and in others wildly overachieving and landing consecutive top-10 finishes. While the Trotters' brand of football has not always won them admiration, it has proved effective.

IN THE PAST

Founded as Christ Church FC in 1874, the club became Bolton Wanderers three years later, the name reflecting the problems they encountered in finding a permanent ground (they used three different venues in their first four years of existence). Bolton's heyday remains the 1920s, when they won the FA Cup three times. Major honours have been thin on the ground since, with the club's darkest days occurring during the 15 years spent outside of the top flight from 1980. In 1995, the Trotters got their first taste of Premiership football, but it was not a happy return to the top tier of the English league. They were bottom for practically the whole season and despite managerial changes halfway through the campaign (Colin Todd taking over from Roy McFarland), the damage was done and Bolton could not avoid relegation. Promotion back to the Premier League would be achieved twice more in the next few years and during their third tenure, from 2001, Bolton determined on a lengthier stay. 'Big' Sam Allardyce surprised everyone by taking the club to four consecutive top-10 finishes, even cementing sixth spot in 2004/05 to bring Bolton their first UEFA Cup qualification.

DID YOU KNOW?
Not qualifying as a city, Bolton is the largest town in Britain. And 'Big' Sam Allardyce is 6ft 3in.

LOOKING FORWARD

Though relegation will be hard to accept, Wanderers have proved on a number of occasions that they have what it takes to bounce back. Having tested themselves against Premier League opposition for more than a decade, manager Owen Coyle will be confident he has the resources to guide them back to top-flight competition at the first time of asking.

★**PREMIER STAR** ■ **Jay-Jay Okocha** ■ **Appearances: 124** ■ **2002-2006**

"So good they named him twice" was the legend emblazoned across many a T-shirt worn by Bolton fans. A great big smiling bag of tricks and stunts and subterfuge and pure footballing joy. Did anyone not love Jay-Jay Okocha?

|||||||||||||||||||||||||||||||||||||||||||||||||||||||||||||||||||||||||||||||||||||||||||||||||||||||||||||||||||

Full name **Fulham Football Club** | Nickname(s) **The Cottagers / The Whites / The Lilywhites** | Founded **1879** | Ground **Craven Cottage** (25,700)

FULHAM

After their Great Escape, the old boys of London have a spring in their step

PREMIER FACTFILE

Club homepage
fulhamfc.com

Rivals Chelsea, QPR

Premier League Seasons 11

Highest position
7th (2008/09)

Lowest position
17th (2007/08)

Biggest victory in Premier League
6-0 v Norwich
15 May 2005*

Biggest defeat in Premier League
0-5 v Manchester Utd
21 December 2011

Biggest transfer paid
£11.5m to Olympique
Lyon for Steve Marlet

Biggest transfer received
£12.8m from
Manchester United
for Louis Saha

Seasons played	**11**
Played	418
Won	130
Drawn	121
Lost	167
Goals for	480
Goals against	552
Goal difference	-72
Points	511
Relegations	0
Average points	46.45

HODGSON HIGHS

Having achieved promotion to the Premier League in 2000/01, the Cottagers initially troubled only the lower regions of the table. Managers such as Jean Tigana, Chris Coleman and Lawrie Sanchez came and went before Roy Hodgson took the helm. He masterminded the 'Great Escape' of 2007/08 (when Fulham were twice mathematically relegated during open play in the closing stages of the season), secured the club's highest league finish the season after (seventh) and took them to the Europa League final in 2009/10, beating Juventus and Shakhtar Donetsk on the way. After Hodgson moved to Liverpool in 2010/11, Mark Hughes took control, but a successful season and eighth place wasn't enough for the Welshman, who preferred ambitious unemployment to managing a top-10 Premier League club – ironically, he was to later wash up at QPR. Dutchman Martin Jol was appointed and his attack-minded game led to another top-10 finish in 2011/12.

DID YOU KNOW?
Fulham are the oldest of London's professional football clubs. Their first pro signing was J H Love

START TO ALMOST FINISHED

Formed in 1879 as Fulham St Andrews Church Sunday School FC, the club turned professional in 1898, having moved to Craven Cottage in 1894. Fulham spent much of their time bouncing between leagues and suffered one of the biggest FA Cup semi-final defeats in 1907/08, losing 6-0 to Newcastle United. But they have produced many England legends over the years, including George Cohen, Bobby Robson and Rodney Marsh, while their greatest player is arguably Johnny Haynes. In 1975 they lost 2-0 to West Ham in the FA Cup final and reached a nadir of being second-bottom in the Football League in the mid-1990s before Mr Al Fayed bought them and pushed for the top flight.

THE FUTURE'S BRIGHT

Oranjeman Jol continues to implement his attacking philosophy at Craven Cottage, but keeping two of the club's star players, Clint Dempsey and Moussa Dembélé, will be crucial for the Whites going forward.

*ONLY FIRST RESULT STATED

★**PREMIER STAR** ■ Clint Dempsey ■ Appearances: 184 ■ 2007-Present

A wonderful goalscoring record from midfield marks Clint Dempsey out as the greatest American ever to have played in the Premier League. Alongside Simon Davies, he is currently the longest-serving player at the Cottage.

||||||||||||||||||||||||||||||||||||||||||||||||||||||||||||||||||||||||||||||||||||||||||||||||||||||||||||||||||||||||||||||||||||||||

Full name **Sunderland Association Football Club** | Nickname **The Black Cats** | Founded **1879** | Ground **Stadium of Light** (48,707)

SUNDERLAND

They're the proverbial yo-yo club, but the Black Cats can still spring a surprise

PREMIER FACTFILE

Club homepage
safc.com

Rivals Newcastle

Premier League Seasons 11

Highest position
7th (1999/2000, 2000/01)

Lowest position
20th (2002/03, 2005/06)

Biggest victory in Premier League
0-5 v Derby
18 September 1999

Biggest defeat in PL
7-1 v Everton
24 November 2007

Biggest transfer paid
£13m to Rennes for Asamoah Gyan

Biggest transfer received
£24m from Aston Villa for Darren Bent

Seasons played	11
Played	418
Won	112
Drawn	104
Lost	202
Goals for	422
Goals against	606
Goal difference	-184
Points	440
Relegations	3
Average points	40.00

CATS ON A HOT TIN ROOF

Sunderland's relationship with the Premier League can only be described as up and down. Promoted for the 1995/96 season, they were instantly relegated, bounced back in 1999/00 and were relegated again in 2002/03. They were back in 2005, but only lasted a season before dropping down again (with a then record low of 15 points) before securing promotion in 2006/07. Phew! The club left Roker Park in 1997 for the Stadium of Light and the team have been through numerous managers since, including Mick McCarthy and Manchester United alumni Roy Keane and Steve Bruce. Former Aston Villa manager Martin O'Neill was appointed in late 2011.

TEACHERS

Formed as Sunderland & District Teachers AFC in 1879, the club dominated the Football League up until 1936, claiming six league titles and the FA Cup (1937). Big money was spent in the post-war years (notably £18,000 for Ivor Broadis, Carlisle's player/manager, who became the first footballer to transfer himself), but the 1950s were marked by financial scandal and relegation (in 1958) was the result. The Black Cats won the FA Cup in 1973 as a second-division team – beating Leeds 1-0, which was no mean feat – but 1987 brought relegation to Division Three. They quickly returned to Division Two and, in 1992, lost the FA Cup final 2-0 to Liverpool. Peter Reid was appointed manager in 1995 and he steered Sunderland clear of relegation and into the Premier League.

> **DID YOU KNOW?**
> Kevin Phillips is the only Englishman to win the European Golden Shoe award, after scoring 30 goals in 1999/00

MID-TABLE FLUX

Sunderland, like a handful of other Premier League clubs, find themselves in a slight state of flux. The league has become so competitive that any teams outside of the perennially successful top four or five sides could easily find themselves relegation fodder without astute leadership and investment. Fortunately, they have O'Neill steering the ship, but – having lost Darren Bent to Aston Villa and Asamoah Gyan on loan to Al Ain in the UAE – recruiting potent goalscoring power before the 2012/13 season starts is crucial to their chances of staying up.

★**PREMIER STAR** ∎ **Kevin Phillips** ∎ **Appearances: 239** ∎ **1997-2003**

A veritable goal machine. Turn him up to full match-day pace and there's not much you could do to stop Kevin Phillips. The tiny terror is currently Sunderland's post-war record goalscorer, with 134 in 239 appearances. Awesome.

Full name **Coventry City Football Club** | Nickname **The Sky Blues** | Founded **1883** | Ground **Ricoh Arena** (32,609)

COVENTRY CITY

From success and glory to gloom and doom, but think of the memories...

THE DUBLINERS

Coventry were relegated from the Premier League in 2001, dropping out of the first tier of English football for the first time in 34 years, but served up an exciting brand of football during their golden era. They seemed destined for a top-10 finish in the Premier League's inaugural year, but slipped to 15th after a barren run. Phil Neal took them to their highest finish (11th) the next season, but was sacked in 1994/95 after poor results.

SKY'S THE LIMIT

Ron Atkinson took over and brought his usual flashes of success and bravado, but Coventry would have been relegated in 1996/97 had Middlesbrough not been deducted points for not fulfilling a fixture. With Gordon Strachan at the helm Coventry finished 11th, 15th and 14th, but couldn't stem the downward slide in 2001. In 2011/12, they dropped to the third tier of English football for the first time in 48 years.

> **DID YOU KNOW?**
> Dion Dublin once invented a percussion instrument called the Dube and played with Ocean Colour Scene

★ **PREMIER STAR**

■ **Dion Dublin** ■ **Appearances: 145** ■ **1994-1998**

Started as a centre-back so knew how to make them suffer. Imposing and dynamic, he scored 23 goals in 1997/98.

*ONLY FIRST RESULT STATED

Seasons played	Played	Won	Drawn	Lost	GF	GA	GD	Pts	Relegated	Average pts
9	354	99	112	143	387	490	-103	409	1	45.40

Full name **Sheffield Wednesday Football Club** | Nickname(s) **The Owls** | Founded **1867** | Ground **Hillsborough Stadium** (39, 732)

SHEFFIELD WEDS

Wednesday didn't used to be Orange

★ **PREMIER STAR**

■ **Des Walker** ■ **Appearances: 309** ■ **1993-2001**

A tough-tackling, pacy centre-back who won the captain's armband and fans' affections in 300-plus appearances.

HISTORY BOYS

One of the oldest football clubs in the world, Sheffield Wednesday have recently begun a climb back to the big time: Dave Jones securing second-tier football on the last day of the 2011/12 season in front of 38,802 home supporters. In 1976, the Owls nearly slipped down to the fourth division, but by 1992 were founding members of the Premier League. In fact, 1992/93 was one of their most successful. With Trevor Francis at the helm, they finished seventh and reached the League Cup and FA Cup finals, losing to Arsenal in both. No silverware or European jaunt, but widespread acclaim.

BYE, BYE

A succession of managers failed to live up to Francis (although David Pleat did get seventh in 1996/97) and the expensively assembled squad of 1999/2000 – which included referee-shoving Paulo Di Canio – were relegated. The Owls haven't been back since.

> **DID YOU KNOW?**
> Sheffield Wednesday was initially a cricket club named after the day of the week on which they played

*ONLY FIRST RESULT STATED

Seasons played	Played	Won	Drawn	Lost	GF	GA	GD	Pts	Relegations	Average pts
8	316	101	89	126	409	453	-44	392	1	49.00

|||||||||||||||||||||||||||||||||||||||||||||||||||||||||||||||||||||||||||||||||||||||||||||||||||||||||||||||||||||||||||||

Full name **Wimbledon Football Club** | Nickname(s) **The Dons / The Wombles / The Crazy Gang** | Founded **1892** | Ground **Stadium mk** (22,000)

WIMBLEDON

Round the bend, up the road and on course for more upsets

★ **PREMIER STAR**

■ **Dean Holdsworth** ■ **Appearances: 169** ■ **1992-1997**

A hugely powerful old-school forward who was perfectly suited to Wimbledon's style of play and reaped the benefits.

MUST BE CRAZY

Wimbledon's Crazy Gang upset many more-fashionable clubs during their time in the top flight, shocking and delighting in equal measure with their approach. They finished a brilliant sixth in the 1993/94 season, ninth in the next campaign and even made their bow in Europe in the Intertoto Cup. The rot started in 1997/98 and the club were relegated on 14 May 2000 after eight years in the Premier League.

DID YOU KNOW?
The Dons' preparation for one game v Man Utd was to play Bulldog – no tactics, just pick up the ball and fight

MK DONS

Wimbledon fans have been put through the mill in the past 20 years. The club moved from Plough Lane in 1991 to ground share with Crystal Palace: a move that lasted 12 years before, in May 2002, the club was given permission to move 56 miles north to Milton Keynes. A large portion of supporters took umbrage at upping sticks and set up their own club, AFC Wimbledon. Wimbledon became the Milton Keynes Dons in June 2004.

| Seasons played 8 | Played 316 | Won 99 | Drawn 94 | Lost 123 | GF 384 | GA 472 | GD -88 | Pts 391 | Relegations 1 | Average pts 48.88 |

|||||||||||||||||||||||||||||||||||||||||||||||||||||||||||||||||||||||||||||||||||||||||||||||||||||||||||||||||||||||||||||

Full name **Charlton Athletic Football Club** | Nickname **The Addicks** | Founded **1905** | Ground **The Valley** (27,111)

CHARLTON

Can *you* remember when they threatened the Champions League spots?

CURB YOUR...

Charlton have had two periods in the Premier League, 1998/99 and 2000-2007. After two games of their first stint they surprised everyone by being top of the pile, but were then sucked into a relegation battle, which they eventually lost. The board kept faith with manager Alan Curbishley though, and the club bounced straight back up as First-Division champions to enjoy a more prolonged spell at the top.

DID YOU KNOW?
The most likely origin of "Addicks" is from a local fishmonger who rewarded the team with haddock and chips

...ENTHUSIASM

Curbishley gently established the club in the top flight to the point where, in 2003/04, they dared to challenge for a Champions League place. The surprise sale of star player Scott Parker to Chelsea didn't help, though, and Charlton had to settle for seventh place. After 15 years in charge, Curbishley left in 2006 and, despite being handed more money than Curbishley ever had, Iain Dowie could not avoid relegation.

★ **PREMIER STAR**

■ **Mark Kinsella** ■ **Appearances: 208** ■ **1996-2002**

One of the top midfielders in the country in 1998/99, Kinsella's loyalty greatly endeared him to fans.

| Seasons played 8 | Played 304 | Won 93 | Drawn 82 | Lost 129 | GF 342 | GA 442 | GD -100 | Pts 361 | Relegations 2 | Average pts 45.13 |

Full name **Leicester City Football Club** | Nickname **The Foxes** | Founded **1884** | Ground **King Power Stadium** (32,269)

LEICESTER

At one point, the Foxes well and truly had their Premier League tails up

DR MARTIN

Rather than a particular star player or a wealthy benefactor, it was the managerial nous of Martin O'Neill that raised the East Midlands club above and beyond anyone's expectations. Under the Northern Irishman's guidance, Leicester City won immediate promotion to the Premier League and four successive top-10 finishes with players such as Tony Cottee, Muzzy Izzet and Neil Lennon.

TINKER TAYLOR

League Cup wins in 1997 and 2000 meant European football for Leicester for the first time in nearly 40 years, and envious looks from so-called bigger clubs. However, O'Neill realised he had achieved all he could with the club and left for Celtic in 2000. Two years later, after Peter Taylor had squandered £23m in transfer money, Micky Adams was at the helm when the club were relegated, the last game of that season also being the last at Filbert Street.

DID YOU KNOW?
There are three foxy characters associated with LCFC: Filbert Fox, Vicky Vixen and, oddly, Cousin Dennis

★ **PREMIER STAR**

■ **Muzzy Izzet** ■ **Appearances: 266** ■ **1996-2004**

A gifted little genius who could carve and concoct while Neil Lennon did his dirty work. A vital cog in O'Neill's machine.

*ONLY FIRST RESULT STATED

PREMIER FACTFILE

Club homepage
lcfc.com

Rivals Notts Forest, Derby, Coventry City

PL Seasons 8

Highest position
8th (1999/2000)

Lowest position
21st (1994/95)

Biggest victory in PL
0-4 v Derby
26 April 1998

Biggest defeat in PL
6-1 v Arsenal
26 December 2000*

Biggest transfer paid
£5.5m to Wolves for Matt Mills

Biggest transfer received
£11m from Liverpool for Emile Heskey

Seasons played 8	Played 308	Won 84	Drawn 90	Lost 134	GF 354	GA 456	GD -102	Pts 342	Relegations 3	Average pts 42.75

Full name **Birmingham City Football Club** | Nickname **Blues** | Founded **1875** | Ground **St Andrew's** (30,009)

BIRMINGHAM CITY

Determined not to spend another lifetime in Villa's shadow

★ **PREMIER STAR**

■ **Christophe Dugarry** ■ **Appearances: 30** ■ **2003-2004**

A class above everyone at Birmingham. Was at AC Milan, Barcelona and Marseille before St Andrew's. Great pedigree.

ON THE UP

Before Steve Bruce was lured from Crystal Palace in 2001/02 to take the Blues to the Premier League via a play-offs final penalty shoot-out, the club had been away from the top flight for 16 years. During that time, Barry Fry had used 47 players in one season; Trevor Francis had taken the club to the League Cup final in 2001; and their ground had been updated. In short, they were ready for a return to the big time.

DID YOU KNOW?
Under Alex McLeish in 2009/10, the Blues finished ninth – their highest English league finish for 50 years

BIG TALK

Signing Christophe Dugarry on loan during their first top-flight season was inspired: the Frenchman's five-in-five goal haul was decisive in retaining Premier League status and in finishing above arch-rivals Villa, in 13th place. Three more Premier League seasons followed before David Gold declared in 2005/06 that it was "time to start talking about being as good as anyone outside the top four" – and Birmingham were relegated.

*ONLY EARLIEST RESULT STATED

PREMIER FACTFILE

Club homepage
bcfc.com

Rivals Aston Villa

PL Seasons 7

Highest position
9th (2009/10)

Lowest position
19th (2007/08)

Biggest victory in Premier League
5-0 v Portsmouth
21 January 2006

Biggest defeat in PL
0-5 v Man Utd
21 January 2011*

Biggest transfer paid
£6m to Valencia for Nikola Zigic

Biggest transfer received
£6.5m from Liverpool for Jermaine Pennant

Seasons played 7	Played 266	Won 73	Drawn 82	Lost 111	GF 273	GA 360	GD -87	Pts 301	Relegations 3	Average pts 43.00

||||||||||||||||||||||||||||||||||||||||||||||||||||||||||||||||||||||||||||||||||||||||||||||||||||||||||

Full name **Wigan Athletic Football Club** | Nickname **The Latics** | Founded **1932** | Ground **DW Stadium** (25,138)

WIGAN

Whelan's club that simply refuse to go down

★ PREMIER STAR

■ **Arjan de Zeeuw** ■ **Apps: 178** ■ **1999-2002 & 2005-2007**

One of the most committed defenders the Premier League has ever seen. Plenty of aggression, never any malice.

JUST A BABY

Formed in 1932 after the demise of Wigan Borough, making them the youngest club in the Premier League, Wigan Athletic's seven-year stay marks the only top-flight run in the club's history. Besides engineering some truly Houdini-esque relegation escapes during this time, the Latics' biggest achievement has been an astonishing 10th-place finish in their first Premier League campaign of 2005/06.

DID YOU KNOW?
Wigan's French defender Pascal Chimbonda was named in the 2005/06 PFA Team of the Season

WHELAN YEARS

Arriving in the Football League in 1978, it wasn't until local millionaire Dave Whelan bought the Division Three club in 1995 that Wigan could mount a serious assault on top-tier football. Tenth place in their inaugural Premier League season and a League Cup runners-up medal was a good start, but the subsequent years have not been easy. Time and again though, Wigan have proved the naysayers wrong. Gutsy stuff.

PREMIER FACTFILE

Club homepage
wiganlatics.co.uk

Rivals Bolton

PL Seasons 7

Highest position
10th (2005/06)

Lowest position
17th (2006/07)

Biggest victory in PL
0-5 v Hull
(30 Aug 2008)

Biggest defeat in PL
9-1 v Spurs
22 November 2009

Biggest transfer paid
£7m to Newcastle for
Charles N'Zogbia

Biggest transfer received
£15m from Man Utd for
Antonio Valencia

Seasons played 7 | **Played** 266 | **Won** 76 | **Drawn** 67 | **Lost** 123 | **GF** 269 | **GA** 409 | **GD** -140 | **Pts** 295 | **Relegations** 0 | **Average pts** 42.14

||||||||||||||||||||||||||||||||||||||||||||||||||||||||||||||||||||||||||||||||||||||||||||||||||||||||||

Full name **Portsmouth Football Club** | Nickname **Pompey** | Founded **1898** | Ground **Fratton Park** (20,224)

PORTSMOUTH

Money doesn't make you happy...

...DOES IT?

Oh, okay, it does a little bit. Without the millions poured into the club by Milan Mandaric, Portsmouth would not have enjoyed the successes of 2003-10, which included winning the FA Cup, a televised 4-1 home win over Southampton and entertaining AC Milan at the dilapidated Fratton Park.

DID YOU KNOW?
Pompey have held the FA Cup for the longest period in history: six years – because of the Second World War

RAILS OFF

Portsmouth needed to move forward off the field to build upon the success on it, but the bloke with the calculator seemed to have taken a sabbatical. By the end of their Premier League stay in 2009/10, Pompey – a team with the England goalkeeper, right-back and strikeforce, and two midfielders who would later play at Real Madrid and Inter Milan – paid the price for their over-extension. They were docked nine points by the FA after becoming the first top-flight club to go into administration and were relegated.

★ PREMIER STAR

■ **David James** ■ **Appearances: 134** ■ **2006-2010**

Kept clean sheets in his first five appearances for the club and enjoyed his finest spells as a Pompey player.

PREMIER FACTFILE

Club homepage
portsmouthfc.co.uk

Rivals Southampton

PL Seasons 7

Highest position
8th (2007/08)

Lowest position
20th (2009/10)

Biggest victory in Premier League
6-1 v Leeds
8 November 2003

Biggest defeat in PL
6-0 v Manchester City
21 September 2008

Biggest transfer paid
£11m to Liverpool for
Peter Crouch

Biggest transfer received
£20m from Real Madrid
for Lassana Diarra

Seasons played 7 | **Played** 266 | **Won** 79 | **Drawn** 65 | **Lost** 122 | **GF** 292 | **GA** 380 | **GD** -88 | **Pts** 293 | **Relegations** 1 | **Average pts** 41.90

Full name **Derby County Football Club** | Nickname **The Rams** | Founded **1884** | Ground **Pride Park** (33,597)

DERBY

The Rams were far from sheepish in the Premier League of the late 90s...

TOUGH AT THE TOP

Derby's most recent attempt at Premier League success was a disaster. Billy Davies was appointed manager in June 2006 and took them up, but left the club by mutual consent in November 2007 and his successor, Paul Jewell, could not prevent the Premier League's earliest relegation to date, in March 2008.

BOOMING 90s

Jim Smith had fared better with his team of the 1990s. Hired in 1995, after Roy McFarland failed in the play-offs final, his early acquisition of Croatian defender Igor Stimac was to prove crucial. Dean Sturridge's goals also played a key part in the 12th-place finish of 1996/97 and the Rams would toast their new 30,000-seater home, Pride Park, with consecutive top-10 finishes. The turn of the millennium wasn't as kind and John Gregory's side were relegated after six years in the top division.

DID YOU KNOW?
Derby are one of 10 clubs to have competed in every season of the Football League since its formation in 1888

★ PREMIER **STAR**

■ Igor Stimac ■ Appearances: 84 ■ 1995-1999

Style, presence, class: Stimac was Jim Smith's best signing. Played for Croatia at World Cup 1998 and finished third.

PREMIER FACTFILE

Club homepage dcfc.co.uk

Rivals Forest

PL Seasons 7

Highest position 8th (1998/99)

Lowest position 20th (2007/08)

Biggest victory in PL 4-0 v Southampton 27 September 1997*

Biggest defeat in PL 6-0 v Liverpool 1 September 2007*

Biggest transfer paid £3.5m to Norwich City for Robert Earnshaw

Biggest transfer received £7m from Leeds United for Seth Johnson

*ONLY FIRST RESULT STATED

| Seasons played 7 | Played 266 | Won 68 | Drawn 70 | Lost 128 | GF 271 | GA 420 | GD -149 | Pts 274 | Relegations 2 | Average pts 39.10 |

Full name **Queens Park Rangers Football Club** | Nickname(s) **QPR / Hoops** | Founded **1882** | Ground **Loftus Road** (18,360)

QPR

Well, that was an uneventful return, wasn't it...

★ PREMIER **STAR**

■ Les Ferdinand ■ Appearances: 163 ■ 1987-1995

Wonderfully resilient and willing target man, with a powerful shot and an incredible leap. A formidable presence.

HOOPS & DOWNS

Founder members of the Premier League, the famous hoops of QPR finished fifth in 1992/93, the highest of all the London sides, with star striker Les Ferdinand topping their goalscoring charts with 20 goals in 37 games. He would score 16 in 36 the next season and 24 in 1994/95 before being tempted away to Newcastle United for £6m. He couldn't be replaced and Rangers went down.

DID YOU KNOW?
QPR have played at 16 different locations throughout northwest London since their formation in 1882

HOOPS, I DID IT...

In 2011/12, QPR were back in the top flight. Adel Taarabt's 19 goals and performances in the Championship had earned him plaudits, but he didn't hit the same heights in the Premier League. However, QPR survived a crazy season that included a change of owner and manager, and escaping relegation by one point on the last day, despite having their captain sent off and losing in the final seconds to title-chasing (and thus title-winning) Manchester City.

PREMIER FACTFILE

Club homepage qpr.co.uk

Rivals Chelsea

PL Seasons 5

Highest position 5th (1992/93)

Lowest position 19th (1995/96)

Biggest victory in Premier League 5-1 v Coventry 23 October 1993

Biggest defeat in PL 6-0 v Fulham 2 October 2011

Biggest transfer paid £6m to Fulham for Bobby Zamora

Biggest transfer received £6m from Newcastle Utd for Les Ferdinand

| Seasons played 5 | Played 202 | Won 69 | Drawn 46 | Lost 87 | GF 267 | GA 298 | GD -31 | Pts 253 | Relegations 1 | Average pts 50.60 |

Full name **Norwich City Football Club** | Nickname **The Canaries** | Founded **1902** | Ground **Carrow Road** (27,033)

NORWICH

Delia gets some icing for her cake, now let's be 'avin' you!

★ **PREMIER STAR**

■ Grant Holt ■ Appearances: 120 ■ 2009-2012

A crafty, lumbering handful, with a surprisingly deft touch – so good in 2011/12 he nearly made the England squad.

RECENT WORK

Norwich have had three spells in the Premier League, their first and last stints garnering the most affection. Under the unerring stewardship of Paul Lambert in 2011/12, Norwich blazed a yellow trail, finishing 12th, with Grant Holt outscoring Edin Dzeko, Mario Balotelli and Luis Suárez along the way.

CITY SLICKERS

Despite selling star striker Robert Fleck to Chelsea when the Premier League started in 1992/93, Norwich led the way with six games to go before dropping behind Aston Villa and Manchester United. Inspired by Bryan Gunn, captain Ian Butterworth and Mark Robins, they were an elegant and effective unit, but never really recovered from the loss of Mike Walker to Everton and Chris Sutton to Blackburn. The next season they finished mid-table before nosediving to relegation misery in 1994/95.

DID YOU KNOW?
Norwich City were originally known as the Citizens and played in blue-and-white shirts

PREMIER FACTFILE

Club homepage
canaries.co.uk

Rivals Ipswich Town

PL Seasons 5

Highest position
3rd (1992/93)

Lowest position
20th (1994/95)

Biggest victory in PL
5-1 v Everton
25 September 1993

Biggest defeat in PL
7-1 v Blackburn
3 October 1992

Biggest transfer paid
£3.5m to West Brom for Robert Earnshaw

Biggest transfer received
£7.5m from West Ham for Dean Ashton

Seasons played 5	Played 202	Won 62	Drawn 62	Lost 78	GF 257	GA 323	GD -66	Pts 248	Relegations 2	Average pts 49.60

Full name **Nottingham Forest Football Club** | Nickname **Forest** | Founded **1865** | Ground **City Ground** (30,576)

NOTT'M FOREST

Sometimes you can't see the wood for the trees at the City Ground

OL' BIG'EAD

Forest legend Brian Clough resigned his 18-year tenure at the club after relegation in the first Premier League season. Striker Teddy Sheringham had left for Spurs and Des Walker for Sampdoria.

STAN THE MAN

Frank Clark, a manager with an unremarkable CV at the time, orchestrated a quick return to the top flight and led Forest to third place in the 1994/95 season. Stan Collymore and Brian Roy forged a fearsome partnership and helped seal a UEFA Cup campaign. Forest were the only English side to reach the last eight of a European competition the following season, but after Collymore left for Liverpool they struggled for goals. Pierre van Hooijdonk couldn't save them, but his partnership with Kevin Campbell brought them back up. However, under 'Big Ron' Atkinson, who only won four out of 16 games, they were swiftly relegated again.

DID YOU KNOW?
Forest donated shirts to Arsenal and Liverpool to help the clubs get established – both still wear red today

★ **PREMIER STAR**

■ Stan Collymore ■ Appearances: 65 ■ 1993-1995

A rampaging goal machine, who used to run riot through defences, pillaging goalmouths and bursting nets.

PREMIER FACTFILE

Club homepage
nottinghamforest.co.uk

Rivals Derby County

PL Seasons 5

Highest position
3rd (1994/95)

Lowest position
22nd (1992/93)

Biggest victory in Premier League
1-7 v Sheffield Weds
1 April 1995

Biggest defeat in PL
8-1 v Manchester Utd
6 February 1999

Biggest transfer paid
£3.5m to Celtic for Pierre van Hooijdonk

Biggest transfer received
£8.5m from Liverpool for Stan Collymore

Seasons played 5	Played 198	Won 60	Drawn 59	Lost 79	GF 229	GA 287	GD -58	Pts 239	Relegations 3	Average pts 47.80

Full name **Ipswich Town Football Club** | Nickname **The Tractor Boys** | Founded **1878** | Ground **Portman Road** (30,311)

IPSWICH

The Tractor Boys made hay while the sun shone

BRIEF HISTORY

Ipswich once scaled the Premier League table to finish in an extraordinary fifth place, but are now in the Championship. They claimed the Division One title in 1962, but the club's most notable era was in the late 1970s and early 80s, when FA Cup and UEFA Cup triumphs were masterminded by the great Sir Bobby Robson.

DID YOU KNOW?
In March 2012, Portman Road's South Stand was renamed after 1966 England boss Sir Alf Ramsey

UP AND DOWN

Ipswich Town's introduction to the newly formed Premier League was not a happy one. Three years of struggle (not to mention a record 9-0 defeat at the hands of Manchester United) ended in their relegation in 1995. But an incredible return in 2000/01 resulted in them grabbing fifth spot. It was not a portent of things to come, however, and in 2002 the club was demoted once more. This led to administration and a downward spiral that the club has done well to recover from.

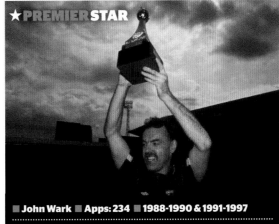

★ **PREMIER STAR**

■ **John Wark** ■ **Apps: 234** ■ **1988-1990 & 1991-1997**

One of four inaugural members of the club's Hall of Fame, the goal-grabbing midfielder is synonymous with Ipswich.

Seasons played	5	Played	202	Won	57	Drawn	53	Lost	92	GF	219	GA	312	GD	-93	Pts	224	Relegations	2	Average pts	44.80

Full name **West Bromwich Albion Football Club** | Nickname **The Baggies** | Founded **1878** | Ground **The Hawthorns** (26,272)

WEST BROM

You never know quite what to expect from the Baggies in the top tier

★ **PREMIER STAR**

■ **Russell Hoult** ■ **Appearances: 190** ■ **2001-2007**

As dependable a keeper as you could hope to have, Hoult's presence inspired the rest of West Brom's backline.

TOP FLIGHT

They have spent the majority of their history playing in the top flight, but when the Premier League was born in 1992, West Bromwich Albion were languishing in English football's third tier. They pulled themselves back up the pyramid, but their relationship with the Premier League has been a turbulent one.

DID YOU KNOW?
West Brom's record victory to date has been their 12-0 league win over Darwen on 4 April 1892

MEGSON YEARS

While historically they have always held a strong league position, it wasn't until 2000 that the Baggies made a realistic, concerted effort to reach the Premier League. Gary Megson would be the man to take them there in 2002, but before West Brom could get too settled they were hit with the ignominy of instant relegation. The archetypal yo-yo club, Albion were promoted and relegated twice more over the next few years, before returning again in 2010. How long they stay for this time is anyone's guess.

*ONLY FIRST RESULT STATED

Seasons played	6	Played	228	Won	52	Drawn	60	Lost	116	GF	233	GA	374	GD	-141	Pts	216	Relegations	3	Average pts	36.00

Full name **Stoke City Football Club** | Nickname **The Potters** | Founded **1863** | Ground **Britannia Stadium** (27,740)

STOKE

Pulis's boys are gonna take some barging off the captain's table

■ **Abdoulaye Faye** ■ **Appearances: 81** ■ **2008-2011**

Took the captaincy after his first year and wore the badge with pride. Gave everything on the pitch, every game.

POT SHOTS

Though relative newbies to the Premier League – arriving on the scene in 2008 – Stoke City are the oldest club in the division, having been founded in 1863. In the 1930s and early 40s, the team featured Stanley Matthews, one of England's greatest players, and they reached the League Cup final in 1964. They lost that game to Leicester, but their first (and, as yet, only) major trophy came eight years later in the same competition, 2-1 against Chelsea.

DID YOU KNOW?
Only Notts County (formed in 1862) are older than Stoke City in the whole of the English football league

TOUGH LOVE

Stoke have started to carve a place for themselves in the Premier League thanks to manager Tony Pulis and a physicality that has become synonymous with the club. Last season they competed in Europe after an FA Cup final appearance and while last season's 14th-place finish was a dip, few expect Stoke to exit the top flight anytime soon.

Seasons played	Played	Won	Drawn	Lost	GF	GA	GD	Pts	Relegations	Average pts
4	152	47	42	63	154	204	-50	183	0	45.75

Full name **Crystal Palace Football Club** | Nickname **Eagles** | Founded **1905** | Ground **Selhurst Park** (26,309)

CRYSTAL PALACE

Eagles climbing and diving, but when will they soar?

FOUR RICHER...

Talk about not knowing what to wear for the party: Crystal Palace have been relegated and promoted to and from the Premier League on four occasions.

...FOUR POORER

In the inaugural Premier League season, they were relegated on goal difference, despite amassing 49 points from 42 games; in 1994/95 they reached the semi-finals of both domestic cups, but again couldn't score enough goals and were relegated on the last day; in 1997/98, despite acquiring the services of 'Bald Eagle' Attilio Lombardo and Tomas Brolin, they nosedived with just 33 points; and in 2004/05, the efforts of Iain Dowie and goal machine Andy Johnson (21 strikes) were not enough to prevent relegation on 15 May 2005 after a nail-biting, final-day 2-2 draw with Charlton Athletic. Palace are the only team to have been relegated from the Premier League four times.

DID YOU KNOW?
Steve Coppell took the Palace manager's job on four occasions: 1984-93, 1995-96, 1997-98 and 1999-2000

★ **PREMIER STAR**

■ **Attilio Lombardo** ■ **Appearances: 43** ■ **1997-1999**

Regarded as the best player ever to wear the shirt. Couldn't keep the Eagles up, but his wizardry almost made up for it.

Seasons played	Played	Won	Drawn	Lost	GF	GA	GD	Pts	Relegations	Average pts
4	160	37	49	74	160	243	-83	160	4	40.00

Full name **Wolverhampton Wanderers Football Club** | Nickname **Wolves** | Founded **1877** | Ground **Molineux** (27,828)

WOLVES

Will they ever replicate the club's truly golden era?

BIG TEETH

Having endured a torrid time in the Premier League last season, the sun finally set on Wolves' three-year stint in the top flight, which had been a marked improvement on their last outing at that level, which lasted for a solitary season. Formed in 1877, Wolves, managed by former player Stan Cullis, made a big noise in the 1950s, winning three Division One titles bookended by FA Cup victories in 1949 and 1960.

NO APPETITE

Such consistent success has not yet been replicated and Wolves' arrival in the Premier League in 2003 signified a return to top-tier football after a 19-year exile. Instant relegation followed and, in 2006, the seemingly Championship-rooted Wolves staged a complete clear-out. Mick McCarthy took up the reins of a bare-bones squad and the move paid dividends when they rejoined the Premier League in 2009.

DID YOU KNOW?
Wolves are the only team to have won titles in five different leagues, and were first to score 7,000 league goals

★ **PREMIER STAR**

■ **Jody Craddock** ■ **Appearances: 215** ■ **2003-2012**

Consistently solid and one of the most dependable centre-backs in the league. A club manager's dream.

ONLY EARLIEST RESULT STATED

Seasons played 4 | **Played** 152 | **Won** 32 | **Drawn** 40 | **Lost** 80 | **GF** 156 | **GA** 281 | **GD** -125 | **Pts** 136 | **Relegations** 2 | **Average pts** 34.00

Full name **Sheffield United Football Club** | Nickname **The Blades** | Founded **1889** | Ground **Bramall Lane** (32,702)

SHEFFIELD UTD

Despite being one of the elite in '92, the Blades have lost their cutting edge

★ **PREMIER STAR**

■ **Phil Jagielka** ■ **Appearances: 254** ■ **2000-2007**

Played in central defence and midfield, but metaphorically always led from the front despite his young age.

FOUNDERS

Relegated in 1994, having been a founding member of the Premier League two years earlier, it would be more than a decade before Sheffield United fought their way back among the elite for the 2006/07 season. But their jubilation was shortlived and the subsequent years have not been kind.

DID YOU KNOW?
Sheffield United were the first English team to take over a Chinese club, Chengdu Wuniu, now Chengdu Blades

KEEPERS

Since the club's heyday at the end of the 19th and start of the 20th centuries, it has been a long hard slog for the Blades to maintain a presence at the top of the English game. In 1990 they returned to Division One after a 14-year exile and this led to a seat at the Premier League table – for a couple of years at least. Although United returned in 2006, they were relegated again and suffered a catastrophic decline that resulted in them being demoted to League One two years ago. They are still there.

ONLY EARLIEST RESULT STATED

Seasons played 3 | **Played** 122 | **Won** 32 | **Drawn** 36 | **Lost** 54 | **GF** 128 | **GA** 168 | **GD** -40 | **Pts** 132 | **Relegations** 2 | **Average pts** 44.00

---

20 SOMETHING Dutch defender Arjan de Zeeuw helped bring Premier League football to two different clubs for the first time: Barnsley and Portsmouth.

Full name **Reading Football Club** | Nickname **The Royals** | Founded **1871** | Ground **Madejski Stadium** (24,169)

READING

The trials and tribulations of the regal Royals.

★ **PREMIER STAR**

■ **Ivar Ingimarsson** ■ **Appearances: 282** ■ **2003-2011**

Formed a rock-solid partnership with Ibrahima Sonko and spent his best years at the club. Played 282 for the Royals.

HIGHS AND LOWS

Topping the Championship table last season, Reading were rewarded with their second promotion to the Premier League in six years. Fans will be hoping to replicate or even improve on the eighth-place finish they managed in 2005, whilst being mindful of the subsequent fall from grace that followed

DEAR JOHN...

Established in 1871 (making them one of the oldest clubs around), Reading's 102-year stay at Elm park never saw much in the way of domestic glory, and it wasn't until John Madejski's takeover in 1991 that the club began to make real strides. Hugely unfortunate not to qualify for Premiership contention in 1995 (owing to the League's new stipulation for a 20, not 22-team competition), Reading eventually made the cut in their Championship-winning 2005/6 season, amassing a record 106 points.

DID YOU KNOW?
Reading's heaviest defeat came in the 1st round of the 1893/94 FA Cup, when Preston North End beat them 18-0.

Seasons played 2	Played 76	Won 26	Drawn 13	Lost 37	GF 93	GA 113	GD -20	Pts 91	Relegated 1	Average pts 45.50

Full name **Oldham Athletic Association Football Club** | Nickname **The Latics** | Founded **1895** | Ground **Boundary Park** (10,638)

OLDHAM

Bloody Mark Hughes...

NASTY '90S

Oldham were on the rise in the early 90s. They'd won the League Cup final in 1990 and secured promotion to the top tier for the inaugural Premier League season. But times were to get rather tough at Boundary Park, though...

DID YOU KNOW?
Nicknamed Ice Station Zebra, Boundary Park is fondly known as the coldest stadium in the Football League

ROYLE RETREAT

Joe Royle's boys ended Big Ron's title challenge by beating his beleaguered side 0-1 at Villa Park, effectively giving Man Utd their first title in 27 years, and then stayed up, courtesy of a 4-3 victory over Southampton on the final day.

Oldham reached the FA Cup semi-final the next year and only an extra-time Mark Hughes goal stopped them from securing a memorable victory and a Wembley appearance. It was a moment that defined their season: they didn't recover, failing to register victories in any of the remaining seven games and dropping into the second tier.

★ **PREMIER STAR**

■ **Andy Ritchie** ■ **Appearances: 250** ■ **1987-1995**

A heart-on-the-sleeve, steely goalscorer who harried and bustled his way into the hearts and minds of Latics fans.

Seasons played 2	Played 84	Won 22	Drawn 23	Lost 39	GF 105	GA 142	GD -37	Pts 89	Relegated 1	Average pts 44.50

Full name **Hull City Association Football Club** | Nickname **The Tigers** | Founded **1904** | Ground **KC Stadium** (25,586)

HULL CITY

They had an airport. And a Geovanni

GEOVANNI GENIUS

Overwhelming favourites for relegation following their promotion, Geovanni scored Hull's first ever Premier League goal as they registered a 2-1 victory over Fulham on the opening day of the 2008/09 season. They would only lose one of their first nine games; in fact, a 2-1 victory at the Emirates and a 1-0 win at White Hart Lane boosted them to joint-top of the league. But early promise

DID YOU KNOW?

Steve Bruce, recently installed as the new manager, has targeted a return to the EPL within three years

quickly faded, the team only winning two more fixtures in the entire campaign.

BROWN AND DOWN

Phil Brown was put on gardening leave in their second season in the EPL, and was replaced by Iain Dowie. But the club remained in a state of flux despite the changes, and were relegated after drawing 2-2 at Wigan in May 2010. Assem Allam, a local businessman, now holds the future of the club in his hands.

★ **PREMIER STAR**

■ **Geovanni** ■ **Appearances: 60** ■ **2008-2010**

Previously at Barcelona, Benfica and Manchester City, his spectacular form kept them in the EPL for a second season.

PREMIER FACTFILE

Club homepage
hullcityafc.net

Rivals Leeds Utd, Sheffield Utd

PL Seasons 2

Highest position
17th (2008-09)

Lowest position
19th (2009-10)

Biggest victory in PL
0-3 v West Brom
(25 Oct 2008)

Biggest defeat in PL
0-5 v Wigan Athletic
(30 Aug 2008)*

Biggest transfer paid
£5m to Fulham for
Jimmy Bullard

Biggest transfer received
£4m from Sunderland
for Michael Turner

*ONLY FIRST RESULT STATED

Seasons played 2	Played 76	Won 14	Drawn 23	Lost 39	GF 73	GA 139	GD -66	Pts 65	Relegated 1	Average pts 32.50

Full name **Bradford City Association Football Club** | Nickname **The Bantams** | Founded **1903** | Ground **Valley Parade** (25,136)

BRADFORD

Brazen owners and bald pundits

★ **PREMIER STAR**

■ **Benito Carbone** ■ **Appearances: 42** ■ **2000-01**

Illuminated Valley Parade during the 2000/01 season with his confident, jinking style, and finished with 10 goals.

GEOFF CHARGES

When chairman Geoffrey Richmond took over Bradford in January 1994, he promised Premier League action at Valley Parade within five years. Chris Kamara got promotion to League One and was then dismissed. Then, in 1998/99, with considerable backing from the chairman, and Paul Jewell in the management hotseat, Bradford made the jump to the top flight for the first time in 77 years.

DID YOU KNOW?

ITV Digital's collapse sent the club into administration, but Carbone waived much of his owed money

HAIRY STUFF

The media mocked Jewell's team, labelling them "Dad's Army" after the signing of Neil Redfearn and Dean Saunders. A final day 1-0 victory over Liverpool, after a solid run of nine games without defeat, ensured survival and Sky Sports pundit Rodney Marsh, who'd betted against it with his hair, shaved his head. Despite the arrival of Benito Carbone, on £40K a week, next season they finished with 26 points and sunk without trace.

PREMIER FACTFILE

Club homepage
bradfordcityfc.co.uk

Rivals Leeds Utd, Huddersfield Town

PL Seasons 2

Highest position
17th (1999/2000)

Lowest position
20th (2000/01)

Biggest victory in PL
3-0 v Wimbledon
(30 April 2000)

Biggest defeat in PL
0-6 v Man Utd
(5 Sept 2000)

Biggest transfer paid
£2m to Leeds Utd for
David Hopkin

Biggest transfer received
£2m from Newcastle for
Des Hamilton

Seasons played 2	Played 76	Won 14	Drawn 20	Lost 42	GF 68	GA 138	GD -70	Pts 62	Relegated 1	Average pts 31.00

Full name **Watford Football Club** | Nickname **The Hornets** | Founded **1898** | Ground **Vicarage Road** (17,477)

WATFORD

Not much EPL history – plenty of gaps...

★ **PREMIER STAR**

■ **Ben Foster** ■ **Appearances: 73** ■ **2005-2007**

Made admirers during his two-year loan spell at Vicarage Road, being a solid and commanding platform.

ROCKET MEN!
Elton John, Graham Taylor, Luther Blissett, John Barnes, the 1984 FA Cup Final, Gianluca Vialli, Gifton Noel-Williams(!): there's no doubt Watford have a memorable modern history... but, sadly, that doesn't really extend to the Premier League.

STUNG HORNETS
The first stint in the top tier, in 1999/00, began nicely as the Hornets returned from Anfield with Liverpool's scalp and beat Chelsea at home. That was as good as it got though, as a dire run of form meant the club was relegated with a record low point-haul of 24. They returned in 2006/07 under boss Aidy Boothroyd and made a similar impression: there were no outrageous victories this time and the club saw in the New Year 10 points adrift of safety. A tall order to stay up then, which, despite closing the gap to three points at the end of March, they couldn't overcome.

DID YOU KNOW?
Watford were initially nicknamed The Brewers, as Benskins Brewery used to own the Vicarage Road freehold

PREMIER FACTFILE

Club homepage watfordfc.com

Rivals Luton Town

PL Seasons 2

Highest position 20th (1999/00, 2006/07)

Lowest position 20th (1999/00, 2006/07)

Biggest victory in PL 4-2 v Portsmouth (9 April 2007)

Biggest defeat in PL 5-0 v Wimbledon (4 December 1999)

Biggest transfer paid £3.25m for Nathan Ellington from West Brom

Biggest transfer received £8m for Ashley Young from Aston Villa

Seasons played 2	Played 76	Won 11	Drawn 19	Lost 46	GF 64	GA 136	GD -72	Pts 52	Relegated 2	Average pts 26.00

Full name **Swansea City Association Football Club** | Nickname(s) **The Swans / The Jacks** | Founded **1912** | Ground **Liberty Stadium** (20,520)

SWANSEA

A breath of Welsh fresh air

WELSH DRAGONS
Sixth position in their first season in the second tier ultimately resulted in unsuccessful play-off drama and, the following season, Kenny Jackett would be replaced by Robert Martinez only for the same thing to happen. An 18-game unbeaten run brought promotion the next season though, and they managed the feat again in 2010/11, beating Reading in the play-offs and opening the gates to the Premier League promised land – the first Welsh team to do so.

DID YOU KNOW?
The last league goal scored at the Vetch, the Swans' old ground, was notched by Adrian Forbes on 30 April, 2005

11TH HEAVEN
They weren't done, though. An incredible season of results in the top tier saw them finish 11th, beating Liverpool 1-0 on the final day and, most importantly of all, showing that even promoted teams on limited budgets can play easy-on-the-eye passing football. Long may "Swansalona" prosper under new manager Michael Laudrup.

★ **PREMIER STAR**

■ **Nathan Dyer** ■ **Appearances: 137** ■ **2009-present**

Smart, tenacious winger who, in Swansea City style, remains direct but never gives the ball away too cheaply.

PREMIER FACTFILE

Club homepage swanseacity.net

Rivals Bristol City, Cardiff City

PL Seasons 1

Highest position 11th (2011/12)

Lowest position 11th (2011/12)

Biggest victory in PL 3-0 v West Brom (17 Sept 2011)

Biggest defeat in PL 0-4 v Man City (15 Aug 2011)

Biggest transfer paid £3.5m for Danny Graham from Watford

Biggest transfer received £2m for Jason Scotland from Wigan Athletic

Seasons played 1	Played 38	Won 12	Drawn 11	Lost 15	GF 44	GA 51	GD -7	Pts 47	Relegated 0	Average pts 47.00

Full name **Blackpool Football Club Ltd** | Nickname(s) **The Seasiders / The Tangerines** | Founded **1887** | Ground **Bloomfield Road** (16,220)

BLACKPOOL

One-season seaside wonders

PIER PRESSURE

When Blackpool were promoted to the Premier League in 2010, there weren't many commentators who gave them a chance, many betting on them not achieving a single victory. But Ian Holloway and his troops had other ideas.

DID YOU KNOW?
In June 2005 a book of Ian Holloway's quotes, *Let's Have Coffee: The Tao Of Ian Holloway* was published

ORANGE-BOOM!

With a squad assembled on a shoestring and a manager with a brilliantly blunt sense of humour, the Tangerines captured the imagination of the Premier League. Utilising an entertaining, attacking style, they beat Wigan away 4-0 on the opening day, put three past Spurs at Bloomfield Road and completed the league double over Liverpool. However, unable to string positive results together in the latter stages of the season, their slide down the table eventually equalled relegation when they succumbed to Man United 4-2 on the final day of the season.

★ PREMIER STAR

■ **Charlie Adam** ■ Appearances: **91** ■ **2009-11**

Such a danger from dead balls and a real threat from the edge of the box. The opposition's tormentor-in-chief.

Seasons played 1	Played 38	Won 10	Drawn 9	Lost 19	GF 55	GA 78	GD -23	Pts 39	Relegated 1	Average pts 39.00

Full name **Barnsley Football Club** | Nickname(s) **The Tykes / The Reds** | Founded **1887** | Ground **Oakwell Stadium** (23,009)

BARNSLEY

Football Club develops acute sense of vertigo

★ PREMIER STAR

■ **Neil Redfearn** ■ Appearances: **292** ■ **1991-1998**

Played 790 matches in the Football League, the fifth highest total of all time, and 292 for Barnsley. A club legend.

SECOND COMING!

Holding the record for spending more seasons in the second tier than any other English club, it's no surprise that Barnsley got a little acrophobic on ascent to the top flight in 1997/98, failing to retain their status. That's not to say the season was a complete washout, though.

DID YOU KNOW?
In 1998 during a match against Sunderland Ashley Ward scored, missed a penalty and got sent off – all in 5 minutes

RED ALL OVER

Their stalwart captain and penalty taker, Neil Redfearn, missed only one game, scored their first ever top-tier goal on the opening day of the season and finished the competition in double figures with ten goals. Despite being hammered 7-0 at Old Trafford, the Tykes got revenge by forcing a replay in the FA Cup and then dumping Fergie's men out. They also managed a 1-0 victory at Anfield, with Ashley Ward getting the winner. Eventually though, they weren't consistent enough, and only one win in their last nine sent them down.

Seasons played 1	Played 38	Won 10	Drawn 5	Lost 23	GF 37	GA 82	GD -45	Pts 35	Relegated 1	Average pts 35.00

Full name **Burnley Football Club** | Nickname **The Clarets** | Founded **1882** | Ground **Turf Moor** (22,546)

BURNLEY

Claret here, Claret there...

★ **PREMIER STAR**

■ **Steven Fletcher** ■ **Appearances: 35** ■ **2009-2010**

Solid all-rounder with a steady touch and a canny eye for goal. Well worth the record transfer fee.

CLARET BLIMMIN' EVERYWHERE!

Burnley marked their 127th year as a club by spending it for the first time in the Premier League. They hadn't been in the top tier for 33 years and, in truth, very little was expected.

They had an up-and-coming manager in Owen Coyle though, and were prepared to break records to stay up – including the club transfer fee: £3m on Hibernian's Steven Fletcher. Beating reigning champions Man Utd 1-0 at Turf Moor ignited their campaign; in fact, Burnley would become the first promoted club to win all of their first four home fixtures.

DID YOU KNOW?
Robbie Blake scored the first home goal and the first away goal ever for Burnley in the Premier League

GIVE US MOOR

Away form was problematic though, and morale dipped further when Coyle left for Bolton Wanderers in January 2010. Burnley taught Spurs a lesson in their final game, winning 4-2 and suggesting a return to the top – but they remain firmly rooted in the Championship.

Seasons played 1 | **Played** 38 | **Won** 8 | **Drawn** 6 | **Lost** 24 | **GF** 42 | **GA** 82 | **GD** -40 | **Pts** 30 | **Relegated** 1 | **Average pts** 30.00

Full name **Swindon Town Football Club** | Nickname(s) **The Robins / The Reds / The Spartans** | Founded **1879** | Ground **The County Ground** (15,728)

SWINDON

From Hoddle to Di Canio via Maurice Malpas...

100 GOAL GLORY

Promoted under Glenn Hoddle, who left for Chelsea before Swindon's singular Premier League campaign got underway, the Robins never really adjusted to the quality of England's top flight. Though they managed a commendable 2-2 draw against Man Utd, they only managed five wins throughout the season and conceded 100 goals, which still remains a record for a 42-game season.

DID YOU KNOW?
Swindon were the first League club to have floodlights installed in 1951. They cost a cool £350

SPARTANS UNITE!

After numerous managers – including Dennis Wise, Paul Sturrock and Maurice Malpas – the enigmatic Paolo Di Canio took the hot seat and led his charges to the League Two Championship title, smashing Port Vale 5-0 on the last day in front of home support and winning a club-record 10 consecutive games along the way. It's been a long time coming, but it looks like Swindon are finally back in business.

★ **PREMIER STAR**

■ **John Moncur** ■ **Appearances: 58** ■ **1992-1994**

A playmaker who never shirked a tackle, Moncur was committed and creative. A great all-round midfielder.

Seasons played 1 | **Played** 42 | **Won** 5 | **Drawn** 15 | **Lost** 22 | **GF** 46 | **GA** 100 | **GD** -54 | **Pts** 30 | **Relegated** 1 | **Average pts** 30.00

All-time Premier League table

Every season's maths added together in one ranked table. Where's your team?

Pos	Goals	Seasons	Played	Won	Drawn	Lost	GF	GA	GD	Pts	Av Pts	Page
1	Manchester United	20	772	500	163	109	1541	660	881	1663	83.15	page 16
2	Arsenal	20	772	415	204	153	1345	717	628	1449	72.45	page 17
3	Chelsea	20	772	401	199	172	1282	741	541	1402	70.10	page 18
4	Liverpool	20	772	380	194	198	1236	753	483	1334	64.20	page 19
5	Aston Villa	20	772	283	240	249	973	923	50	1089	54.45	page 20
6	Tottenham Hotspur	20	772	294	204	274	1072	1020	52	1086	54.30	page 21
7	Everton	20	772	272	218	282	974	979	-5	1034	51.70	page 22
8	Newcastle United	18	692	277	186	229	996	885	111	1017	56.50	page 23
9	Blackburn Rovers	18	696	262	184	250	927	907	20	970	53.89	page 24
10	Manchester City	15	582	211	151	220	771	736	35	784	52.27	page 25
11	West Ham United	16	616	202	158	256	723	880	-157	764	47.75	page 26
12	Leeds United	12	468	189	125	154	641	573	68	692	57.66	page 27
13	Middlesbrough	14	536	160	156	220	621	741	-120	633	45.20	page 28
14	Southampton	13	506	150	137	219	598	738	-140	587	45.15	page 29
15	Bolton Wanderers	13	494	149	128	217	575	745	-170	575	44.23	page 30
16	Fulham	11	418	130	121	167	480	552	-72	511	46.45	page 31
17	Sunderland	11	418	112	104	202	422	606	-184	440	40.00	page 32
18	Coventry City	9	354	99	112	143	387	490	-103	409	45.40	page 33
19	Sheffield Wednesday	8	316	101	89	126	409	453	-44	392	49.00	page 33
20	Wimbledon	8	316	99	94	123	384	472	-88	391	48.88	page 34
21	Charlton Athletic	8	304	93	82	129	129	442	-100	361	45.13	page 34
22	Leicester City	8	308	84	90	134	354	456	-102	342	42.75	page 35
23	Birmingham City	7	266	73	82	111	273	360	-87	301	43.00	page 35
24	Wigan Athletic	7	266	76	67	123	269	409	-140	295	42.14	page 36
25	Portsmouth	7	266	79	65	122	292	380	-88	293	41.90	page 36
26	Derby County	7	266	68	70	128	271	420	-149	274	39.10	page 37
27	Queens Park Rangers	5	202	69	46	87	267	298	-31	253	50.60	page 37
28	Norwich City	5	202	62	62	78	257	323	-66	248	49.60	page 38
29	Nottingham Forest	5	198	60	59	79	229	287	-58	239	47.80	page 38
30	Ipswich Town	5	202	57	53	92	219	312	-93	224	44.80	page 39
31	West Bromwich Albion	6	228	52	60	116	233	374	-141	216	36.00	page 39
32	Stoke City	4	152	47	42	63	154	204	-50	183	45.75	page 40
33	Crystal Palace	4	160	37	49	4	160	243	-83	160	40.00	page 40
34	Wolverhampton Wanderers	4	152	32	40	80	156	281	-125	136	34.00	page 41
35	Sheffield United	3	122	32	36	54	128	168	-40	132	44.00	page 41
36	Reading	2	76	26	13	37	93	113	-20	91	45.50	page 42
37	Oldham Athletic	2	84	84	23	39	105	142	-37	89	44.50	page 42
38	Hull City	2	76	14	23	39	73	139	-66	65	32.50	page 43
39	Bradford City	2	76	14	20	42	68	138	-70	62	31.00	page 43
40	Watford	2	76	11	19	46	64	136	-72	52	26.00	page 44
41	Swansea City	1	38	12	11	15	44	51	-7	47	47.00	page 44
42	Blackpool	1	38	10	9	19	55	78	-23	39	39.00	page 45
43	Barnsley	1	38	10	5	23	37	82	-45	35	35.00	page 45
44	Burnley	1	38	8	6	24	42	82	-40	30	30.00	page 46
45	Swindon Town	1	42	5	15	22	22	100	-53	30	30.00	page 46

THE HISTORY

1992/93

The inaugural season bids farewell to Clough and hello to Cantona – and Manchester United begin an enduring love affair with the trophy

Steve Bruce, left, and Bryan Robson lift the new Premiership trophy for the first time

▼ 1992/93 PREMIER LEAGUE STATS

Champions Manchester United (1st Premiership title, 8th title)

Top at Christmas Norwich City (finished 3rd)

Total goals scored 1,222

Average goals/game 2.65

Biggest home win Blackburn 7-1 Norwich City

Biggest away win Man City 2-5 Everton / Blackburn 2-5 Coventry City

Longest winning run 7 (Man Utd) (Sheff Wed)

Longest unbeaten run 11 (Man Utd)

Highest attendance 44,619 (Liverpool v Everton)

Lowest attendance 3,039 (Wimbledon v Everton)

Average attendance 21,126

Champions League Man Utd

UEFA Cup Aston Villa, Norwich City

UEFA Cup Winners' Cup Arsenal

▼ TOP GOALSCORERS

1	**Teddy Sheringham** (Forest, Spurs)	22
2	**Les Ferdinand** (QPR)	20
3	**Dean Holdsworth** (Wimbledon)	19
4	**Micky Quinn** (Coventry City)	17
5	**Alan Shearer** (Blackburn)	16
	David White (Man City)	16

20 SOMETHING The most successful English managers in the EPL are Ron Atkinson (1993) and Kevin Keegan (1996), who both achieved second place.

PREMIER LEAGUE TEAM OF THE YEAR

Forward — Ian Wright — Arsenal
Forward — Alan Shearer — Blackburn
Midfielder — Ryan Giggs — Man Utd
Midfielder — Roy Keane — Forest
Midfielder — Paul Ince — Man Utd
Midfielder — Gary Speed — Leeds Utd
Defender — Gary Pallister — Man Utd
Defender — Paul McGrath — Aston Villa
Defender — Tony Dorigo — Leeds Utd
Defender — David Bardsley — QPR
Goalkeeper — Peter Schmeichel — Man Utd

Manchester United endured a similarly turbulent opening, conceding the Premiership's first goal to Sheffield United at Brammall Lane, with Brian Deane grabbing his second in a 2-1 victory for the Blades.

After seven games, a balanced Norwich City side sat atop the league on 16 points and Coventry City, spearheaded by a £200,000 acquisition from Newcastle United, Micky Quinn, were second on 15. Elsewhere, Ian Rush would shortly break Roger Hunt's longstanding Liverpool scoring record of 286 goals.

Unfortunately for the high-flying Canaries, the irrepressible Shearer brought them back to Earth with a feathery bump on 3 October, scoring twice in a thumping 7-1 victory. But his and, effectively, Blackburn's challenge came to an end on Boxing Day, when the Geordie striker was ruled out for the season with a knee injury sustained in a robust clash with Leeds.

The enigmatic Dalian Atkinson's fearsome partnership with Dean Saunders at Villa – known as the Deadly Duo or D-Men – was also snuffed out because of injury, and Villa's plentiful goal supply eventually dried up.

A turning point not involving cartilage or ligaments took place at Manchester United and would be the catalyst for the club's first title in 26 years. Having slipped to 10th place after 15 games, Alex Ferguson freshened up his squad with an audacious move for Leeds United striker Eric Cantona. With a newfound attacking impulse and

confidence, United lost only two of their remaining 27 games.

Elsewhere, Sheffield Wednesday, beset by injury problems, switched Paul Warhurst from being a defender to an attacker, and he finished the season with 18 goals, helping the Owls to two cup finals in the process; Brian Clough, in his last season as Nottingham Forest boss, lost his final game 2-0 to Sheffield United and retired a relegated manager; QPR finished the highest of all the London clubs, in fifth; Liverpool's Ronnie Rosenthal concocted *that* miss; and the new backpass rule caused all sorts of tactical kerfuffle.

But at the end of its first season, the Premiership spotlight rested firmly on Old Trafford – it has rarely deviated since.

And so it began. After months of negotiation, procrastination and bigwigs in expensive suits collectively daydreaming of prawn sandwiches, the Premiership was born. The suckling behemoth quickly signed a broadcasting-rights contract with British Sky Broadcasting for the hitherto unheard of sporting sum of £304m and the teams prepared for the inaugural dogfight.

Blackburn bought Alan Shearer from Southampton for a British record transfer fee of £3.5m and Dean Saunders waved goodbye to a gloomy career at Anfield to embrace the claret and blue of 'Big Ron' Atkinson's rejuvenated Aston Villa.

Arsenal, installed as title favourites by the bookies, sold David Rocastle to Leeds and lost their first two games of the season: the first 2-4, after being 2-0 up at home to Norwich City; and the second to a goal from Blackburn's new number 9, Shearer, at Ewood Park.

1992/93 DID YOU KNOW?

■ **Jack Wilshere, Neymar and Mario Götze were all born in 1992.**
■ **The new Premiership trophy took a whole 10 months to make.**
■ **Sir Bobby Moore, England's inspirational World Cup-winning captain, died in 1993 from cancer. A 20ft statue of Moore was erected outside the new Wembley when it opened 14 years later, in 2007. He was the first of the '66 team to perish.**

Neymar da Silva: born the year the Premier League began

	FINAL POSITIONS	P	W	D	L	F	A	GD	Pts
1	Manchester United (C)	42	24	12	6	67	31	36	84
2	Aston Villa	42	21	11	10	57	40	17	74
3	Norwich City	42	21	9	12	61	65	-4	72
4	Blackburn Rovers	42	20	11	11	68	46	22	71
5	Queens Park Rangers	42	17	12	13	63	55	8	63
20 ▼	Crystal Palace	42	11	16	15	48	61	-13	49
21 ▼	Middlesbrough	42	11	11	20	54	75	-21	44
22 ▼	Nottingham Forest	42	10	10	22	41	62	-21	40

▼ AWARDS

PFA Player of the Year
Paul McGrath (Aston Villa)

PFA Young Player of the Year
Ryan Giggs (Man Utd)

FWA Player of the Year
Chris Waddle (Sheff Wed)

LMA Manager of the Year
Dave Bassett (Sheff Utd)

▼ ALSO IN 1992/93

■ **Ballon d'Or**
Marco van Basten (Milan)
■ **Mercury Music Prize**
Screamadelica
■ **BBC Sports Personality of the Year** Liz McColgan
■ **Oscar for best film**
Unforgiven

1993/94

Roy Keane makes his bow for Manchester United, who see off a spirited challenge by Blackburn Rovers to win the Premiership for a second time

Manchester United celebrate winning their second Premiership title after being pushed all the way by Kenny Dalglish's Blackburn Rovers side

▼ 1993/94 PREMIER LEAGUE STATS

Champions Manchester United (2nd Premiership title, 9th title)
Top at Christmas Man Utd (1st)
....
Total goals scored 1,195
Average goals/game 2.58
Biggest home win
Aston Villa 5-0 Swindon
Manchester United 5-0 Sheff Weds
Sheff Weds 5-0 Ipswich

Sheff Weds 5-0 West Ham
Biggest away win
Swindon Town 0-5 Leeds Utd
Swindon Town 0-5 Liverpool
Longest winning run
8 (Manchester United)
Longest unbeaten run
22 (Manchester United)
....
Highest attendance 44,751

(Manchester United v Liverpool)
Average attendance 23,044
....
Champions League Man Utd
Cup Winners' Cup Arsenal, Chelsea
UEFA Cup Aston Villa, Blackburn
Rovers, Newcastle Utd

▼ TOP GOALSCORERS

1	**Andy Cole** (Newcastle United)	34
2	**Alan Shearer** (Blackburn)	31
3	**Matt Le Tissier** (Southampton)	25
	Chris Sutton (Norwich City)	25
5	**Ian Wright** (Arsenal)	23
6	**Peter Beardsley** (Newcastle United)	21
7	**Mark Bright** (Sheffield Wednesday)	19
8	**Eric Cantona** (Manchester United)	18

PREMIER LEAGUE TEAM OF THE YEAR

Forward
Peter Beardsley
Newcastle Utd

Forward
Eric Cantona
Man Utd

Forward
Alan Shearer
Blackburn

Midfielder
David Batty
Blackburn

Midfielder
Gary McAllister
Leeds Utd

Midfielder
Paul Ince
Man Utd

Defender
Tony Adams
Arsenal

Defender
Gary Pallister
Man Utd

Defender
Denis Irwin
Man Utd

Defender
Gary Kelly
Leeds Utd

Goalkeeper
Tim Flowers
Blackburn

In the twilight of his memorable Old Trafford career, Manchester United made it a priority to replace their 36-year-old 'Captain Marvel' Bryan Robson at the start of the 114th season of competitive football in England. Alex Ferguson looked towards relegated Nottingham Forest and their buccaneering 22-year-old Irish midfielder Roy Keane, and backed his instincts to the tune of a record-breaking £3.75m.

"If they can retain the hunger, these players can achieve whatever they want to achieve," Fergie stated, "because they're good enough."

Keane's star would burn brightly as the season progressed and United signalled their desire with a hard-fought penalty shoot-out victory over Arsenal in the Charity Shield curtain-raiser. An early championship marker came against Aston Villa, at Villa Park, on 23 August. The Villains had run Ferguson's men close for the title in 1992/93, but Lee Sharpe's brace proved decisive in a 2-1 win for United.

Elsewhere in the league things were not so rosy. Arsenal were expected to push Fergie's men hard, but lacked United's cohesion and firepower; Spurs chairman Alan Sugar sacked manager Terry Venables amid accusations of financial irregularities; Graeme Souness was given the push by Liverpool in January after an alarming run of form; and Manchester City grew tired of Peter Reid's colourful language only four games into the season, replacing him with Oxford United's Brian Horton.

Newly promoted Newcastle United, revitalised under Kevin Keegan (who based his side on the Liverpool team he once graced), would echo their manager's never-say-die spirit and finish the season in a creditable third place – Peter Beardsley and Andy Cole proving to the lacklustre England boss, Graham Taylor, that Englishmen could play with attacking flair.

But it would be Kenny Dalglish's Blackburn Rovers, spearheaded by the irresistible Alan Shearer, who would push Manchester United hardest for the Premiership crown.

By March, the gap between the sides had shrunk from 16 points to seven. Fergie's men would lose to Chelsea and Eric Cantona would receive a five-match ban after a malicious stamp on Swindon Town's John Moncur, and another red card four days later against Arsenal.

Blackburn drew level on points at the top of the table after a stunning double by Shearer secured a 2-0 Easter win over United, and another

goal from the striker gave Rovers a 1-0 victory over Villa. But the title race ended when Blackburn lost 2-1 away to Coventry City. "The lads have given us a lot of enjoyment and a lot of pride, and you can't ask for more than that," said a dejected Dalglish.

A well-known beer brand had become the league's first title sponsors in the 1993/94 season and it was Manchester United who were raising a glass at its denouement. To cap it all, Alex Ferguson's men beat Chelsea 4-0 in the FA Cup final to become only the fourth team in the 20th century to achieve the double.

Andy Cole scored a Premiership record 34 goals for Newcastle United and Swindon Town were relegated after conceding 100 goals in 42 games, and recording just five wins.

PREMIER LEAGUE GOAL OF THE SEASON

■ Rod Wallace ■ 17 April 1994
■ **Leeds** v Tottenham Hotspur

Picking the ball up 20 yards inside his own half, Wallace wriggles past three opponents on the touchline, dribbles to the edge of the 18-yard box and curls a shot into the far corner of the net. As Gerald Sinstadt noted: "That was perfection!"

1993/94 DID YOU KNOW?

■ England manager, Graham Taylor, resigned in November 1993 after his team's abject failure to qualify for the 1994 World Cup in the USA. He was branded a Turnip by the English media after his team's awful performance against Sweden, the headline reading: "Swedes 2 Turnips 1".
■ Legendary Manchester United manager Sir Matt Busby died of cancer on 20 January 1994 at the age of 84.

ITV's *An Impossible Job* documentary made for some painful viewing

▼ FINAL POSITIONS

		P	W	D	L	F	A	GD	Pts
1	Manchester United (C)	42	27	11	4	80	38	42	92
2	Blackburn Rovers	42	25	9	8	63	36	27	84
3	Newcastle United	42	23	8	11	82	41	41	77
4	Arsenal	42	18	17	7	53	28	25	71
5	Leeds United	42	18	16	8	65	39	26	70
20	▼ Sheffield United	42	8	18	16	42	60	-18	42
21	▼ Oldham Athletic	42	9	13	20	42	68	-26	40
22	▼ Swindon Town	42	5	15	22	47	100	-53	30

▼ AWARDS

PFA Player of the Year
Eric Cantona (Manchester United)

PFA Young Player of the Year
Andy Cole (Newcastle United)

FWA Player of the Year
Alan Shearer (Blackburn)

FA Premier League Manager of the Year Alex Ferguson

▼ ALSO IN 1993/94

■ **Ballon d'Or**
Hristo Stoichkov
(Barcelona)
■ **Mercury Music Prize**
Suede
■ **BBC Sports Personality of the Year** Linford Christie
■ **Oscar for best film**
Schindler's List

1994/95

Blackburn Rovers end their long wait for another league title after a season of record-breaking scorelines, high excitement and shocking revelations

Kenny Dalglish managed Blackburn Rovers to their first league title in 81 years after a nail-biting final day of the season

▼ 1994/95 PREMIER LEAGUE STATS

Champions Blackburn
(1st Premiership title, 3rd title)

Top at Christmas Blackburn (1st)

Goals scored 1,195

Average goals/game 2.58

Biggest home win
Manchester United 9-0
Ipswich Town

Biggest away win

Sheffied Wednesday 1-7
Nottingham Forest

Longest winning run
7 (Blackburn Rovers)

Longest unbeaten run
13 (Nottingham Forest)

Highest attendance 43,868
(Manchester United v Sheffield
Wednesday)

Average attendance 26,698

Champions League Blackburn
Cup Winners' Cup Everton
UEFA Cup Leeds United,
Liverpool, Man Utd, Notts Forest

▼ TOP GOALSCORERS

1	**Alan Shearer** (Blackburn)	34
2	**Robbie Fowler** (Liverpool)	25
3	**Les Ferdinand** (QPR)	24
4	**Stan Collymore** (Nottingham Forest)	22
5	**Andy Cole** (Newcastle/Manchester Utd)	21
6	**Jürgen Klinsmann** (Tottenham)	21
7	**Matt Le Tissier** (Southampton)	19
8	**Teddy Sheringham** (Tottenham)	18

PREMIER LEAGUE **TEAM OF THE YEAR**

Forward
Alan Shearer
Blackburn

Forward
Chris Sutton
Blackburn

Forward
Jürgen Klinsmann
Spurs

Midfielder
Paul Ince
Man Utd

Midfielder
Matthew Le Tissier
Southampton

Midfielder
Tim Sherwood
Blackburn

Defender
Colin Hendry
Blackburn

Defender
Gary Pallister
Man Utd

Defender
Graeme Le Saux
Blackburn

Defender
Rob Jones
Liverpool

Goalkeeper
Tim Flowers
Blackburn

Jürgen Klinsmann arrived at Tottenham from Monaco.

The league was infiltrated by foreign stars after the 1994 USA World Cup – Romania's Gheorghe Popescu (also Spurs), Holland's Bryan Roy (Forest) and Sweden's Stefan Schwarz (Arsenal) to name but a few.

The pairing of Sutton and Alan Shearer provided the springboard for Blackburn's title challenge, while Eric Cantona made a scoring return from suspension for Manchester United. But few could have predicted the ignominy with which the Frenchman would end his season or the vulnerability of the champions early in the campaign, which was outlined by their 3-2 defeat away to Ipswich Town.

United quickly got over their slump, beating Blackburn 4-2 at Ewood Park and then blasting Newcastle's unbeaten record by winning 2-0 at Old Trafford. After 12 games, Newcastle, Manchester United, Forest, Blackburn, Liverpool and Leeds occupied the top six spots, and they would do so at the end of the season.

Revelations rocked the game, though. There were match-fixing allegations against former Liverpool keeper Bruce Grobbelaar; the suspect temperament of Cantona exploded when he kung-fu kicked a Crystal Palace fan and received a lengthy suspension; Arsenal's Paul Merson admitted to an addiction to drugs and gambling, but made an incredible comeback just weeks later; and the Gunners' manager, George Graham, denied any personal gain from the

A fter this season, the Premiership would be reduced to 20 clubs to trim the bulky fixture list, so in the 1994/95 campaign there were four relegation places to try to avoid, while only two clubs would be promoted from Division One.

After successive Premiership titles, Manchester United were bidding to become only the fourth club in the 20th century (alongside Huddersfield Town, Arsenal and Liverpool) to win three championships in a row. Blackburn broke the English transfer record again, acquiring Chris Sutton from Norwich for £5m, a record then broken by Manchester United in January, when they paid £6m for Newcastle's Andy Cole.

Elsewhere, Frank Clark's Nottingham Forest were the surprise package, their forward, Stan Collymore, setting the top flight alight; Liverpool looked to be on the rise under Roy Evans; and theatrical German striker

1994/95 **DID YOU KNOW?**

■ **Andy Cole scored a Premiership record five goals in Manchester United's 9-0 defeat of Ipswich Town at Old Trafford, which was also a record scoreline for the league.**
■ **Former Spurs player Nayim put a smile on Tottenham fans' faces when he scored the winner for Real Zaragoza in the Cup Winners' Cup final against Arsenal with a freak last-minute goal from 40 yards out.**

Nayim: capable of the sporadically sublime

transfers of Pål Lydersen and John Jensen, but was sacked in February.

The Premiership became a two-horse race and with one game to go, only two points separated Blackburn and Manchester United. After much mathematical toing and froing over an amazing 90 minutes, Blackburn lost 2-1 to Liverpool, but Manchester United could only draw 1-1 away to West Ham and so relinquished their crown.

United keeper Peter Schmeichel had conceded only four goals in 21 home Premiership fixtures, but Kenny Dalglish ended Blackburn's 81-year wait for the league title to become only the third manager – alongside Herbert Chapman (Huddersfield and Arsenal) and Brian Clough (Derby and Forest) – to win it with different clubs, having done so with Liverpool.

▼ FINAL POSITIONS	P	W	D	L	F	A	GD	Pts
1 Blackburn Rovers (C)	42	27	8	7	80	39	41	89
2 Manchester United	42	26	10	6	77	28	49	88
3 Nottingham Forest	42	22	11	9	72	43	29	77
4 Liverpool	42	21	11	10	65	37	28	74
5 Leeds United	42	20	13	9	59	38	21	73
19 ▼ Crystal Palace	42	11	12	19	34	49	-15	45
20 ▼ Norwich City	42	10	13	19	37	54	-17	43
21 ▼ Leicester City	42	6	11	25	45	80	-35	29
22 ▼ Ipswich Town	42	7	6	29	36	93	-57	27

▼ AWARDS

PFA Player of the Year
Alan Shearer (Blackburn)

PFA Young Player of the Year
Robbie Fowler (Liverpool)

FWA Player of the Year
Jürgen Klinsmann (Spurs)

Premier League Manager of the Year Kenny Dalglish (Blackburn)

▼ ALSO IN 1994/95

■ **Ballon d'Or**
George Weah
(AC Milan)
■ **Mercury Music Prize**
Elegant Slumming
■ **BBC Sports Personality of the Year** Jonathan Edwards
■ **Oscar for best film**
Forrest Gump

1995/96

Kevin Keegan will "love it if we beat them – love it!" But his Newcastle United side are left heartbroken as Manchester United win the Premiership again

Manchester United prove it is possible to win something with kids, their young side clinching a league-and-cup double to silence the doubters

▼ 1995/96 PREMIER LEAGUE STATS

Champions Manchester United (3rd Premiership title, 10th title)

Top at Christmas Newcastle (2nd)

Goals scored 988

Average goals/game 2.6

Biggest home win
Blackburn 7-0 Notts Forest

Biggest away win
Bolton 0-6 Man Utd

Longest winning run
6 (Manchester United)

Longest unbeaten run
15 (Liverpool)

Highest attendance 53,926
(Manchester United v
Nottingham Forest)

Average attendance 27,550

Champions League
Manchester United

Cup Winners' Cup Liverpool

UEFA Cup Arsenal, Aston Villa,
Newcastle United

▼ TOP GOALSCORERS

1	**Alan Shearer** (Blackburn)	31
2	**Robbie Fowler** (Liverpool)	28
3	**Les Ferdinand** (Newcastle Utd)	25
4	**Dwight Yorke** (Aston Villa)	17
5	**Andrei Kanchelskis** (Everton)	16
	Teddy Sheringham (Tottenham Hotspur)	16
7	**Chris Armstrong** (Tottenham Hotspur)	15
	Ian Wright (Arsenal)	15

PREMIER LEAGUE TEAM OF THE YEAR

Forward
Alan Shearer
Blackburn

Forward
Les Ferdinand
Newcastle Utd

Midfielder
David Ginola
Newcastle Utd

Midfielder
Steve Stone
Forest

Midfielder
Ruud Gullit
Chelsea

Midfielder
Rob Lee
Newcastle Utd

Defender
Ugo Ehiogu
Aston Villa

Defender
Tony Adams
Arsenal

Defender
Alan Wright
Aston Villa

Defender
Gary Neville
Man Utd

Goalkeeper
David James
Liverpool

The start of the 1995/96 season signalled an £80m transfer merry-go-round dubbed the Summer of Madness. Stan Collymore arrived at Anfield for £8.4m, the third time the English transfer record had been broken in 12 months, Newcastle forked out £6m for Les Ferdinand, David Ginola touched down on Tyneside and Arsenal paid a club record £7.5m for the unsettled Dutch master Dennis Bergkamp.

Journalists and pundits alike couldn't understand Alex Ferguson's preparations for the season. He sold key assets Paul Ince, Andrei Kanchelskis and Mark Hughes, and put his faith in young players such as the Neville brothers, David Beckham, Paul Scholes and Nicky Butt. When United lost their opening match 3-1 to a game Aston Villa side, Alan Hansen made the now infamous declaration on *Match of the Day*: "You can't win anything with kids." How wrong could one pundit be?

Despite having to do without the services of Eric Cantona, suspended for the first seven games of the season, the kids would hold their own and found themselves second in the table in October.

Kevin Keegan's Newcastle became the team to watch. In exhilarating early form, with Ginola, Peter Beardsley, Robert Lee and Keith Gillespie feeding a voracious Ferdinand, they won nine of their first 10 games.

Big things were also happening on Teesside. Middlesbrough's player-manager Bryan Robson, who had orchestrated automatic promotion to the Premiership, pulled off the transfer coup of the season by persuading much-coveted Brazilian playmaker Juninho Paulista to play at the Riverside, where he became known as TLF (The Little Fella).

Villa invested shrewdly in the summer and put the previous season's failures far behind them, with likeable Trinidadian Dwight Yorke forming a fruitful strike partnership with Savo Milosevic. Villa would eventually finish a praiseworthy fourth.

Liverpool only took one point in November to effectively end any semblance of a title challenge.

In December, a legal challenge in the European Court of Justice by little-known Belgian midfielder Jean-Marc Bosman gave out-of-contract players aged 23 or more the right to become free agents and move to other EU clubs for no fee. Clubs could no longer prevent players from leaving – player power had begun.

Nottingham Forest were the only English club still in Europe after Christmas, an on-field scuffle between team-mates David Batty and Graeme Le Saux summing up Blackburn's miserable showing.

Back in the league, Newcastle's 10-point lead was reduced to seven when Manchester United beat them 2-0 at Old Trafford. Despite the gap being increased again, United lost just one game before the sides met once more on 4 March, at St James' Park, where Ferguson's side won 1-0 to reduce the gap to a single point.

Newcastle had to beat Tottenham on the last day of the season to have any chance of overturning the champions. They couldn't – and, a week later, Ferguson, Cantona and the United kids completed the double by beating Liverpool in the FA Cup final.

1995/96 DID YOU KNOW?

- Bob Paisley died on 14 February 1996 at the age of 77. He won a record 20 trophies during his reign at Liverpool between 1974-83.
- Alex Ferguson, Howard Kendall, Steve Coppell, Gerry Francis and Kevin Keegan were all linked with the England job after Euro '96 but it eventually went to Glenn Hoddle.
- Newcastle's Peter Beardsley received an MBE in 1995 for his services to football.

Bob Paisley: the most successful club manager ever in European competition

PREMIER LEAGUE GOAL OF THE SEASON

- Tony Yeboah
- 23 September 1995
- Wimbledon v **Leeds United**

Controlling a clearance on his chest then instep, the big Ghanaian surges past two defenders with the ferocity of a tsunami and lashes in an unbelievable shot from distance, stinging the crossbar in doing so.

▼ FINAL POSITIONS

		P	W	D	L	F	A	GD	Pts
1	**Manchester United**	38	25	7	6	73	35	38	82
2	**Newcastle United**	38	24	6	8	66	37	29	78
3	**Liverpool**	38	20	11	7	70	34	36	71
4	**Aston Villa**	38	18	9	11	52	35	17	63
5	**Arsenal**	38	17	12	9	49	32	17	63
18	▼ **Manchester City**	38	9	11	18	33	58	-25	38
19	▼ **Queens Park Rangers**	38	9	6	23	38	57	-19	33
20	▼ **Bolton Wanderers**	38	8	5	25	39	71	-32	29

▼ AWARDS

PFA Player of the Year
Les Ferdinand (Newcastle Utd)

PFA Young Player of the Year
Robbie Fowler (Liverpool)

FWA Player of the Year
Eric Cantona (Manchester Utd)

Premier League Manager of the Year Alex Ferguson (Manchester Utd)

▼ ALSO IN 1995/96

- **Ballon d'Or** Matthias Sammer (Borussia Dortmund)
- **Mercury Music Prize** Dummy
- **BBC Sports Personality of the Year** Jonathan Edwards
- **Oscar for best film** Braveheart

1996/97

Liverpool would top the table at Christmas only to leave the Kop wanting as they, and the rest of the league, surrendered to Manchester United once more

Why not pop a cork or two when you win yet another Premier League title? Why not indeed

▼ 1996/97 PREMIER LEAGUE STATS

Champions Manchester Utd
(4th Premiership title, 11th title)

Top at Christmas Liverpool (4th)

Total goals scored 970

Average goals/game 2.55

Biggest home win
Newcastle Utd 7-1 Spurs
Everton 7-1 Southampton

Biggest away win

Sunderland 0-4 Spurs
Nottingham Forest 0-4 Man Utd
Leeds Utd 0-4 Man Utd

Longest winning run 7
(Newcastle Utd)

Longest unbeaten run 16
(Man Utd)

Highest attendance 55,314
(Man Utd v Wimbledon)

Lowest attendance 17,525

(Nottingham Forest v Blackburn)

Average attendance 28,471

Champions League Man Utd,
Newcastle Utd

Cup Winners' Cup Chelsea

UEFA Cup Arsenal, Aston Villa,
Leicester City, Liverpool

▼ TOP GOALSCORERS

1	**Alan Shearer** (Newcastle Utd)	25
2	**Ian Wright** (Arsenal)	23
3	**Robbie Fowler** (Liverpool)	18
	Ole Gunnar Solskjaer (Manchester Utd)	18
5	**Dwight Yorke** (Aston Villa)	17
6	**Les Ferdinand** (Newcastle Utd)	16
	Fabrizio Ravanelli (Middlesbrough)	16

20 SOMETHING Emile Heskey was the first ever Wigan player to appear for England when he played in a European Championship qualifier against Israel in 2007.

PREMIER LEAGUE **TEAM OF THE YEAR**

Forward
Ian Wright
Arsenal

Forward
Alan Shearer
Newcastle Utd

Midfielder
Steve McManaman
Liverpool

Midfielder
David Beckham
Man Utd

Midfielder
David Batty
Newcastle Utd

Midfielder
Roy Keane
Man Utd

Defender
Mark Wright
Liverpool

Defender
Tony Adams
Arsenal

Defender
Stig Inge Bjørnebye
Liverpool

Defender
Gary Neville
Man Utd

Goalkeeper
David Seaman
Arsenal

After the success of Euro '96, club supporters and converted football fans barely had time to draw breath before the new Premiership season began.

To the chagrin of many Gunners fans, Arsenal had appointed the little-known Arsène Wenger to begin a rebuilding process in north London, while Ruud Gullit became player-manager of Chelsea after Glenn Hoddle was selected as England manager. Liverpool's talented young team would begin to realise their potential this season, but also cultivate their 'Spice Boys' reputation, while Alan Shearer swapped Ewood Park for St James' Park, and the club he supported as a boy, in a world-record £15m deal.

After helping Manchester United to overcome Newcastle 4-0 in the Charity Shield, David Beckham announced his intentions for the season with a lobbed goal from 52m out in a 3-0 victory over Wimbledon on the opening day.

But United would draw their next three games in a muted start to the season. Sheffield Wednesday, on the other hand, enjoyed a 100% start, beating Aston Villa, Leeds, Newcastle and Leicester. Manager David Pleat wasn't buying into the hype, though: "If you speak to too many people too much, sometimes you say things you don't really want to say. I would like to say nothing at the moment, get on with things and see how well we can do."

Blackburn's era as title-challengers was rapidly fading: Kenny Dalglish had moved on and Ray Harford's time as coach came to an abrupt end when, after 11 Premiership games without a win, they were knocked out of the Coca-Cola Cup by Stockport County.

Meanwhile, at Stamford Bridge, Gullit had used his superb international reputation and connections to acquire French centre-back Franck Leboeuf and Italian superstars Gianluca Vialli, Roberto Di Matteo and Gianfranco Zola. They were to win the FA Cup with a 2-0 victory over Middlesbrough and dedicate their victory to Matthew Harding, the Chelsea chairman who died in a helicopter crash in October.

Liverpool, with Steve McManaman continuing to excel, topped the table after Christmas, five points ahead of Manchester United, who had a game in hand. Instead of gathering momentum, though, they stumbled badly. And Robbie Fowler's suspension for the last four games put the final nail in the Reds' title hopes and they finished fourth on goal difference.

Despite a 5-0 drubbing by

PREMIER LEAGUE **GOAL OF THE SEASON**

■ Gianfranco Zola ■ 26 Feb 1997
■ **Chelsea** v Manchester United

Dan Petrescu slides Zola in behind Denis Irwin on the right channel, the Italian dummies the cross, Irwin commits and he cuts inside, dummies another, Gary Pallister commits, and he comes inside again and blasts past Schmeichel. Wizardry.

Newcastle and a humiliating 6-3 defeat away to Southampton, Alex Ferguson's men regained top spot in late January and retained it until the end. Their fourth Premiership title was confirmed when Liverpool failed to beat Wimbledon in the penultimate series of matches. The only thing that spoilt the party was Eric Cantona's shock decision to retire from football.

Middlesbrough, despite investing in foreign stars such as Emerson, Fabrizio Ravanelli and Gianluca Festa, were relegated. They had been deducted three points by the FA for cancelling a fixture against Blackburn in December, when Boro claimed they had 23 ill or injured players. If they had gone ahead with the game, using youth and reserve players, they would have stayed up. Football, eh?

1996/97 **DID YOU KNOW?**

■ **Ruud Gullit became the first overseas and first black manager to win the FA Cup when Chelsea beat Middlesbrough 2-0.**
■ **In November, Manchester United lost at home in the European Cup for the first time in 40 years, 1-0 to Fenerbahce.**
■ **On 18 May Eric Cantona announced his retirement from football. He would never be tempted to play again.**

Gullit also coined the phrase "sexy football"

▼ **FINAL POSITIONS**	P	W	D	L	F	A	GD	Pts
1 **Manchester United (C)**	38	21	12	5	76	44	32	75
2 **Newcastle United**	38	19	11	8	73	40	33	68
3 **Arsenal**	38	19	11	8	62	32	30	68
4 **Liverpool**	38	19	11	8	62	37	25	68
5 **Aston Villa**	38	17	10	11	47	34	13	61
18 ▼ **Sunderland**	38	10	10	18	35	53	-18	40
19 ▼ **Middlesbrough**	38	10	12	16	51	60	-9	39
20 ▼ **Nottingham Forest**	38	6	16	16	31	59	-28	34

▼ AWARDS

PFA Player of the Year
Alan Shearer (Newcastle Utd)

PFA Young Player of the Year
David Beckham (Manchester Utd)

FWA Player of the Year
Gianfranco Zola (Chelsea)

Premier League Manager of the Year Alex Ferguson (Manchester Utd)

▼ ALSO IN 1996/97

■ **Ballon d'Or**
Ronaldo (Inter Milan)
■ **Mercury Music Prize**
Different Class
■ **BBC Sports Personality of the Year** Damon Hill
■ **Oscar for best film**
The English Patient

1997/98

Arsène Wenger leads a French revolution in north London as Arsenal do the double – and a young striker called Michael Owen emerges on Merseyside

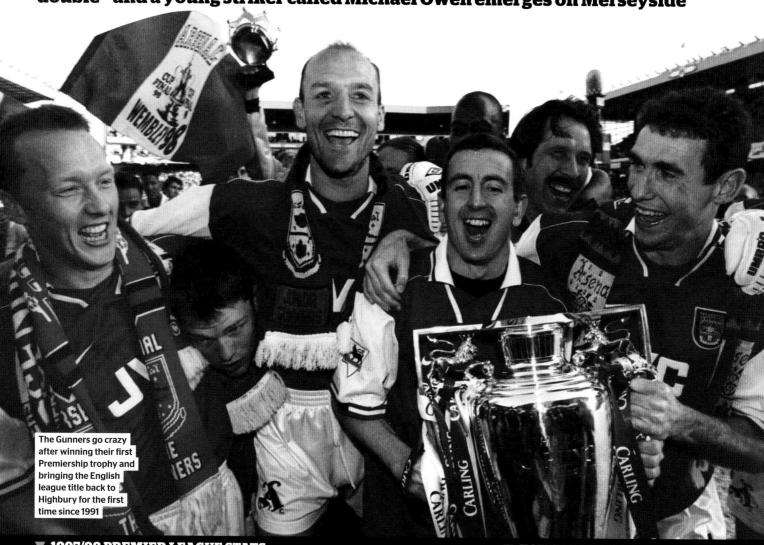

The Gunners go crazy after winning their first Premiership trophy and bringing the English league title back to Highbury for the first time since 1991

▼ 1997/98 PREMIER LEAGUE STATS

Champions Arsenal
(1st Premiership title, 11th title)
Top at Christmas
Manchester United (2nd)

Total goals scored 1019
Average goals/game 2.68
Biggest home win
Manchester United 7-0 Barnsley
Biggest away win

Barnsley 0-6 Chelsea
Longest winning run
10 (Arsenal)
Longest unbeaten run
18 (Arsenal)
Highest attendance 55,306
(Manchester United v Wimbledon)
Lowest attendance 14,410
(Crystal Palace v Wimbledon)
Average attendance 29,212

Champions League
Arsenal, Man Utd, Newcastle Utd
UEFA Cup Aston Villa, Blackburn,
Leeds Utd, Liverpool
UEFA Intertoto Cup Crystal Palace

▼ TOP GOALSCORERS

1	**Dion Dublin** (Coventry City)	18
	Michael Owen (Liverpool)	18
	Chris Sutton (Blackburn)	18
4	**Dennis Bergkamp** (Arsenal)	16
	Kevin Gallacher (Blackburn)	16
	Jimmy Floyd Hasselbaink (Leeds Utd)	16
7	**Andy Cole** (Manchester Utd)	15
	John Hartson (West Ham)	15

The first ever substitute in the EPL was Mike Phelan, who replaced Paul Ince after just five minutes of Man Utd's opening game in 1992.

PREMIER LEAGUE TEAM OF THE YEAR

Forward — **Dennis Bergkamp** — Arsenal

Forward — **Michael Owen** — Liverpool

Midfielder — **Ryan Giggs** — Man Utd

Midfielder — **David Beckham** — Man Utd

Midfielder — **David Batty** — Newcastle Utd

Midfielder — **Nicky Butt** — Man Utd

Defender — **Colin Hendry** — Blackburn

Defender — **Gary Pallister** — Man Utd

Defender — **Nigel Winterburn** — Arsenal

Defender — **Gary Neville** — Man Utd

Goalkeeper — **Nigel Martyn** — Leeds Utd

PREMIER LEAGUE GOAL OF THE SEASON

■ Dennis Bergkamp
■ 27 August 1997
■ Leicester City v **Arsenal**

Bergkamp, the Premiership's most artful demolition unit, receives the ball on the full, juggles it past a clueless defender before flicking it onto his right foot and slotting beyond the equally clueless goalkeeper.

So far so good for Alex Ferguson in the Premiership. Kenny Dalglish, Alan Shearer and Jack Walker's millions had prised the title from him in 1994/95, but his bitter Merseyside rivals had yet to mount a credible challenge and no one from the capital seemed to have the required nous to overthrow his empire... until now.

Arsène Wenger was appointed manager of Arsenal on 30 September 1996. Those who knew little of the global game grunted and groaned when he arrived at Highbury, but in little more than two seasons he would mould one of the greatest sides the top flight has ever seen.

Early on it was Blackburn and Roy Hodgson – who had done a sterling job reinvigorating the ex-title winners – who emerged as title contenders, with Liverpool, Leeds, Aston Villa and Chelsea also putting in strong bids.

Chelsea had signed moustachioed Dutch international goalkeeper Ed de Goey in a bid to halt their defensive lapses, and the Uruguayan Gus Poyet to break forward from what was a particularly defensive midfield. Ken Bates' sacking of Ruud Gullit in January – after the Chelsea manager had bemoaned the lack of transfer funds – galvanised the Blues and 33-year-old player-manager Gianluca Vialli led them to Cup Winners' Cup and Coca-Cola Cup triumphs, and fourth place in the league.

Again, Liverpool seemed to have the ingredients for success, but not the recipe. Another striking sensation would emerge from the Anfield Academy, though: Michael Owen had impressed in a handful of appearances the previous year and, when Robbie Fowler broke his leg and was ruled out for much of the campaign, Owen stepped up to the plate, scoring 18 goals in 36 Premiership games.

On the blue side of the Mersey things weren't so compelling. Everton had their most difficult season for 50 years, only avoiding relegation thanks to a better goal difference than Bolton. Howard Kendall's third reign at the Toffees would soon end, with Walter Smith waiting in the wings to replace him.

Football was put into perspective when Justin Fashanu, the only English footballer ever to disclose his homosexuality, committed suicide in a lock-up in Shoreditch, east London. Fashanu believed a warrant to be out for his arrest in the USA for sexual assault, but an inquest in London on 9 September 1998 established that US police had dropped the investigation because of a lack of evidence.

Back on the pitch, Manchester United were 11 points clear at the top of the table, but Arsenal had three games in hand. By mid-March, when Wenger's men won 1-0 at Old Trafford, the gap had been reduced to three and, in April, the lead changed hands. The Gunners never looked back and clinched their first league title since 1991 with a 4-0 victory over Everton at Highbury. Wenger became the first manager from outside the British Isles to win the English top flight and Arsenal became only the second English club to repeat the double, having first won it in 1971.

All three promoted teams – Bolton Wanderers, Barnsley and Crystal Palace – were relegated after just one season in the Premiership.

1997/98 DID YOU KNOW?

■ Billy Bremner, the combative midfielder who starred for Leeds in the Don Revie era, died on 7 December after suffering a heart attack at the age of 54.

■ Seventeen-year-old striker Robbie Keane scored twice on his debut for Wolves against Norwich in Division One. He would go on to score on his full debuts for Coventry City, West Ham, LA Galaxy and Aston Villa. Some record.

Billy Bremner: Liked a tackle. And then another one. And then...

	FINAL POSITIONS	P	W	D	L	F	A	GD	Pts
1	**Arsenal (C)**	38	23	9	6	68	33	35	78
2	**Manchester United**	38	23	8	7	73	26	47	77
3	**Liverpool**	38	18	11	9	68	42	26	65
4	**Chelsea**	38	20	3	15	71	43	28	63
5	**Leeds Utd**	38	17	8	13	57	46	11	59
18	▼ **Bolton Wanderers**	38	9	13	16	41	61	-20	40
19	▼ **Barnsley**	38	10	5	23	37	82	-45	35
20	▼ **Crystal Palace**	38	8	9	21	37	71	-34	33

▼ AWARDS

PFA Player of the Year
Dennis Bergkamp (Arsenal)

PFA Young Player of the Year
Michael Owen (Liverpool)

FWA Player of the Year
Dennis Bergkamp (Arsenal)

Premier League Manager of the Year Arsène Wenger (Arsenal)

▼ ALSO IN 1997/98

■ **Ballon d'Or**
Zinedine Zidane (Juventus)

■ **Mercury Music Prize**
New Forms

■ **BBC Sports Personality of the Year** Greg Rusedski

■ **Oscar for best film**
Titanic

1998/99

Manchester United see off opposition at home and abroad to clinch an unprecedented treble – the Premiership, FA Cup and Champions League

Joy unconfined as Manchester United celebrate their fifth Premiership title after coming from behind to beat Spurs on the final day

▼ 1998/99 PREMIER LEAGUE STATS

Champions Manchester Utd (5th Premiership title, 12th title)	Notts Forest 1-8 Man Utd	
Top at Christmas Aston Villa (6th)	**Longest winning run** 7 (Leeds Utd)	**Champions League** Man Utd, Arsenal, Chelsea
	Longest unbeaten run 21 (Chelsea)	**UEFA Cup** Newcastle Utd, Spurs, Leeds Utd
Total goals scored 963	**Highest attendance** 55,316 (Man Utd v Southampton)	**UEFA Intertoto Cup** West Ham
Average goals/game 2.53		
Biggest home win Liverpool 7-1 Southampton	**Lowest attendance** 20,480 (Notts Forest v Sheff Wed)	
Biggest away win	**Average attendance** 30,591	

▼ TOP GOALSCORERS

1	**Jimmy Floyd Hasselbaink** (Leeds Utd)	18
	Michael Owen (Liverpool)	18
	Dwight Yorke (Manchester Utd)	18
4	**Nicolas Anelka** (Arsenal)	17
	Andy Cole (Manchester Utd)	17
6	**Hamilton Ricard** (Middlesbrough)	15

Forward
Nicolas Anelka
Arsenal

Forward
Dwight Yorke
Man Utd

Midfielder
David Ginola
Spurs

Midfielder
David Beckham
Man Utd

Midfielder
Patrick Vieira
Arsenal

Midfielder
Emmanuel Petit
Arsenal

Defender
Jaap Stam
Man Utd

Defender
Sol Campbell
Spurs

Defender
Denis Irwin
Man Utd

Defender
Gary Neville
Man Utd

Goalkeeper
Nigel Martyn
Leeds Utd

His trophy rehomed on the red side of north London, nearly 200 miles south, Alex Ferguson decided to reinvigorate his squad ahead of the 1998/99 season. In came Jesper Blomqvist as backup for Ryan Giggs; Jaap Stam, for £10.6m from PSV Eindhoven; and Dwight Yorke from Aston Villa for a whopping £12.6m. David Beckham, stupidly sent off while playing for England against Argentina in a pivotal 1998 World Cup clash, would establish himself as a major star during the season.

The loss of Yorke to United seemed to undermine Villa's chances of a top-four finish, but John Gregory's astute procurement of Paul Merson and Dion Dublin revitalised the club, and they spent much of the season's first half perched on the top spot.

Blackburn's paradoxical form continued. This time, with expectations high, they soon found themselves in a relegation battle. Roy Hodgson was relieved of his duties in November, but a change of manager didn't help. Brian Kidd's men were relegated on the penultimate day of the season after failing to beat Manchester United at Ewood Park.

World Cup-winning Frenchman Marcel Desailly joined cup kings Chelsea, who felt they were ready for a genuine title challenge and who had the diminutive Gianfranco Zola in the form of his life. Liverpool, despite the deadly duo of Michael Owen and Robbie Fowler, looked like a team in transition under new manager Gérard Houllier. In January, Steve McManaman, their principle playmaker, announced his move to Real Madrid (weakening the club's credibility significantly) and, in doing so, signalled the break-up of the Reds' so-called 'Spice Boys'. Liverpool would have to settle for a poor seventh place.

As Christmas came and went, so too did Villa's form – at one point, they endured 10 games without a win. The rest of the season would become a three-horse race between Manchester United, Arsenal and Chelsea.

Nwankwo Kanu joined the Gunners after Christmas, while West Ham manager Harry Redknapp brought in Paulo Di Canio from Sheffield Wednesday. Chelsea's first defeat in 22 matches came in January, at the hands of defending champions Arsenal, and United beat Charlton 1-0 – so, with 15 games to go, there were only two points between the top four.

But Manchester United were just warming up. They knocked eight past

1998/99 DID YOU KNOW?

■ During his time out of the game because of injury, Manchester United's Jesper Blomqvist did media work for MUTV and presented his own cookery show called *Cooking With Jesper*.
■ Glenn Hoddle's reign as England manager came to end in February after he appeared to insinuate in an interview that disabled people are being punished for sins in a former life.

Glenn Hoddle: better when he used to let his feet do the talking

PREMIER LEAGUE GOAL OF THE SEASON

■ Nwankwo Kanu ■ 4 April 1999
■ **Arsenal** v **Middlesbrough**

Lee Dixon, marauding down the right, sweeps a cross into the Middlesbrough box and Nwankwo Kanu, tightly marked and over ten yards out, flicks it across the bewildered keeper with his trailing foot and into the goal. Wonderful piece of invention.

Forest at the City Ground, Ole Gunnar Solskjaer scoring four in 14 minutes, and by mid-March they had opened up a four-point gap.

Arsenal fought back and after beating their north-London rivals Tottenham 3-1 – while United drew 2-2 with Liverpool – looked set to regain the title. However, United took full advantage of Arsenal's 1-0 defeat away to Leeds, coming back from 1-0 down at Spurs on the final day to win 2-1 and clinch their fifth Premiership title, having lost only three games.

The following weekend they beat Newcastle 2-0 at Wembley to lift the FA Cup and, on 26 May, secured the Champions League trophy by beating Bayern Munich 2-1 in the Camp Nou to claim a historic treble. Quite a season for the Red Devils.

	FINAL POSITIONS	P	W	D	L	F	A	GD	Pts
1	**Manchester United**	38	22	13	3	80	37	43	79
2	**Arsenal**	38	22	12	4	59	17	42	78
3	**Chelsea**	38	20	15	3	57	30	27	75
4	**Leeds United**	38	18	13	7	62	34	28	67
5	**West Ham United**	38	16	9	13	46	53	-7	57
18	▼ **Charlton Athletic**	38	8	12	18	41	56	-15	36
19	▼ **Blackburn Rovers**	38	7	14	17	38	52	-14	35
20	▼ **Nottingham Forest**	38	7	9	22	35	69	-34	30

▼ AWARDS

PFA Player of the Year
David Ginola (Spurs)

PFA Young Player of the Year
Nicolas Anelka (Arsenal)

FWA Player of the Year
David Ginola (Spurs)

FA Premier League Manager of the Year Alex Ferguson (Man Utd)

▼ ALSO IN 1998/99

■ **Ballon d'Or**
Rivaldo (Barcelona)
■ **Mercury Music Prize**
Bring It On
■ **BBC Sports Personality of the Year**
Michael Owen
■ **Oscar for best film**
Shakespeare In Love

1999/00

Thierry Henry brought some 'va-va-voom' to Highbury and Kevin Phillips couldn't stop scoring – but there was no halting Manchester United's march to the top

Teddy Sheringham leads the celebrations after Manchester United romped home to win their sixth Premiership title in eight seasons

▼ 1999/00 PREMIER LEAGUE STATS

Champions Manchester United
(6th Premiership title, 13th title)

Top at Christmas Leeds Utd (3rd)

Total goals scored 1060

Average goals/game 2.79

Biggest home win
Newcastle Utd 8-0 Sheff Weds

Biggest away win
Derby County 0-5 Sunderland

Longest winning run
11 (Man Utd)

Longest unbeaten run
14 (Man Utd)

Highest attendance 61,619
(Man Utd v Derby County)

Lowest attendance 15,511
(Watford v Wimbledon)

Average attendance 30,755

Champions League
Man Utd, Arsenal, Leeds Utd

UEFA Cup Chelsea, Liverpool,
Leicester City

Intertoto Cup Aston Villa
Bradford City

▼ TOP GOALSCORERS

1	**Kevin Phillips** (Sunderland)	30
2	**Alan Shearer** (Newcastle Utd)	23
3	**Dwight Yorke** (Manchester Utd)	20
4	**Michael Bridges** (Leeds Utd)	19
	Andy Cole (Manchester Utd)	19
6	**Thierry Henry** (Arsenal)	17
7	**Paulo Di Canio** (West Ham)	16

PREMIER LEAGUE TEAM OF THE YEAR

Forward
Kevin Phillips
Sunderland

Forward
Andy Cole
Man Utd

Midfielder
Harry Kewell
Leeds Utd

Midfielder
David Beckham
Man Utd

Midfielder
Patrick Vieira
Arsenal

Midfielder
Roy Keane
Man Utd

Defender
Sami Hyypia
Liverpool

Defender
Jaap Stam
Man Utd

Defender
Ian Harte
Leeds Utd

Defender
Gary Kelly
Leeds Utd

Goalkeeper
Nigel Martyn
Leeds Utd

Nigel Winterburn, Tony Adams, Martin Keown, Steve Bould and Lee Dixon was spent. Bould left for Sunderland at the start of the campaign and – after being replaced by Sylvinho at Christmas and failing to regain his position – Dixon left for West Ham at the end of the year. Arsène Wenger was making waves in the transfer market, though: Thierry Henry was brought to north London from Juventus for £11m.

Sunderland frontman Kevin Phillips could not stop hitting the net. In a spectacular season, the Black Cats finished a hugely creditable seventh and Phillips scored 30 goals, seven more than the prolific Alan Shearer at Newcastle United.

Expected to mount a serious title challenge, Chelsea reserved their most consistent displays for Europe, their league form largely erratic despite the acquisition of France captain Didier Deschamps. Gianluca Vialli did lift his fourth trophy in two-and-a-half seasons, though, when his team beat Aston Villa 1-0 in the FA Cup.

Leeds United's exciting new team – incorporating players such as Harry Kewell, Jonathan Woodgate and Alan Smith – entered the new millennium on top of the English footballing pyramid and, despite falling 22 points adrift of Manchester United by the end of the season, had a campaign that was deemed a huge success.

Two points behind Leeds and two ahead of Chelsea, Liverpool were in their second season under Gérard Houllier. The forerunners of his largely

n 1998/99, a season-long struggle ended in Manchester United winning the Premiership by one point. The conclusion? Their rivals were closing on them and this time around the title could be anyone's.

Wrong! United won 28 of their 38 matches in 1999/2000 to beat their nearest rivals, Arsenal, to the title by 18 points.

With his team facing a busy fixture schedule and the impending FIFA World Club Championship, Sir Alex Ferguson was accused of arrogance and disrespect when he pulled the holders out of the FA Cup, Andy Townsend even suggesting in *The Sun* newspaper that they should never be allowed back into the tournament. When they were knocked out of

Europe by Real Madrid, 3-2 in the quarter-finals, most of the country's media smugly declared the Red Devils' season a relative failure.

Arsenal were in a period of change again. Their legendary backline of

1999/00 DID YOU KNOW?

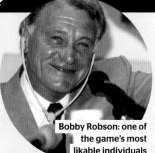

■ Despite finishing 11th, Newcastle were the third-highest scoring club under Bobby Robson this season, with 63 goals in 38 games.
■ Matt Le Tissier scored only three goals for Southampton this term, but became the first midfielder to reach 100 Premiership goals.
■ Wimbledon's 14-year run in the top flight ended when Bradford beat Liverpool 1-0 on the last day.

Bobby Robson: one of the game's most likable individuals

disappointing foreign contingent – Vladimir Smicer, Titi Camara and Sami Hyypia – were brought in, but it was local talent (Steven Gerrard, Robbie Fowler and Michael Owen) that kept the Reds in the race for a Champions League place. This was surrendered on the last day, however, after a shock defeat by Bradford City.

Watford were relegated with a Premiership low of 24 points, Shearer quit the international scene and Bobby Robson succeeded Ruud Gullit as manager of Newcastle United.

This season was all about Manchester United, though. At a time when their rivals were going through transitional periods, Ferguson's men dominated the competition after Christmas and deserved their sixth title in eight seasons.

▼ FINAL POSITIONS

		P	W	D	L	F	A	GD	Pts
1	**Manchester United (C)**	38	28	7	3	97	45	+52	91
2	**Arsenal**	38	22	7	9	73	43	+30	73
3	**Leeds United**	38	21	6	11	58	43	+15	69
4	**Liverpool**	38	19	10	9	51	30	+21	67
5	**Chelsea**	38	18	11	9	53	34	+19	65
18	▼ **Wimbledon**	38	7	12	19	46	74	-28	33
19	▼ **Sheffield Wednesday**	38	8	7	23	38	70	-32	31
20	▼ **Watford**	38	6	6	26	35	77	-42	24

▼ AWARDS

PFA Player of the Year
Roy Keane (Manchester Utd)

PFA Young Player of the Year
Harry Kewell (Leeds Utd)

FWA Player of the Year
Roy Keane (Manchester Utd)

Premier League Manager of the Year Alex Ferguson (Man Utd)

▼ ALSO IN 1999/00

■ **Ballon d'Or**
Luís Figo
(Real Madrid)
■ **Mercury Music Prize**
OK
■ **BBC Sports Personality of the Year** Lennox Lewis
■ **Oscar for best film**
American Beauty

2000/01

Sir Alex claims a hat-trick of consecutive Premiership titles, but has to concede manager of the year to George Burley with his overachieving Tractor Boys

The champagne is once again in full flow as Manchester United's players celebrate the club's third title in a row – but Fergie was already looking to next season

CARLING CHAMPIONS 2001

▼ 2000/01 PREMIER LEAGUE STATS

Champions Manchester Utd
(7th Premiership title, 14th title)
Top at Christmas Man Utd (1st)

....

Total goals scored 992
Average goals/game 2.61
Biggest home win
Man Utd 6-0 Bradford City
Biggest away win
Charlton Athletic 0-4 Liverpool

Man City 0-4 Arsenal
Derby County 0-4 Chelsea
Man City 0-4 Leeds Utd
Derby County 0-4 Liverpool
Longest winning run
8 (Man Utd)
Longest unbeaten run
13 (Leeds Utd)
Highest attendance 67,637
(Man Utd v Coventry City)

Lowest attendance 15,523
(Bradford City v Coventry City)
Average attendance 32,905

....

Champions League Man Utd,
Arsenal, Liverpool (3rd qualifying)
UEFA Cup Leeds United, Chelsea,
Ipswich Town
UEFA Intertoto Cup Aston Villa,
Newcastle Utd

▼ TOP GOALSCORERS

1	**Jimmy Floyd Hasselbaink** (Chelsea)	23
2	**Marcus Stewart** (Ipswich Town)	19
3	**Thierry Henry** (Arsenal)	17
	Mark Viduka (Leeds Utd)	17
5	**Michael Owen** (Liverpool)	16
6	**Teddy Sheringham** (Man Utd)	15
7	**Emile Heskey** (Liverpool)	14
	Kevin Phillips (Sunderland)	14

PREMIER LEAGUE TEAM OF THE YEAR

Forward
Thierry Henry
Arsenal

Forward
Teddy Sheringham
Man Utd

Midfielder
Ryan Giggs
Man Utd

Midfielder
Steven Gerrard
Liverpool

Midfielder
Patrick Vieira
Arsenal

Midfielder
Roy Keane
Man Utd

Defender
Wes Brown
Man Utd

Defender
Jaap Stam
Man Utd

Defender
Sylvinho
Arsenal

Defender
Stephen Carr
Spurs

Goalkeeper
Fabien Barthez
Man Utd

At the Premiership's inception, nobody believed one team would dominate in quite the way Manchester United have. The start of a new millennium didn't curb the club's ambitions and Sir Alex Ferguson's men retained their crown, Fergie becoming the first manager to win three successive English league titles. But this wasn't enough to secure the Manager of the Year award. That was given to George Burley, whose astonishing season at Ipswich Town was too hard for the judges to ignore.

Burley took over at Ipswich in 1994, when they were at the foot of the Premiership. He went down with the club, rebuilt the team, suffered three gruelling play-off defeats, re-emerged in the top flight in 2000 and, despite nationwide predictions of relegation, secured fifth spot and a UEFA Cup berth, nearly 20 years after the club's last jaunt on the continent. A fairytale, secured on a limited budget and truly

worthy of the praise bestowed upon it.

For the third year running, Arsenal finished second to United and with no silverware. The Gunners were trounced 6-1 by United in February, at which point their title dream was practically over, and, despite leading 1-0 with five minutes to go, they were beaten by two Michael Owen goals in the FA Cup final. Gérard Houllier's revitalised Liverpool also won the League Cup and UEFA Cup, and finished third in the Premiership to secure European Cup qualification for the first time since the Heysel stadium disaster of 1985. Jari Litmanen and Dietmar Hamman added more continental flavour to their play and the marauding Steven Gerrard won PFA Young Player of the Year after one of the club's most successful seasons.

Despite having won five trophies since February 1998, Gianluca Vialli was sacked by Chelsea after a poor start to the season. His successor was Claudio Ranieri, whose big signing, Jimmy Floyd Hasselbaink, forged a lucrative partnership with Gianfranco Zola to help secure sixth place in the table, UEFA Cup football and the top goalscorer accolade, with 23.

Leeds, on a fantastic European Cup adventure, teetered above the relegation places at Christmas, but fought their way up to fourth; Paul Gascoigne failed to make a real difference in an unremarkable Everton side; Glenn Hoddle caused more outrage by walking out on Southampton in March and taking the reins at Spurs the next day;

Manchester City had risen in 2000, but fell in 2001, manager Joe Royle being dismissed within days of their relegation, to be replaced by Kevin Keegan, who had resigned as England manager in October after losing a World Cup qualifier to Germany. Sven-Göran Eriksson became the first foreign manager of England, winning his first match 3-0 against Spain.

After 10 close shaves, Coventry City were finally relegated and Bradford equalled Swindon's low of five league wins to also go down.

At the end of the season, Ferguson broke Manchester United's transfer record twice for Ruud van Nistelrooy (£19m) and Juan Sebastián Verón (£28.1m). It was believed 2001/02 would be his last season at United's helm – how wrong we were!

▼ FINAL POSITIONS	P	W	D	L	F	A	GD	Pts
1 Manchester United	38	24	8	6	79	31	48	80
2 Arsenal	38	20	10	8	63	38	25	70
3 Liverpool	38	20	9	9	71	39	32	69
4 Leeds United	38	20	8	10	64	43	21	68
5 Ipswich Town	38	20	6	12	57	42	15	66
18 ▼ Manchester City	38	8	10	20	41	65	-24	34
19 ▼ Coventry City	38	8	10	20	36	63	-27	34
20 ▼ Bradford City	38	5	11	22	30	70	-40	26

▼ AWARDS

PFA Player of the Year
Teddy Sheringham (Manchester Utd)

PFA Young Player of the Year
Steven Gerrard (Liverpool)

FWA Player of the Year
Teddy Sheringham (Manchester Utd)

Premier League Manager of the Year George Burley (Ipswich Town)

▼ ALSO IN 2000/01

■ **Ballon d'Or**
Michael Owen (Liverpool)
■ **Mercury Music Prize**
The Hour Of Bewilderbeast
■ **BBC Sports Personality of the Year** Steve Redgrave
■ **Oscar for best film** Gladiator

2001/02

Top-scoring Thierry Henry fires Arsenal to their second Premiership title, the Gunners snatching the trophy from Manchester United at Old Trafford

Arsenal revel in stealing back the Premiership crown at Old Trafford to complete the double, having beaten Chelsea four days earlier to win the FA Cup

▼ 2001/02 PREMIER LEAGUE STATS

Champions Arsenal
(2nd Premiership title, 12th title)
Top at Christmas
Newcastle Utd (4th)

Total goals scored 1,000
Average goals/game 2.63
Biggest home win
Blackburn 7-1 West Ham
Biggest away win

Ipswich Town 0-6 Liverpool
Longest winning run
13 (Arsenal)
Longest unbeaten run
24 (Manchester United)
Highest attendance 67,683
(Man Utd v Middlesbrough)
Lowest attendance 15,412
(Leicester City v Middlesbrough)
Average attendance 34,249

Champions League
Arsenal, Liverpool, Man Utd,
Newcastle Utd
UEFA Cup
Leeds Utd, Chelsea, Blackburn,
Fulham, Ipswich Town

▼ TOP GOALSCORERS

1	**Thierry Henry** (Arsenal)	24
2	**Jimmy Floyd Hasselbaink** (Chelsea)	23
	Ruud van Nistelrooy (Manchester Utd)	23
	Alan Shearer (Newcastle Utd)	23
5	**Michael Owen** (Liverpool)	19
6	**Ole Gunnar Solskjaer** (Manchester Utd)	17
7	**Robbie Fowler** (Liverpool)	15
8	**Eidur Gudjohnsen** (Chelsea)	14

PREMIER LEAGUE TEAM OF THE YEAR

Forward
Thierry Henry
Arsenal

Forward
Ruud van Nistelrooy
Man Utd

Midfielder
Ryan Giggs
Man Utd

Midfielder
Robert Pires
Arsenal

Midfielder
Patrick Vieira
Arsenal

Midfielder
Roy Keane
Man Utd

Defender
Sami Hyypia
Liverpool

Defender
Rio Ferdinand
Leeds Utd

Defender
Wayne Bridge
Southampton

Defender
Steve Finnan
Fulham

Goalkeeper
Shay Given
Newcastle Utd

Arsenal – allowed Ferguson's side to claim top spot for the first time this season. By March, though, Arsenal were strong favourites for the title and lived up to the bookies' expectations at Old Trafford on 8 May, when they lifted the trophy. Liverpool snuck into second place with a 4-3 win over Graeme Souness' Blackburn Rovers.

Elsewhere in the league, Fulham – backed by multi-millionaire Mohamed Al Fayed, the owner of Harrods in London – had spent £34m and planned to attack their first season in the Premiership with fresh-faced vigour. Rather optimistically, Al Fayed predicted title glory in the first year, but the west London club finished 43 points behind champions Arsenal.

After the jubilations of the previous season, George Burley's Ipswich nosedived in 2001/02. Despite having the Premier League Manger of the Year and travelling into Europe for the first time in 20 years after finishing fifth the previous season, Ipswich made a diabolical start to this campaign, winning just one of their first 17 Premiership matches. It looked like Burley had turned a corner when his side won seven of their next eight games, but a 5-0 walloping by Liverpool on the last day of the season condemned the Tractor Boys to relegation.

Leicester City were already down by then. In their final season at the 111-year-old Filbert Street stadium, they finished rock bottom with just five wins. (The loss of essential TV revenue, coupled with the cost of a new ground

PREMIER LEAGUE GOAL OF THE SEASON

- **Dennis Bergkamp**
- **Newcastle Utd v Arsenal**
- **2 March 2002**

Receiving the ball with his back to goal, Bergkamp's first touch, pirouette around the bamboozled Nikos Dabizas and finish are all part of one fluid, joyous movement. Pure brilliance from the Dutch master.

Welcome to the spotlight, Messrs Wenger and Henry. After three years of living in the shadow of Manchester's Red Devils, it was Arsenal's turn for title glory. Not only that, but the crown was snatched from Sir Alex Ferguson and Co with a 1-0 victory at Old Trafford in the penultimate game of the season. Galling isn't the word...

The 10th season of the Premier League was a close-run thing, though, with Leeds, Liverpool and Newcastle joining Arsenal in exerting pressure on the champions and each other.

After back-to-back away victories over Arsenal and Leeds, Newcastle United topped the table over the Christmas period. Liverpool had been

eight points clear of a struggling Manchester United at the beginning of December, but fell away terribly. Bizarrely, however, their form in January – beating United at Old Trafford and salvaging a point against

2001/02 DID YOU KNOW?

- Unusually, Arsenal secured their double in reverse, winning the title four days *after* the FA Cup.
- At the end of the season, Wimbledon were given the all-clear for the move to Milton Keynes.
- The collapse of ITV Digital in May 2002 plunged many clubs into turmoil: Bradford City, Forest, Watford, Barnsley, Lincoln City and Port Vale all filed for administration.

ITV Digital: the scourge of many Football League clubs

– The Walkers Stadium – resulted in the club entering administration; but, remarkably, they returned to the Premiership just a year later.) Derby County also went down, which meant, for the first time in the history of the league, all three promoted teams – Fulham, Bolton Wanderers and Blackburn Rovers – avoided relegation.

Barclaycard replaced Carling as the official sponsor of the Premiership; Claudio Ranieri signed Frank Lampard for Chelsea; two of Arsenal's longest-serving players, Tony Adams and Lee Dixon, called time on their Arsenal careers, as did Blackburn's effervescent Mark Hughes.

But this was Arsenal's and Thierry Henry's season – and the new-look Gunners were to develop into something very special indeed.

▼ FINAL POSITIONS

		P	W	D	L	F	A	GD	Pts
1	Arsenal (C)	38	26	9	3	79	36	43	87
2	Liverpool	38	24	8	6	67	30	37	80
3	Manchester United	38	24	5	9	87	45	42	77
4	Newcastle United	38	21	8	9	74	52	22	71
5	Leeds United	38	18	12	8	53	37	16	66
18	▼ Ipswich Town	38	9	9	20	41	64	-23	36
19	▼ Derby County	38	8	6	24	33	63	-30	30
20	▼ Leicester City	38	5	13	20	30	64	-34	28

▼ AWARDS

PFA Player of the Year
Ruud van Nistelrooy (Man Utd)

PFA Young Player of the Year
Craig Bellamy (Newcastle Utd)

FWA Player of the Year
Robert Pires (Arsenal)

FA Premier League Manager of the Year Arsène Wenger (Arsenal)

▼ ALSO IN 2001/02

- **Ballon d'Or** Ronaldo (Real Madrid)
- **Mercury Music Prize** Stories From The City, Stories From The Sea
- **BBC Sports Personality of the Year** David Beckham
- **Oscar for best film** A Beautiful Mind

2002/03

If there's one thing you can expect from an Alex Ferguson team it's that they will never give up. Case in point: the Premier League's 2002/03 campaign...

Keane and Neville lead the celebrations, as United demolish Arsenal's lead to take their eighth EPL title

▼ 2002/03 PREMIER LEAGUE STATS

Champions
Man Utd (8th Premiership title, 15th English title)

Top at Christmas Man Utd (1st)

Total goals scored 1000
Average goals/game 2.63
Biggest home win
Chelsea 5-0 Man City
Arsenal 6-1 Southampton

Biggest away win
West Bromwich Albion 0-6 Liverpool

Longest winning run
7 (Liverpool)

Longest unbeaten run
18 (Man Utd)

Highest attendance 67,721
(Man Utd 4-1 Charlton Athletic)

Lowest attendance 14,017

(Fulham 0-4 Blackburn)
Average attendance 35,470

Champions League
Man Utd, Arsenal, Newcastle Utd, Chelsea

UEFA Cup
Southampton, Blackburn, Liverpool, Man City

▼ TOP GOALSCORERS

1	**Ruud van Nistelrooy** (Man Utd)	25
2	**Thierry Henry** (Arsenal)	24
3	**James Beattie** (Southampton)	23
4	**Mark Viduka** (Leeds Utd)	20
5	**Michael Owen** (Liverpool)	19
6	**Alan Shearer** (Newcastle)	17

PREMIER LEAGUE TEAM OF THE YEAR

Forward
Alan Shearer
Newcastle Utd

Forward
Thierry Henry
Arsenal

Midfielder
Kieron Dyer
Newcastle Utd

Midfielder
Robert Pires
Arsenal

Midfielder
Paul Scholes
Man Utd

Midfielder
Patrick Vieira
Arsenal

Defender
William Gallas
Chelsea

Defender
Sol Campbell
Arsenal

Defender
Ashley Cole
Arsenal

Defender
Stephen Carr
Spurs

Goalkeeper
Brad Friedel
Blackburn

Rarely does a season begin in the Premier League when it's Alex Ferguson out looking for revenge, but such was the case in 2002/03. Arsenal, his closest foe, would lead the way by a full eight points come the start of March, looking certainties to retain their crown, but United's drive, stamina and never-say-die attitude would serve them well come the seasonal denouement.

As part of his preparations for the season, on July 22 Man Utd announced the capture of Rio Ferdinand from Leeds for £29m, breaking the English transfer record for a third time in just over a year; Dwight Yorke left Old Trafford for Graeme Souness and Ewood Park, where he would ply his trade

alongside Andy Cole once again; David O'Leary, who spent over £100m on players during his time at Elland Road but didn't manage to secure a major trophy, was sacked by Leeds Utd; and Juninho signed for Middlesbrough for a third time from Atlético Madrid.

Tottenham and Glenn Hoddle top the table after the first month of games, the Spurs boss digging £7m deep to lure the talents of Robbie Keane from Leeds Utd. The Lilywhites of north London would enjoy a brief taste of league success and later slip to 10th and the usual mid-table anonymity. Manchester United endured a dismal start to proceedings by their high standards, but a 1-0 home win over Spurs, Ruud van Nistelrooy scoring from the spot, would put them back on track.

Good things are beginning to happen in the red half of Merseyside, too. Liverpool leapfrog Arsenal into pole position at the end of October, leaving some commentators convinced that their 12-year wait for a league title is about to end.

Come Christmas, though, and Manchester United are starting to find their title-winning feet. They beat holders Arsenal 2-0 at Old Trafford and West Ham 3-0 to edge closer to the top, bypassing a Liverpool team on a by now rather predictable decline, beaten by Sunderland 2-1 at the Stadium of Light. Come January, and Houllier's Reds are red-faced and deemed far too inconsistent to challenge. Everton, on the other hand, find themselves just three points off the top spot. How the Premiership tides doth turn...

United would come back, though – and in some style. Despite a demoralising 2-0 defeat to Liverpool

2002/03 DID YOU KNOW?

- David Beckham suffered a gash to his face after his infuriated gaffer kicked a box of football boots in the changing room.
- Sunderland broke the record for a relegated team's lowest goal tally.
- Wayne Rooney became the youngest ever goalscorer in EPL history on 19 October 2002, when he netted a fine winner against Arsenal five days prior to his 17th birthday.

Bold, powerful, terrier-like: welcome to the Prem, Mr Rooney

PREMIER LEAGUE GOAL OF THE SEASON

- Thierry Henry
- 16 November 2002
- Spurs v Arsenal

The French maestro picks up a clearance 35 yards inside his own half, gets the ball out of his feet and gallops, shaking off one defender, coming inside two more before slotting into the net with his weaker foot. Pace and precision.

in the League Cup Final, by 15 March they closed the Gunners' gap to just two points by beating struggling Leeds and then capitalising on Arsenal's surprise slip-up at Blackburn by scraping past Villa 1-0. Sweet revenge against Liverpool, 4-0 at Old Trafford, and Paul Scholes in imperious form against Newcastle and Blackburn sees the Red Devils ascend to the summit.

And so to 4 May 2003, and the completion of another intense and noteworthy United comeback. Arsenal lose 3-2 at home to a resurgent Leeds and relinquish their title to the Red Devils. They'd looked a dead-cert for the honours just a month before, but the pressure from Old Trafford proved too much, and Wenger's men blew it on the run-in.

FINAL POSITIONS

		P	W	D	L	F	A	GD	Pts
1	Manchester United	38	25	8	5	74	34	40	83
2	Arsenal	38	23	9	6	85	42	43	78
3	Newcastle United	38	21	6	11	63	48	15	69
4	Chelsea	38	19	10	9	68	38	30	67
5	Liverpool	38	18	10	10	61	41	20	64
18 ▼	West Ham United	38	10	12	16	42	59	-17	42
19 ▼	West Bromwich Albion	38	6	8	24	29	65	-36	26
20 ▼	Sunderland	38	4	7	27	21	65	-44	19

AWARDS

PFA Player of the Year
Thierry Henry (Arsenal)

PFA Young Player of the Year
Jermaine Jenas (Newcastle Utd)

FWA Player of the Year
Thierry Henry (Arsenal)

FA Premier League Manager of the Year Alex Ferguson

ALSO IN 2002/03

- **Ballon d'Or** Pavel Nedvěd (Juventus)
- **Mercury Music Prize** A Little Deeper
- **BBC Sports Personality of the Year** Paula Radcliffe
- **Oscar for best film** Chicago

2003/04

Arsenal's team were unbeatable, Chelsea's finances unmatchable and Sir Alex Ferguson's eye for talent undiminished in a heated and historic season

Arsenal's Invincibles celebrate with the Premiership trophy, which they won by going through the whole 38-game season without losing a game

▼ 2003/04 PREMIER LEAGUE STATS

Champions Arsenal
(3rd Premiership title, 13th title)
Top at Christmas Manchester United (3rd)

....

Total goals scored 1,012
Average goals/game 2.66
Biggest home win
Arsenal 5-0 Leeds Utd
Chelsea 5-0 Newcastle Utd

Portsmouth 6-1 Leeds Utd
Biggest away win
Wolves 0-5 Chelsea
Leicester City 0-5 Aston Villa
Longest winning run
9 (Arsenal)
Longest unbeaten run
38 (Arsenal)
Highest attendance 67,758
(Man Utd v Southampton)

Lowest attendance 13,981
(Fulham v Blackburn Rovers)

....

Champions League Arsenal, Chelsea, Man Utd, Liverpool
UEFA Cup Newcastle Utd, Middlesbrough

▼ TOP GOALSCORERS

1	**Thierry Henry** (Arsenal)	30
2	**Alan Shearer** (Newcastle Utd)	22
3	**Louis Saha** (Man Utd, Fulham)	20
	Ruud van Nistelrooy (Man Utd)	20
5	**Mikael Forssell** (Birmingham City)	17

PREMIER LEAGUE **TEAM OF THE YEAR**

Forward
Ruud van Nistelrooy
Man Utd

Forward
Thierry Henry
Arsenal

Midfielder
Robert Pires
Arsenal

Midfielder
Steven Gerrard
Liverpool

Midfielder
Patrick Vieira
Arsenal

Midfielder
Frank Lampard
Chelsea

Defender
John Terry
Chelsea

Defender
Sol Campbell
Arsenal

Defender
Ashley Cole
Arsenal

Defender
Lauren
Arsenal

Goalkeeper
Tim Howard
Man Utd

T he first victory of the 2003/04 season was for the competition itself. On 30 July 2003, the Premiership was officially declared the richest football league in Europe – and a season of records ended with one of considerable note: Arsenal went through the entire campaign undefeated, the first team to do so in a 38-game season and only the second team to do so in the history of the English top flight (Preston North End had done it in 1889, but only had to play 22 fixtures).

After the hottest recorded summer, Chelsea turned up the heat on their Premiership rivals with the arrival of Russian oligarch Roman Abramovich. He cleared £100m of debts and ordered the club to recruit the world's best players: Claude Makelele, Juan Sebastián Verón, Joe Cole, Alexei Smertin, Hernan Crespo and Scott Parker all arrived at Stamford Bridge.

German international goalkeeper Jens Lehmann was the only arrival at Arsenal, Arsène Wenger hoping this new 6ft 3in blockade, plus a gradually developing team spirit and footballing philosophy, would be enough to overcome Chelsea's millions and Manchester United's experience.

Sir Alex Ferguson's and David Beckham's differences came to a head in pre-season, when the England captain was sold to Real Madrid for £25m. The relatively unknown Cristiano Ronaldo came from Sporting Lisbon for £12.24m to fill the gap.

Arsenal, United and Chelsea all won their first three games to occupy the top spots early on, and the predicted three-horse race had begun.

Passions were at boiling point during the first Arsenal v United game at the end of September. Patrick Vieira was sent off for lunging at Ruud van Nistelrooy and when the Dutchman missed a late penalty, the Gunners exacted unruly revenge live on TV. Six Arsenal players served bans that could have wrecked the club's season, but another ruling played arguably a bigger part in deciding the title. Manchester United defender Rio Ferdinand missed the last four months of the season after being banned by the FA for missing a drugs test.

Elsewhere during the season, Peter Reid was sacked by rock-bottom, administration-threatened Leeds; Steve McClaren guided Middlesbrough to their first major trophy, the League Cup, thanks to a 2-1 win over Bolton; David Seaman announced his retirement at the age of 40; Newcastle's Gary Speed became

2003/04 DID YOU KNOW?

■ Columbian striker, Juan Pablo Angel, became the first Aston Villa player to score 20 goals in a league season since 1996.
■ Combative Cameroonian international Marc-Vivien Foe, who scored nine goals in 35 games while on loan at Manchester City, including their last one at Maine Road, collapsed and died during a Confederations Cup tie for his country, aged 28.

There can be only Juan: a South American success story

PREMIER LEAGUE GOAL OF THE SEASON

■ Dietmar Hamann
■ 17 March 2004
■ Liverpool v Portsmouth

From the left wing, Michael Owen crosses towards the edge of the penalty area, where the on-rushing Hamann meets the ball on the full with a volley that would smash a hole through next week such is its power.

the first Premiership player to play 400 games; and Gérard Houllier and Claudio Ranieri would be sacked by Liverpool and Chelsea respectively.

Back to the title race, and on 21 February Arsenal came from behind to beat Chelsea 2-1 at Stamford Bridge, while Leeds equalised late on at Old Trafford. With nine games to go, Arsenal were still unbeaten and a win or draw against United at Highbury would set a new record for league games without defeat from the start of a season. The game ended 1-1.

On 25 April, Newcastle beat Chelsea 2-1 at home and gave Arsenal the chance to clinch the Premiership title away to bitter rivals Tottenham Hotspur, which the Gunners did with a 2-2 draw. Four games later they became 'the Invincibles'.

▼ FINAL POSITIONS

		P	W	D	L	F	A	GD	Pts
1	**Arsenal (C)**	38	26	12	0	73	26	47	90
2	**Chelsea**	38	24	7	7	67	30	37	79
3	**Manchester United**	38	23	6	9	64	35	29	75
4	**Liverpool**	38	16	12	10	55	37	18	60
5	**Newcastle United**	38	13	17	8	52	40	12	56
18	▼ **Leicester City**	38	6	15	17	48	65	-17	33
19	▼ **Leeds United**	38	8	9	21	40	79	-39	33
20	▼ **Wolves**	38	7	12	19	38	77	-39	33

▼ AWARDS

PFA Player of the Year
Thierry Henry (Arsenal)

PFA Young Player of the Year
Scott Parker (Charlton Athletic, Chelsea)

FWA Player of the Year
Thierry Henry (Arsenal)

Premier League Manager of the Year Arsène Wenger

▼ ALSO IN 2003/04

■ **Ballon d'Or**
Andriy Shevchenko (AC Milan)
■ **Mercury Music Prize** Boy In Da Corner
■ **BBC Sports Personality of the Year** Jonny Wilkinson
■ **Oscar for best film** TLOTR: Return Of The King

2004/05

The Special One took advantage of Chelsea's millions, and the increasingly bitter rivalry between Arsenal and Manchester United, to steal the title...

José Mourinho, backed by Roman Abramovich's chequebook, delivered Chelsea's first Premier League title in style, finishing 12 points clear of nearest rivals Arsenal

▼ 2004/05 PREMIER LEAGUE STATS

Champions Chelsea
(1st Premiership title, 2nd title)
Top at Christmas Chelsea
....

Total goals scored 974
Average goals/game 2.56
Biggest home win
Arsenal 7-0 Everton
Biggest away win
West Brom 0-5 Liverpool

Longest winning run
8 (Chelsea)
Longest unbeaten run
29 (Chelsea)
Highest attendance 67,989
(Man Utd v Portsmouth)
Lowest attendance 16,180
(Fulham v West Brom)
Average attendance 33,893
....

Champions League
Chelsea, Arsenal, Manchester United, Everton, Liverpool
UEFA Cup Everton, Bolton, Middlesbrough

▼ TOP GOALSCORERS

1	**Thierry Henry** (Arsenal)	25
2	**Andy Johnson** (Crystal Palace)	21
3	**Robert Pires** (Arsenal)	14
4	**Jermain Defoe** (Spurs)	13
	Jimmy Floyd Hasselbaink (Middlesbrough)	13
	Frank Lampard (Chelsea)	13
	Yakubu Aiyegbeni (Portsmouth)	13

PREMIER LEAGUE TEAM OF THE YEAR

Forward
Thierry Henry
Arsenal

Forward
Andrew Johnson
Crystal Palace

Midfielder
Arjen Robben
Chelsea

Midfielder
Shaun Wright-Phillips
Man City

Midfielder
Frank Lampard
Chelsea

Midfielder
Steven Gerrard
Liverpool

Defender
Rio Ferdinand
Man Utd

Defender
John Terry
Chelsea

Defender
Ashley Cole
Arsenal

Defender
Gary Neville
Man Utd

Goalkeeper
Petr Cech
Chelsea

Undoubtedly a three-horse race in 2003/04, this season's Premiership would see Arsène Wenger and Sir Alex Ferguson joined by the self-appointed 'Special One', José Mourinho. Another new manager with a big reputation, Rafael Benítez, took over at Liverpool.

Patrick Vieira pledged his short-term future to Arsenal and 20-year-old Robin van Persie arrived from Feyenoord. After being 3-1 behind to Middlesbrough in the early season, Arsenal won 5-3 to go 43 league games undefeated and beat Nottingham Forest's record. Could they reach 50?

At Chelsea, new signings Petr Cech, Arjen Robben, Mateja Kezman and Ricardo Carvalho were soon joined by Ivorian man-mountain Didier Drogba, and the Mourinho era got off to a great start when the Blues beat Manchester United in front of their home support. United's reaction? To make Wayne Rooney football's most expensive teenager, handing over the princely sum of £27m to secure his services from Everton.

Norwich, back in the top flight, drew their opening fixture at home to Crystal Palace, Andrew Johnson scoring the equaliser to begin a revelatory season for the striker, despite the Eagles' eventual relegation.

Southampton's manager, Paul Sturrock, was given the chop after two games and was quickly followed by Sir Bobby Robson at St James' Park. He was replaced at Newcastle by Graeme Souness, who dragged the Geordie club out of the relegation mire with a five-game unbeaten run. Success was also instant for Mark Hughes, who took over at Blackburn, though his season would prove much more of a struggle. Meanwhile, manager-of-the-month Harry Redknapp turned his back on Portsmouth and took charge at Southampton 14 days later.

At the end of September, Manchester United were seven points off the pace, with Arsenal making a 100% start to the campaign. But Ferguson's men halted the Gunners' unbeaten run at 49, with a 2-0 victory at Old Trafford that included a contentious penalty. Later in the season, United would complete the double over Wenger's team at Highbury to inflict Arsenal's first home defeat since they were beaten 3-2 by Leeds in May 2003.

Mourinho, with Chelsea owner Roman Abramovich's millions, was steamrolling all before him. The Blues led the table at Christmas and only got stronger as they moved into 2004. When Arsenal and Manchester United met at Highbury on 1 February, both managers admitted the loser would be out of the title race. In an extremely tense affair, John O'Shea sealed the 4-2 win for United with a deft chip. Meanwhile, against Blackburn Rovers, Cech's penalty save from Paul Dickov helped him surpass Peter Schmeichel's record of 694 minutes without conceding a Premiership goal.

On 30 April, Chelsea secured their first Premier League title with two goals from Frank Lampard against Bolton Wanderers. United and Arsenal's increasingly volcanic rivalry had played into the Special One's hands. Chelsea finished the season 12 points above the champions, and 18 above United.

PREMIER LEAGUE GOAL OF THE SEASON

■ Erik Edman ■ 16 April 2005
■ Liverpool v **Tottenham**

Liverpool comfortably clear their area and the ball falls to Spurs's least threatening player, left-back Erik Edman, who controls it, pushes it ahead of himself and then unleashes the shot of the season with his left boot. An unstoppable screamer.

2004/05 DID YOU KNOW?

■ Having served a 30 day prison sentence (for driving offences), Birmingham City player Jermaine Pennant was cleared to play against spurs with an electronic tag.
■ Green-jumpered Nottingham Forest legend Brian Clough sadly died on 20 September 2004, aged 69.
■ Emirates airlines handed Arsenal a cool £100m for the naming rights of their new north London stadium.

Ol' Big 'Ed: bright, barmy and totally brilliant

▼ FINAL POSITIONS

		P	W	D	L	F	A	GD	Pts
1	Chelsea (C)	38	29	8	1	72	15	57	95
2	Arsenal	38	25	8	5	87	36	51	83
3	Manchester United	38	22	11	5	58	26	32	77
4	Everton	38	18	7	13	45	46	-1	61
5	Liverpool	38	17	7	14	52	41	11	58
18	▼ Crystal Palace	38	7	12	19	41	62	-21	33
19	▼ Norwich City	38	7	12	19	42	77	-35	33
20	▼ Southampton	38	6	14	18	45	66	-21	32

▼ AWARDS

PFA Player of the Year
John Terry (Chelsea)

PFA Young Player of the Year
Wayne Rooney (Manchester Utd)

FWA Player of the Year
Frank Lampard (Chelsea)

Premier League Manager of the Year José Mourinho (Chelsea)

▼ ALSO IN 2004/05

■ **Ballon d'Or**
Ronaldinho (Barcelona)
■ **Mercury Music Prize** Franz Ferdinand
■ **BBC Sports Personality of the Year** Kelly Holmes
■ **Oscar for best film** Million Dollar Baby

Franz Ferdinand

2005/06

Arsenal changed colour, 'Arry changed allegiance (again) and Wigan took the top flight by surprise – but no one could loosen Mourinho's grip on the trophy

Chelsea had become a formidable force under José Mourinho and they proved it with another Premier League crown

▼ 2005/06 PREMIER LEAGUE STATS

Champions Chelsea
(2nd Premiership title, 3rd title)
Top at Christmas Chelsea (1st)
....
Total goals scored 944
Average goals/game 2.48
Biggest home win
Arsenal 7-0 Middlesbrough
Biggest away win
Middlesbrough 0-4 Aston Villa

Everton 0-4 Bolton
Fulham 0-4 Arsenal
Longest winning run
10 (Chelsea)
Longest unbeaten run
13 (Chelsea)
Highest attendance 73,006
(Man Utd v Charlton Athletic)
Lowest attendance 16,550
(Fulham v Birmingham City)

Average attendance 33,875
....
Champions League
Chelsea, Manchester United,
Liverpool, Arsenal
UEFA Cup
Spurs, Blackburn, Newcastle Utd

▼ TOP GOALSCORERS

1	**Thierry Henry** (Arsenal)	27
2	**Ruud van Nistelrooy** (Manchester Utd)	21
3	**Darren Bent** (Charlton)	18
4	**Robbie Keane** (Spurs)	16
	Frank Lampard (Chelsea)	16
	Wayne Rooney (Manchester Utd)	16
7	**Marlon Harewood** (West Ham)	14

PREMIER LEAGUE **TEAM OF THE YEAR**

Forward
Wayne Rooney
Man Utd

Forward
Thierry Henry
Arsenal

Midfielder
Joe Cole
Chelsea

Midfielder
Cristiano Ronaldo
Man Utd

Midfielder
Frank Lampard
Chelsea

Midfielder
Steven Gerrard
Liverpool

Defender
Jamie Carragher
Liverpool

Defender
John Terry
Chelsea

Defender
William Gallas
Chelsea

Defender
Pascal Chimbonda
Wigan Athletic

Goalkeeper
Shay Given
Newcastle Utd

If Chelsea and José Mourinho hadn't announced themselves with enough pomp in 2004/05, they rubberstamped their authority on the English top flight in 2005/06, changing the order of Premiership football for good.

In preparation, they sought the talents of Manchester City's diminutive Shaun Wright-Phillips, for a cool £21m, while a club-record fee of £24.4m, was paid to Lyon for the services of Ghanaian all-round powerhouse, Michael Essien. Chelsea signalled their intent by winning 14 of their first 16 matches, giving them a crucial headstart over the chasing pack.

Manchester United's early-season form was stuttering and although they picked up a frightening head of steam towards the end of the season

– reducing Chelsea's 18-point lead to a mere seven at one point – a surprising 0-0 draw against bottom club Sunderland, at Old Trafford, on 14 April effectively put paid to their hopes of a last-gasp fightback. Malcolm Glazer's

£800m summer takeover of the country's biggest club had become an unwelcome distraction during preparations to win back their crown. Edwin van der Sar had proved an adept signing, but United didn't show any real unity until the title race was nearly over.

Everton, who had enjoyed such a fruitful campaign the previous season, struggled under new expectation and were unceremoniously dumped out of Champions League qualifying by a Román Riquelme-inspired Villareal. A season that had promised much was to deliver very little.

In stark contrast to the Toffees' failings, Paul Jewell's newly promoted Wigan staggered top-flight opposition with their style and sheer resilience. They began without fear, neutering the champions in their opening fixture until a last-minute wonder strike from Hernan Crespo, with 40 seconds remaining. "I think it's not fair," remarked Mourinho after the match. "They didn't deserve to lose."

To mark their last season at Highbury, Arsenal reverted to wearing the same colour (redcurrant) shirts worn when they first moved to north London in 1913. But their influential skipper Patrick Vieira had departed for Juventus and, barely a week into the season, a 1-0 defeat by Chelsea set the tone for their campaign.

Harry Redknapp's south-coast pendulum rocked back to Blue when he left relegated Southampton to rejoin Portsmouth; Darren Bent and Danny Murphy forged an exciting axis

at Charlton Athletic; European Cup winners Liverpool again failed to make an impact in the Premiership; and Alan Shearer became Newcastle United's highest goalscorer – his 201st strike, against Portsmouth at St James' Park in February breaking Jackie Milburn's 200-goal haul that had stood for 49 years. (Unfortunately, on 17 April, Shearer played his last competitive match in Newcastle's 4-1 victory away to Sunderland after he suffered a knee injury from a tackle by Julio Arca.)

Meanwhile, Spurs missed out on Champions League football because of a bout of food poisoning, and Steve McClaren became England manager.

But the season again belonged to Mourinho and Chelsea, and on 29 April they retained the Premiership title after beating Manchester United 3-0.

PREMIER LEAGUE GOAL OF THE SEASON

- Anton Ferdinand ■ 23 Jan 2006
- **West Ham** v Fulham

A Hammers corner is half cleared by Fulham and a retreating Anton Ferdinand swivels superbly on a headed knockdown to volley home from outside the box with the aplomb of a South American striker. Di Canio would've been proud.

2005/06 DID YOU KNOW?

- In its 14th season, Manchester United became the first team to score 1,000 Premier League goals.
- Legendary Manchester United forward George Best died on 25 November 2005, after suffering multiple organ failure.
- Middlesbrough's 3-0 victory over Chelsea on 11 February was the first time José Mourinho's Chelsea had lost by more than a single goal.

George Best: a bit good on his day, apparently

▼ FINAL POSITIONS

		P	W	D	L	F	A	GD	Pts
1	Chelsea	38	29	4	5	72	22	50	91
2	Manchester United	38	25	8	5	72	34	38	83
3	Liverpool	38	25	7	6	57	25	32	82
4	Arsenal	38	20	7	11	68	31	37	67
5	Tottenham Hotspur	38	18	11	9	53	38	15	65
18	▼ Birmingham City	38	8	10	20	28	50	-22	34
19	▼ West Bromwich Albion	38	7	9	22	31	58	-27	30
20	▼ Sunderland	38	3	6	29	26	69	-43	15

▼ AWARDS

PFA Player of the Year
Steven Gerrard (Liverpool)

PFA Young Player of the Year
Wayne Rooney (Manchester Utd)

FWA Player of the Year
Thierry Henry (Arsenal)

Premier League Manager of the Year José Mourinho (Chelsea)

▼ ALSO IN 2005/06

- **Ballon d'Or** Fabio Cannavaro (Real Madrid)
- **Mercury Music Prize** I Am A Bird Now
- **BBC Sports Personality of the Year** Andrew Flintoff
- **Oscar for best film** Crash

---

20 SOMETHING Aussie stickman Mark Schwarzer was the first overseas player to make 400 Premier League appearances. He did so for Fulham in 2009/10.

2006/07

Chelsea bid for a hat-trick of titles, Reading prove no pushovers, Liverpool and Villa get taken over, and the Premiership has its first glimpse of Carlos Tevez

The Special One, José Mourinho, was left feeling a little ordinary after Sir Alex Ferguson and Manchester United pipped Chelsea to the post for their ninth title

▼ 2006/07 PREMIER LEAGUE STATS

Champions Manchester United
(9th Premiership title, 16th title)

Top at Christmas Man Utd (1st)

....

Total goals scored 931

Average goals/game 2.45

Biggest home win
Reading 6-0 West Ham Utd

Biggest away win
Middlesbrough 0-4 Portsmouth

Reading 0-4 Arsenal
Bolton Wanderers 0-4 Man Utd
Wigan Athletic 0-4 Liverpool
Tottenham Hotspur 0-4 Man Utd

Longest winning run
9 (Chelsea)

Longest unbeaten run
14 (Chelsea)

Highest attendance 76,398
(Manchester United v Blackburn)

Lowest attendance 13,760
(Watford v Blackburn Rovers)

Average attendance 34,402

....

Champions League Man Utd,
Chelsea, Liverpool, Arsenal

UEFA Cup Bolton Wanderers,
Spurs, Everton

Intertoto Cup Blackburn

....

▼ TOP GOALSCORERS

1	**Didier Drogba** (Chelsea)	20
2	**Benni McCarthy** (Blackburn Rovers)	18
3	**Cristiano Ronaldo** (Man Utd)	17
4	**Wayne Rooney** (Man Utd)	14
	Mark Viduka (Middlesbrough)	14
6	**Darren Bent** (Charlton Athletic)	13
	Kevin Doyle (Reading)	13

PREMIER LEAGUE TEAM OF THE YEAR

Forward — Dimitar Berbatov (Spurs)
Forward — Didier Drogba (Chelsea)
Midfielder — Ryan Giggs (Man Utd)
Midfielder — Cristiano Ronaldo (Man Utd)
Midfielder — Paul Scholes (Man Utd)
Midfielder — Steven Gerrard (Liverpool)
Defender — Nemanja Vidic (Man Utd)
Defender — Rio Ferdinand (Man Utd)
Defender — Patrice Evra (Man Utd)
Defender — Gary Neville (Man Utd)
Goalkeeper — Edwin van der Sar (Man Utd)

Manchester United's Wayne Rooney and Cristiano Ronaldo kissed and made up after a spat at the 2002 World Cup, and a new supply line for their talents arrived in the form of £18.6m Michael Carrick from Tottenham. A 5-1 opening-day victory over Fulham and a menacing 100% record in August put the Red Devils top of the pile.

West Ham shocked the footballing world on transfer-deadline day by capturing two world-class Argentinians, Javier Mascherano and Carlos Tevez. The latter kept West Ham up by scoring a vital winning goal against Manchester United on the final day. Financial irregularities overshadowed the celebrations, though, as Sheffield United contested Tevez's eligibility to play.

William Gallas and Ashley Cole swapped clubs, with Chelsea paying the Gunners an additional £5m. Arsenal ended Manchester United's 100% start and Portsmouth went top after a 1-0 win over Charlton.

Reading won the Championship with a record 106 points, but were still expected to struggle in the top flight. However, when they completed a purposeful 3-2 comeback against Middlesbrough in their opening match, it was clear Steve Coppell's men were to be no pushovers.

So to the run-in, and a two-horse race between Chelsea and Manchester United. John Terry missed the whole of January because of injury, and United's mix of experience and youth was proving potent on the pitch. They

PREMIER LEAGUE GOAL OF THE SEASON

- Wayne Rooney
- Man Utd v Bolton
- 17 March 2007

A lesson in the art of the counter-attack. Defending a long throw deep in their own area, Rooney exchanges passes with Cristiano Ronaldo before dinking the ball delicately over Jaaskelainen just over 10 seconds later.

Could José Mourinho's Chelsea make it a hat-trick of Premiership titles? How would Monsieur Wenger be celebrating his 10th year in the Arsenal hotseat – away from Highbury for the first time in nearly 100 years?

Andriy Shevchenko arrived at Stamford Bridge for a whopping £30m and German captain Michael Ballack also took up residence in the capital. "They are not arriving in a team that needs them to be champions," responded Mourinho. "They are arriving into a team who are already champions." Thanks, José.

Just two days after defeat by Barcelona in the Champions League final, Thierry Henry dispelled rumours of his departure from Arsenal by

putting pen to paper on a new four-year contract. Despite his number 7 shirt, Tomas Rosicky found it difficult to fill the boots of Robert Pires and, with Dennis Bergkamp also gone, Arsenal's attacking threat diminished.

won all of their February fixtures to extend their lead to nine points.

To March, and a season-ending injury to Thierry Henry effectively ends Arsenal's challenge, while a very late winner from Manchester United's John O'Shea at Anfield did the same for Rafa Benítez's Liverpool.

The final weekend in April proved decisive. United came from behind to beat Everton 4-2 and Chelsea were held 2-2 at home by Bolton. With three games to go, there was a five-point gap and it was too much for the champions to bridge. On 6 May, United lifted their ninth title in 15 years.

Elsewhere, Randy Lerner took over from Doug Ellis at Aston Villa and George Gillett and Tom Hicks started their lamentable incumbency at Anfield...

2006/07 DID YOU KNOW?

- Reading were playing in the top-flight for the first time in their 135-year history.
- In August, Ben Thatcher viciously elbowed Pedro Mendes during a game at Fratton Park, knocking the Portuguese midfielder unconscious and leaving him requiring hospital treatment.
- Peter Cech fractured his skull in a clash with Reading's Stephen Hunt.

Hope he Mendes well: a pre-hospitalised Pedro

▼ FINAL POSITIONS	P	W	D	L	F	A	GD	Pts
1 Manchester United (C)	38	28	5	5	83	27	56	89
2 Chelsea	38	24	11	3	64	24	40	83
3 Liverpool	38	20	8	10	57	27	30	68
4 Arsenal	38	19	11	8	63	35	28	68
5 Tottenham Hotspur	38	17	9	12	57	54	3	60
18 ▼ Sheffield United	38	10	8	20	32	55	-23	38
19 ▼ Charlton Athletic	38	8	10	20	34	60	-26	34
20 ▼ Watford	38	5	13	20	29	59	-30	28

▼ AWARDS

PFA Player of the Year
Cristiano Ronaldo (Man Utd)

PFA Young Player of the Year
Cristiano Ronaldo (Man Utd)

FWA Player of the Year
Cristiano Ronaldo (Man Utd)

FA Premier League Manager of the Year Sir Alex Ferguson (Man Utd)

▼ ALSO IN 2006/07

- **Ballon d'Or** Kaká (AC Milan)
- **Mercury Music Prize** Whatever People Say I Am, That's What I'm Not
- **BBC Sports Personality of the Year** Zara Phillips
- **Oscar for best film** The Departed

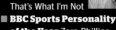

2007/08

Cristiano Ronaldo can't stop scoring, Chelsea give the Special One the old heave-ho, Fulham do a Harry Houdini – and the champions look familiar

Manchester United celebrate taking their total number of Premier League title wins into double figures after a final-day victory over Wigan Athletic

▼ 2007/08 PREMIER LEAGUE STATS

Champions Manchester United (10th Premier League title, 17th title)

Top at Christmas Arsenal (3rd)

....

Total goals scored 1,002

Average goals/game 2.64

Biggest home win
Middlesbrough 8-1 Manchester City

Biggest away win
Derby County 0-6 Aston Villa

Longest winning run
8 (Manchester United)

Longest unbeaten run
21 (Chelsea)

Highest attendance 76,013
(Man Utd v West Ham)

Lowest attendance 14,007
(Wigan v Middlesbrough)

Average attendance 36,076

....

Champions League Man Utd, Chelsea, Arsenal, Liverpool

UEFA Cup Portsmouth, Everton, Spurs, Man City

Intertoto Cup Aston Villa

▼ TOP GOALSCORERS

1	**Cristiano Ronaldo** (Manchester Utd)	31
2	**Fernando Torres** (Liverpool)	24
	Emmanuel Adebayor (Arsenal)	24
4	**Roque Santa Cruz** (Blackburn)	19
5	**Benjani** (Portsmouth, Manchester City)	15
	Dimitar Berbatov (Tottenham Hotspur)	15
	Robbie Keane (Spurs)	15
	Yakubu (Everton)	15

PREMIER LEAGUE TEAM OF THE YEAR

Forward
Fernando Torres
Liverpool

Forward
Emmanuel Adebayor
Arsenal

Midfielder
Ashley Young
Aston Villa

Midfielder
Cristiano Ronaldo
Man Utd

Midfielder
Cesc Fàbregas
Arsenal

Midfielder
Steven Gerrard
Liverpool

Defender
Nemanja Vidic
Man Utd

Defender
Rio Ferdinand
Man Utd

Defender
Gaël Clichy
Arsenal

Defender
Bacary Sagna
Arsenal

Goalkeeper
David James
Portsmouth

A 'Big Four' was becoming prominent in the newly renamed Premier League – Manchester United, Chelsea, Arsenal and Liverpool – and 2007/08 was to be the third season in which this powerful quadrangle would secure the top spots and Champions League status for another campaign.

United had the outstanding individual: Cristiano Ronaldo would score 31 goals, predominantly from midfield, to equal Alan Shearer's Premier League record.

Hungry for continued success, Sir Alex Ferguson had invested £50m in his team over the summer, bringing in Owen Hargreaves, Nani and the controversial Argentinian Carlos Tevez. United weren't the only ones spending

big, though. Liverpool unveiled £27m Spaniard Fernando Torres, who immediately endeared himself to the Kop by scoring in the 1-1 draw with Chelsea on his League debut.

Thaksin Shinawatra, the then-prime minister of Thailand, bought Manchester City and, despite a good start, would suffer the ignominy of the biggest defeat of the season, 8-1 at Middlesbrough. Manager Sven-Göran Eriksson was axed in the summer.

After a 2-0 defeat away to Aston Villa, a goalless draw with Blackburn and a 1-1 stalemate with Rosenborg in the Champions League, hostilities at Chelsea boiled over: the 'Special One', José Mourinho, was shown the door and Abramovich installed Avram Grant as his replacement.

Thierry Henry's summer departure rattled the Arsenal faithful, but with Emmanuel Adebayor, Cesc Fàbregas and Robin van Persie stepping up, the loss of the Frenchman wasn't the catastrophe some had predicted.

At Christmas, with Liverpool's owners Tom Hicks and George Gillett apparently courting German World Cup-winning coach Jürgen Klinsmann, Rafa Benítez was not a happy gaffer – and it began to show on the pitch, with Liverpool unable to slipstream a genuine title challenge.

Tottenham brought in a new back four in January, Jermain Defoe rolled up at Fratton Park, and Nicolas Anelka would forge a new partnership with Didier Drogba at Chelsea.

Arsenal, after losing 4-0 in the Cup to United, lost Eduardo da Silva to an horrific injury against Birmingham City and then conceded a converted penalty in the last seconds to forgo three points. It was a match that changed the course of their season.

A Drogba double against Arsenal

signalled a late charge from Chelsea, while Roy Hodgson's Fulham won their first away match in 34 games, at Reading, to begin their amazing escape from relegation.

Ferguson's bizarre decision to bench Ronaldo for the away clash with Chelsea, and his team's subsequent defeat, meant the title would be decided on the final day for the first time in nine years. Inevitably, it was United who held their nerve as they beat Wigan Athletic 2-0 and Chelsea could only draw with Bolton.

Finally, Derby County finished the season with the worst record since the Premier League was founded. They secured only one win, while Ronaldo, Torres and Adebayor all scored more goals individually than Derby managed as a team.

2007/08 DID YOU KNOW?

- On 29 September 2007, Portsmouth beat Reading 7–4 at Fratton Park in the highest-scoring match in Premier League history.
- On 29 March 2008, Derby's 2-2 draw with Fulham meant they suffered the earliest ever relegation from the Premier League.
- Mark Schwarzer's co-authored children's football book, *Megs Morrison*, was published in 2007.

Robbie Savage: couldn't save the Rams

PREMIER LEAGUE GOAL OF THE SEASON

- Emmanuel Adebayor
- Spurs v Arsenal
- 15 September 2007

He flicks the ball up with his first touch on the edge of the penalty area and then volleys it into the top left of the net with his second. Goals don't come much sweeter, or more spectacular, than this.

▼ FINAL POSITIONS

		P	W	D	L	F	A	GD	Pts
1	Manchester United (C)	38	27	6	5	80	22	58	87
2	Chelsea	38	25	10	3	65	26	39	85
3	Arsenal	38	24	11	3	74	31	43	83
4	Liverpool	38	21	13	4	67	28	39	76
5	Everton	38	19	8	11	55	33	22	65
18	▼ Reading	38	10	6	22	41	66	-25	36
19	▼ Birmingham City	38	8	11	19	46	62	-16	35
20	▼ Derby County	38	1	8	29	20	89	-69	11

▼ AWARDS

PFA Player of the Year
Cristiano Ronaldo (Man Utd)

PFA Young Player of the Year
Cesc Fàbregas (Arsenal)

FWA Player of the Year
Cristiano Ronaldo (Man Utd)

FA Premier League Manager of the Year Sir Alex Ferguson (Man Utd)

▼ ALSO IN 2007/08

- **Ballon d'Or** Cristiano Ronaldo (Man Utd)
- **Mercury Music Prize** Myths Of The Near Future
- **BBC Sports Personality of the Year** Joe Calzaghe
- **Oscar for best film** No Country For Old Men

2008/09

Liverpool would fight them tooth and nail, but Manchester United – with the Reds' record of 18 league titles in their sights – were an irresistible force

Another victory for United and another decisive mind game won by Sir Alex

▼ 2008/09 PREMIER LEAGUE STATS

Champions
Manchester United
(11th Premier League title, 18th title)
Top at Christmas Liverpool (2nd)

Total goals scored 942
Average goals/game 2.48
Biggest home win
Manchester City 6-0 Portsmouth
Biggest away win

Hull City 0-5 Wigan Athletic
Middlesbrough 0-5 Chelsea
West Brom 0-5 ManchesterUtd
Longest winning run
11 (Manchester United)
Longest unbeaten run
21 (Arsenal)
Highest attendance 75,569
(Man Utd v Liverpool)
Lowest attendance 16,550

(Fulham v Birmingham City)
Average attendance 33,875

Champions League Man Utd,
Liverpool, Chelsea, Arsenal
Europa League Everton, Fulham,
Aston Villa

▼ TOP GOALSCORERS

1	**Nicolas Anelka** (Chelsea)	19
2	**Cristiano Ronaldo** (Man Utd)	18
3	**Steven Gerrard** (Liverpool)	16
4	**Robinho** (Man City)	14
	Fernando Torres (Liverpool)	14

PREMIER LEAGUE TEAM OF THE YEAR

Forward
Fernando Torres
Liverpool

Forward
Nicolas Anelka
Chelsea

Midfielder
Ashley Young
Aston Villa

Midfielder
Cristiano Ronaldo
Man Utd

Midfielder
Ryan Giggs
Man Utd

Midfielder
Steven Gerrard
Liverpool

Defender
Nemanja Vidic
Man Utd

Defender
Rio Ferdinand
Man Utd

Defender
Patrice Evra
Man Utd

Defender
Glen Johnson
Portsmouth

Goalkeeper
Edwin van der Sar
Man Utd

R umours and speculation abounded ahead of the 2008/09 season: Sir Alex Ferguson succeeded in retaining the services of Footballer of the Year Cristiano Ronaldo, Luiz Felipe Scolari arrived to take over at Chelsea and Mark Hughes assumed the hotseat at Manchester City. Meanwhile, for the first time in their 105-year history, Hull City entered the top flight of English football.

Deco, Chelsea's big new signing, was in full pomp early on, helping the Blues to two wins and a draw in August and securing the Player of the Month award. Manchester City became the wealthiest football club in the world after the takeover by super-rich Abu Dhabi United Group and captured Robinho from Real Madrid for a British transfer record of £32.5m.

Kevin Keegan's second resignation from Newcastle prompted renewed calls for owner Mike Ashley's head and, despite Emmanuel Adebayor free-scoring for the Gunners, Arsenal

fans remained sceptical of achieving success after a summer of flirting with European heavyweights.

Hull, the league's surprise package early on, took three points at the Emirates and White Hart Lane, the latter result encouraging Spurs' board to part company with Juande Ramos at the end of October and appoint Harry Redknapp as manager 24 hours later. Redknapp would change the club's fortunes by immediately achieving something Ramos hadn't all season – a Tottenham win.

Chelsea's 86-game unbeaten record came to an end when they lost 1-0 to Liverpool, who went three points clear at the top. Arsenal lost 2-0 at home to Aston Villa and, afterwards, William Gallas publicly criticised his teammates and was promptly stripped of his captaincy. Cesc Fábregas took over and led the Gunners to a 2-1 victory at once-impregnable Stamford Bridge.

In December, Roy Keane resigned as Sunderland manager, with the Black Cats locked in the bottom three. Back-to-back 4-0 and 4-1 wins earned his caretaker replacement, Ricky Sbragia, an 18-month deal. Blackburn's Paul Ince followed Keane on to the managerial scrapheap, after recording a mere three wins in 17 games.

After Christmas, Hull's plummet down the table resulted in a dressing-down on the pitch by manager Phil Brown at half-time in their 5-1 defeat away to Manchester City, while table-toppers Liverpool demolished Newcastle 5-1 at St James' Park. But pressure was getting to the Reds,

2008/09 DID YOU KNOW?

- **Paul Ince became the first black British manager in the Premier League, with Blackburn, and started with a 3-2 win over Everton.**
- **Harry Redknapp recorded the best start to a management career at Tottenham for 110 years.**
- **Aston Villa's Gabriel Agbonlahor scored the Premier League's second-fastest hat-trick (seven minutes) in his side's 4-2 win over Manchester City.**

Paul Ince: sacked after just 177 days as Blackburn gaffer

as Benitez illustrated nicely via an explosive rant at Sir Alex Ferguson.

By February, Manchester United were five points clear at the top and looking unshakeable, while World Cup-winner Scolari was sacked, leaving his successor, Guus Hiddink, to resuscitate Chelsea's title challenge.

Liverpool's 4-1 victory at Old Trafford in March suggested the title race was far from over and when Fulham beat United 2-0 at Craven Cottage – and the Reds beat Villa 5-0 – the margins were once again reduced.

But it was not to be for Liverpool. Teenage debutant Federico Macheda scored a stunning winner for United against Villa and they lifted their 11th title with a 0-0 draw with Arsenal at Old Trafford to equal Liverpool's record of 18 top-flight titles.

▼ FINAL POSITIONS

		P	W	D	L	F	A	GD	Pts
1	Manchester United	38	28	6	4	68	24	44	90
2	Liverpool	38	25	11	2	77	27	50	86
3	Chelsea	38	25	8	5	68	24	44	83
4	Arsenal	38	20	12	6	68	37	31	72
5	Everton	38	17	12	9	55	37	18	63
18	▼ Newcastle United	38	7	13	18	40	59	-19	34
19	▼ Middlesbrough	38	7	11	20	28	57	-29	32
20	▼ West Bromwich Albion	38	8	8	22	36	67	-31	32

▼ AWARDS

PFA Player of the Year
Ryan Giggs (Manchester Utd)

PFA Young Player of the Year
Ashley Young (Aston Villa)

FWA Player of the Year
Steven Gerrard (Liverpool)

Premier League Manager of the Year Sir Alex Ferguson (Man Utd)

▼ ALSO IN 2008/09

- **Ballon d'Or**
Lionel Messi (Barcelona)
- **Mercury Prize**
The Seldom Seen Kid
- **BBC Sports Personality of the Year** Chris Hoy
- **Oscar for best film** Slumdog Millionaire

2009/10

Cash-strapped Portsmouth are docked points but reach the Cup final, while Chelsea bring their shooting boots to clinch their third title in style

The Blues hit eight goals past a luckless Wigan on the last day of the season to make Carlo Ancelotti the first Italian manager to win the Premier League title

▼ 2009/10 PREMIER LEAGUE STATS

Champions Chelsea
(3rd Premier League title, 4th title)
Top at Christmas Chelsea (1st)

Total goals scored 1,053
Average goals/game 2.77
Biggest home win
Tottenham Hotspur 9-1
Wigan Athletic
Biggest away win

Everton 1-6 Arsenal
Longest winning run
6 (Chelsea)
Longest unbeaten run
12 (Birmingham City)
Highest attendance 75,316
(Man Utd 4-0 Stoke City)
Lowest attendance 14,323
(Wigan Athletic 0-0 Portsmouth)
Average attendance 34,150

Champions League
Chelsea, Manchester United,
Arsenal, Spurs
Europa League
Manchester City, Aston Villa,
Liverpool

▼ TOP GOALSCORERS

1	**Didier Drogba** (Chelsea)	29
2	**Wayne Rooney** (Manchester Utd)	26
3	**Darren Bent** (Sunderland)	24
4	**Carlos Tevez** (Manchester City)	23
	Frank Lampard (Chelsea)	22
6	**Fernando Torres** (Liverpool)	18
	Jermain Defoe (Tottenham)	18
8	**Cesc Fábregas** (Arsenal)	15

In 2008 only one EPL side made to the FA Cup semi-finals: Portsmouth. Both Chelsea *and* Liverpool were dumped out by Barnsley.

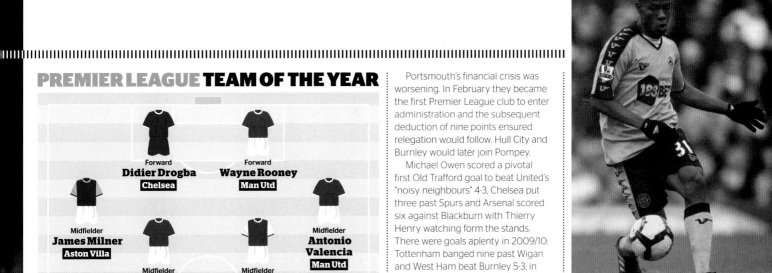

PREMIER LEAGUE **TEAM OF THE YEAR**

Forward
Didier Drogba
Chelsea

Forward
Wayne Rooney
Man Utd

Midfielder
James Milner
Aston Villa

Midfielder
Antonio Valencia
Man Utd

Midfielder
Darren Fletcher
Man Utd

Midfielder
Cesc Fábregas
Arsenal

Defender
Richard Dunne
Aston Villa

Defender
Thomas Vermaelen
Arsenal

Defender
Patrice Evra
Man Utd

Defender
Branislav Ivanovic
Chelsea

Goalkeeper
Joe Hart
Birmingham City

Portsmouth's financial crisis was worsening. In February they became the first Premier League club to enter administration and the subsequent deduction of nine points ensured relegation would follow. Hull City and Burnley would later join Pompey.

Michael Owen scored a pivotal first Old Trafford goal to beat United's "noisy neighbours" 4-3, Chelsea put three past Spurs and Arsenal scored six against Blackburn with Thierry Henry watching form the stands. There were goals aplenty in 2009/10: Tottenham banged nine past Wigan and West Ham beat Burnley 5-3; in fact, the net rippled more times in this Premier League season than in any of the previous nine.

Ryan Giggs secured his century of Premier League goals in United's 4-1 win over Portsmouth in November, and Roberto Mancini replaced Mark Hughes as manager of Manchester City, despite the Welshman taking his team to within six points of a Champions League place.

Snow put paid to some league ties at the beginning of 2010 and John Terry's personal life threatened to undermine Chelsea's hot streak, which included a 7-2 demolition of Sunderland. Despite errant handshakes and a dreadful 4-2 home defeat by Manchester City, Chelsea were still top at the end of February, but it remained a three-horse race with United and a rejuvenated Arsenal.

A 1-1 wobble at Blackburn was quickly rectified when Ancelotti's men put five past Pompey on the south

PREMIER LEAGUE GOAL OF THE SEASON

■ **Maynor Figueroa**
■ **12 December 2009**
■ **Stoke City v Wigan Athletic**

An innocuous free-kick inside the Wigan half turns goal of the season when Figueroa notices keeper Thomas Sørensen off his line. The defender smashes the ball 60 yards upfield and into the back of Stoke's net.

Sir Alex Ferguson was going in search of a record fourth consecutive title without Cristiano Ronaldo, who was sold to Real Madrid for £80m, or Carlos Tevez, who joined fierce rivals Manchester City for an undisclosed fee.

Carlo Ancelotti arrived from Milan to take charge at Chelsea, their fourth manager in 21 months after José Mourinho, Avram Grant and Luiz Felipe Scolari. The cuddly Italian's new charges got out of the blocks well, winning all of their games in August.

Manchester United won their first clash with Arsenal and had the bonus of seeing Arsène Wenger sent to the Old Trafford stands for kicking a water bottle. Manchester City's Emmanuel Adebayor added salt to the Gunners'

wounds two weeks later, scoring in a 4-2 win over Arsenal and then sprinting the length of the pitch to celebrate in front of his old club's fans. "We have to do a big mistake to be better tomorrow," he said afterwards.

2009/10 **DID YOU KNOW?**

■ **Chelsea finished the season with an incredible 103 goals to become the first team to score more than 100 goals in a season in the top flight of English football since the Tottenham side of 1962/63.**
■ **Five days before he dies, the brilliant, wheelchair-bound Sir Bobby Robson attends an England XI v Germany XI at St James' Park to raise money for his cancer charity.**

Danny Blanchflower:
Spurs legend

coast and seven past Aston Villa at Stamford Bridge. Birmingham's Kevin Phillips, meanwhile, put a dent in Arsenal's hopes with a late equaliser in March, when Phil Brown departed from Hull City.

In a tense finale to one of the most eagerly contested title races in recent times, Arsenal's fire was extinguished by Wigan, 3-2 at the DW Stadium, but United kept in the hunt with a dramatic late winner at the Etihad and a 3-1 victory over Spurs.

It wasn't to be, though. Chelsea's seven-goal thrashing of Stoke and a stunning 8-0 home win over Wigan emphatically sealed the title. Ancelotti became the fifth manager, and the first Italian, to win the Premier League. He secured the double a week later with a 1-0 FA Cup win over Portsmouth.

▼ FINAL POSITIONS

		P	W	D	L	F	A	GD	Pts
1	Chelsea (C)	38	27	5	6	103	32	71	86
2	Manchester United	38	27	4	7	86	28	58	85
3	Arsenal	38	23	6	9	83	41	42	75
4	Tottenham Hotspur	38	21	7	10	67	41	26	70
5	Manchester City	38	18	13	7	73	45	28	67
18	▼ Burnley	38	8	6	24	42	82	-40	30
19	▼ Hull City	38	6	12	20	34	75	-41	30
20	▼ Portsmouth	38	7	7	24	34	66	-32	19

▼ AWARDS

PFA Player of the Year
Wayne Rooney (Manchester Utd)

PFA Young Player of the Year
James Milner (Aston Villa)

FWA Player of the Year
Wayne Rooney (Manchester Utd)

Premier League Manager of the Year Harry Redknapp (Spurs)

▼ ALSO IN 2009/10

■ **FIFA Ballon d'Or** Lionel Messi (Barcelona)
■ **Mercury Music Prize** Speech Therapy
■ **BBC Sports Personality of the Year** Ryan Giggs
■ **Oscar** for best film The Hurt Locker

2010/11

Blackpool came, saw and were relegated, 'King' Kenny returned to Anfield at the expense of Roy and Balotelli made a splash on the Blue side of Manchester

Manchester United left Liverpool behind to become the team with the most English league titles after winning their 12th Premier League crown and 19th League title

▼ 2010/11 PREMIER LEAGUE STATS

Champions Manchester United
(12th Premier League title, 19th title)
Top at Christmas Man Utd (1st)

....

Total goals scored 1,063
Average goals/game 2.8
Biggest home win
Man Utd 7-1 Blackburn
Arsenal 6-0 Blackpool,
Chelsea 6-0 West Bromwich Albion,

Newcastle United 6-0 Aston Villa
Biggest away win
Wigan Athletic 0-6 Chelsea
Longest winning run
5 (Chelsea)
Longest unbeaten run
24 (Man Utd)
Highest attendance 75,486
(Man Utd v Bolton Wanderers)
Lowest attendance 14,042

(Wigan Athletic v Wolverhampton
Wanderers)
Average attendance 35,190

....

Champions League Man Utd,
Chelsea, Man City, Arsenal
Europa League Spurs, Fulham
Birmingham City, Stoke City

▼ TOP GOALSCORERS

1	**Dimitar Berbatov** (Manchester Utd)	20
	Carlos Tevez (Manchester City)	20
3	**Robin van Persie** (Arsenal)	18
4	**Darren Bent** (Sunderland, Aston Villa)	17
5	**Peter Odemwingie** (West Brom)	15

PREMIER LEAGUE TEAM OF THE YEAR

Forward
Dimitar Berbatov
Man Utd

Forward
Carlos Tevez
Man City

Midfielder
Gareth Bale
Spurs

Midfielder
Nani
Man Utd

Midfielder
Jack Wilshere
Arsenal

Midfielder
Samir Nasri
Arsenal

Defender
Vincent Kompany
Man City

Defender
Nemanja Vidic
Man Utd

Defender
Ashley Cole
Chelsea

Defender
Bacary Sagna
Arsenal

Goalkeeper
Edwin van der Sar
Man Utd

1-0 victory over Spurs, but West Ham would prop up the division virtually from the start, signalling a long and arduous campaign for the Hammers.

Manchester United were looking strong, especially their Bulgarian forward Dimitar Berbatov, who reacquainted himself with the headlines when he became the first United player in 64 years to score a hat-trick against Liverpool; Darren Bent and Asamoah Gyan were forming an exciting strike partnership at Sunderland; and Gérard Houllier returned to English football in September as boss of Aston Villa – but he was to leave in June after suffering a serious illness.

Back at United, Javier Hernández was proving something of a sensation, scoring with an astonishing back-header against Stoke to keep his side hot on Chelsea's heels. Despite losing to Manchester City in the clash of the Italian bosses, the Blues remained top of the table by three points at the end of September. Ray Wilkins' surprise sacking left an empty spot next to Carlo Ancelotti at Stamford Bridge, though, and brought an alarming downturn in form for Chelsea that would eventually result in the manager's departure, despite the team recovering to secure second place.

Wayne Rooney's much-publicised wage spat with United came to an end and his emergence from the bench galvanised the Red Devils as they edged to the top of the table.

Arsenal's 3-1 win over Chelsea in late December sent more jitters up the

PREMIER LEAGUE GOAL OF THE SEASON

- Wayne Rooney
- 12 February 2011
- Man Utd v Man City

This is why he gets paid top dollar: Nani's deflected cross loops high and Rooney, adjusting fiendishly quickly, leaps to bicycle-kick the ball beyond the best goalkeeper in the land. A wonderful, wonderful finish.

spine of owner Roman Abramovich, while Chris Baird's first goals in three years helped Fulham to their first win on the road in more than 16 months, 2-0 against Stoke.

Liverpool surrendered more pride at home to Wolves, losing 1-0, and after only six months in charge, Roy Hodgson left Anfield with 'King' Kenny Dalglish assigned to rally the troops. Within six weeks, the Reds – having flirted with the relegation places for much of the early season – were more comfortably in the top half of the table.

United, meanwhile, ploughed on and, despite losing to Dalglish's team and Arsenal in the final month, they cantered to their 19th English league crown to surpass Liverpool as the club with most title wins – one of Sir Alex Ferguson's biggest achievements.

On arrival in the Premier League, Blackpool looked a safe bet to be the whipping boys of the division. But they registered their first top-flight win since 1970 in style – 4-0 against Wigan at the DW Stadium. Ian Holloway's men would eventually lose their battle against relegation, but added some colour to the competition along the way.

Martin O'Neill made a shock departure from Aston Villa; Yaya Touré joined Manchester City, for "about £24m" from Barcelona, along with Aleksandar Kolarov, James Milner and Mario Balotelli; and the much-travelled Roy Hodgson signed a three-year deal to manage Liverpool, making Joe Cole his first major signing.

Chelsea began as they finished the previous season, winning all three matches in August, scoring 14 goals and conceding none. Wigan exacted revenge for last season's 9-1 thrashing at White Hart Lane by registering a

2010/11 DID YOU KNOW?

- This was the first season in 12 that Liverpool failed to qualify for any European competition.
- On 15 January, Nat Lofthouse, the 'Lion of Vienna', died aged 85. He scored 30 times in 33 games for England and spent his whole career at Bolton Wanderers.
- As the Noughties drew to a close Chelsea sat atop the Premier League, with Man Utd nestled in second.

Nat Lofthouse: a proper Englishman

	FINAL POSITIONS	P	W	D	L	F	A	GD	Pts
1	Manchester United	38	23	11	4	78	37	41	80
2	Chelsea	38	21	8	9	69	33	36	71
3	Manchester City	38	21	8	9	60	33	27	71
4	Arsenal	38	19	11	8	72	43	29	68
5	Tottenham Hotspur	38	16	14	8	55	46	9	62
18	▼ Birmingham City	38	8	15	15	37	58	-21	39
19	▼ Blackpool	38	10	9	19	55	78	-23	39
20	▼ West Ham United	38	7	12	19	43	70	-27	33

▼ AWARDS

PFA Player of the Year
Gareth Bale (Spurs)

PFA Young Player of the Year
Jack Wilshere (Arsenal)

FWA Player of the Year
Scott Parker (West Ham)

Premier League Manager of the Year Sir Alex Ferguson (Man Utd)

▼ ALSO IN 2010/2011

- **FIFA Ballon d'Or** Lionel Messi (Barcelona)
- **Mercury Music Prize** The xx
- **BBC Sports Personality of the Year** Tony McCoy
- **Oscar for best film** The King's Speech

2011/12

While 'Arry blows it and van Persie plays a blinder, Mancini's Kompany of giants turn Manchester blue for the first time – with the last kick of the last day

Aguero's 94th-minute goal secured Mancini's men their first Premier League title in dramatic fashion

▼ 2011/12 PREMIER LEAGUE STATS

Champions	Fulham 6-0 QPR	**Lowest attendance** 15,195
Manchester City (1st Premier	**Biggest away win**	(QPR v Bolton Wanderers)
League title, 3rd title)	Man Utd 1-6 Man City	**Average attendance** 34,486
Top at Christmas Man City (1st)	Norwich 1-6 Man City	
....	**Longest winning run**	**Champions League**
Total goals scored 1,066	8 (Man Utd)	Man City, Man Utd, Arsenal,
Average goals/game 2.81	**Longest unbeaten run**	Chelsea
Biggest home win	14 (Man City)	**Europa League**
Man Utd 8-2 Arsenal	**Highest attendance** 75,627	Spurs, Newcastle, Liverpool
Arsenal 7-1 Blackburn	(Man Utd v Wolves)	

▼ TOP GOALSCORERS

1	**Robin van Persie** (Arsenal)	30
2	**Wayne Rooney** (Man Utd)	27
3	**Sergio Aguero** (Manchester City)	23
4	**Clint Dempsey** (Fulham)	17
	Emmanuel Adebayor (Spurs)	17
	Yakubu (Blackburn Rovers)	17

PREMIER LEAGUE TEAM OF THE YEAR

Forward
Wayne Rooney
Man Utd

Forward
Robin van Persie
Arsenal

Midfielder
Gareth Bale
Spurs

Midfielder
David Silva
Man City

Midfielder
Scott Parker
Spurs

Midfielder
Yaya Touré
Man City

Defender
Fabricio Coloccini
Newcastle Utd

Defender
Vincent Kompany
Man City

Defender
Leighton Baines
Everton

Defender
Kyle Walker
Spurs

Goalkeeper
Joe Hart
Man City

And finally here we are 20 years on in our beloved Premier League. Many players and managers have come and gone; new grounds have been built and filled; and beach balls, kung-fu and prawn sandwiches have filtered into the public consciousness through the beautiful game. But one thing has remained the same – the best football played week-in, week-out by the oldest, most competitive league in the world.

The 20th season was no different. In fact, it raised the bar. It was recently voted Best Season by an FA panel, and with good reason: it was the first time the Premier League was won on goal difference, it was the first time a previously relegated team had won the Premier League and it was the first time that Manchester City, courtesy of an injury-time Sergio Aguero goal, managed to lift the Premier League trophy. Unforgettable stuff, indeed.

It all began in earnest on 13 August 2011, and the opening month gave a good preview of the two-horse race that was about to follow: the blue and red sides of Manchester both won their first four fixtures, Sergio Aguero announcing his arrival by scoring two goals in 32 minutes as a substitute against Swansea, and Wayne Rooney netting nine times in his first five fixtures. In north London, Robin Van Persie started more serenely but would go on to notch 30 goals from 38 appearances in, for him at least, a remarkably injury-free season.

The usual Premier League protagonists carved their way into the frame early on with Liverpool disappointing and Newcastle United, Norwich City and Swansea City compelling in fairly equal measure.

After a decent run in the league, soaring clear of Arsenal by 10 clear points, Tottenham were impressively overhauled by their north-London rivals and forced out of an automatic Champions League spot due to fifth-placed Chelsea beating Bayern in the final in Munich. Harry's head had been turned by the England vacancy left by Fabio Capello on 8 February and his team won only three times in the next 11 games. Daniel Levy was not impressed and sacked the cockney gaffer, going from hero to zero in under four months.

This season was all about one north-western city though, and when a Vincent Kompany header won the crucial Manchester derby 1-0, on 31 March 2012, despite Roberto Mancini's protestations that it was already over, the title race was very much back on.

In fact, it went to the final day. And changed hand a few times during the afternoon, too: Wayne Rooney's 27th goal of the season in the 20th minute away at Sunderland gave United the edge, but Pablo Zabaleta's first of the season put City back on top at half-time. Second half, and Djibril Cissé equalised for QPR, putting United on top, and then Joey Barton was sent off at Loftus Road but the 10 men went on to take the lead with a surprise Jamie Mackie strike after 66 minutes. Phew!

It wasn't over yet, though. With three minutes left to play and the engraver preparing to etch the words Manchester United on to the trophy once again, Edin Dzeko scored in the 92nd minute and Aguero in the 94th. Job done. And so the 20th title went to Kompany, Mancini, the Etihad and the Abu Dhabi United Group.

2011/12 DID YOU KNOW?

■ On 21 December Aston Villa winger Marc Albrighton scored the Premier League's 20,000th goal in a 2-1 defeat to Arsenal at Villa Park.
■ Luis Suarez scored the first Premier League goal of the season for Liverpool at Sunderland; Sergio Aguero's (have we mentioned that yet?) was the last.
■ Manchester City's David Silva topped the assists chart with a fruitful 17.

Marc Albrighton celebrates a benchmark EPL goal

FINAL POSITIONS

		P	W	D	L	F	A	GD	Pts
1	**Manchester City**	38	28	5	5	93	29	64	89
2	**Manchester United**	38	28	5	5	89	33	56	89
3	**Arsenal**	38	21	7	10	74	49	25	70
4	**Tottenham Hotspur**	38	20	9	9	66	41	25	69
5	**Newcastle Utd**	38	19	8	11	56	51	5	65
18	▼ **Bolton Wanderers**	38	10	6	22	46	77	-31	36
19	▼ **Blackburn Rovers**	38	8	7	23	48	78	-30	31
20	▼ **Wolves**	38	5	10	23	40	82	-42	25

▼ AWARDS

PFA Player of the Year
Robin van Persie (Arsenal)

PFA Young Player of the Year
Kyle Walker (Spurs)

FWA Player of the Year
Robin van Persie (Arsenal)

FA Premier League Manager of the Year Alan Pardew (Newcastle)

▼ ALSO IN 2011/12

■ **FIFA Ballon d'Or**
Lionel Messi (Barcelona)
■ **Mercury Music Prize**
Let England Shake
■ **BBC Sports Personality of the Year** Mark Cavendish
■ **Oscar for best film** The Artist

FINAL WHISTLE

TOP 10
PREMIER LEAGUE MEMORABLE MOMENTS

Acts of madness, tragedy, glory, inspiration and sheer embarrassment

Cantona kung-fu kick
Crystal Palace v Manchester Utd, 1994/95

1 Eric Cantona's unique talent was matched only by his unpredictable temperament. During the 1994/95 season, the latter culminated in a foot-first lunge at Crystal Palace fan Matthew Simmons, followed by a series of punches. "It was a mistake," admitted Cantona to the BBC. "But that's life. That's me. You can feel very quickly a prisoner of your past, of the memories. I prefer to be free and think about tomorrow."

Bullard team talk
Manchester City v Hull City, 2009/10

5 The last time Hull had visited Eastlands – on Boxing Day 2008 – they not only endured an embarrassing 5-1 defeat, but, at half-time, manager Phil Brown sat them in the corner of the pitch, in front of their fans, for a half-time lecture. Awkward times. Fast-forward a year, to November 2009. Hull – still in the top flight – are one down at Eastlands, but Jimmy Bullard is about to relieve the tension by equalising and then mimicking his boss' public antics during the ensuing celebrations.

Di Canio done good
Everton v West Ham, 2000/01

6 Paulo Di Canio's sportsmanship away to Everton was a moment of genuine good nature in times of mounting sporting pressures. Trevor Sinclair crossed the ball in the dying minutes, but Di Canio, with a glaring opportunity to seal the points, caught it and indicated an injury to Everton goalkeeper Paul Gerrard rather than attempt to score. Goodison Park rewarded him with sustained applause – and deservedly so.

Black Cats beach ball
Sunderland v Liverpool, 2009/10

7 A moment unlikely to be repeated should the Premier League run for a millennia. In a gesture of support for Liverpool, Callum Campbell, 16, punched a branded beach ball on to the pitch. At the same time, Sunderland's Darren Bent hit a very saveable shot, which hit the beach ball, changed direction and whistled past Pepe Reina. "My mum tells me it wasn't my fault," Callum said. "The referee should never have allowed the goal. I hope the real fans understand and forgive me."

Keegan loses it
Middlesbrough v Manchester Utd, 1995/96

2 Kevin Keegan's exciting Newcastle team had built up a 12-point lead over perennial champions Manchester United. Sensing danger and Keegan's increasingly fragmented temperament, Alex Ferguson cranked up the mind games, insinuating that teams didn't try as hard against Newcastle as they did against his men. With the title slipping away, and the Red Devils needing something against Boro, Keegan lost it. "I will love it if we beat them," he ranted, "*love* it!" They didn't.

The Alcock wobble
Sheffield Wednesday v Arsenal, 1998/99

3 **After taking umbrage at Patrick Vieira pushing Wim Jonk, Di Canio threatens Arsenal's captain, then raises his hands to well-known north-London pacifier Martin Keown. Paul Alcock issues the number 11 with a red card and the fuming Roman reacts by shoving the referee in the chest with both hands. A comical fall, an 11-match ban and a £10,000 fine follow, as does a mummy's boy tantrum from flinching Nigel Winterburn.**

Becks' halfway hoof
Wimbledon v Manchester Utd, 1996/97

4 Not just a "phenomenal" strike, as John Motson said at the time, but also the start of a phenomenon. In 1996, as part of Alex Ferguson's much-derided 'kids' approach to winning titles, David Beckham lined up on the right of midfield away to the Crazy Gang. The ball at his feet, the 21-year-old – with a quick glance up – sees the poor position of Neil Sullivan and, from behind the halfway line, smashes a lob over the keeper and into the goal. Swiftly calculated, wonderfully executed.

Muamba collapse
Spurs v Bolton Wanderers, 2011/12

8 **Saturday 17 March, 2012. A routine game descends into chaos after Bolton midfielder Fabrice Muamba collapses on the pitch after suffering a cardiac arrest. A consultant cardiologist, in the ground as a Spurs fan, comes to his aid and Muamba is taken to hospital. Despite his heart stopping for 78 minutes, he makes a full recovery. On 2 May, Muamba attends Bolton's home game against Spurs and pays tribute to those who helped him.**

Delia's half-time rant
Norwich City v Manchester City, 2004/05

9 Was there too much brandy in the half-time cakes? Whether you saw it as a cringeworthy rally cry or spontaneous passion, Delia Smith's outburst is lodged firmly in the Premier League's teeth. Worried her team didn't have the gumption to rise to their more illustrious visitors, she made an impromptu plea. "This is a message for possibly the best supporters in the world," she yelled. "We need a 12th man. Where are you? WHERE ARE YOU?" Mostly cowering at the back, Delia.

Gooooooaaaaaalllllllll!
Manchester City v QPR, 2011/12

10 **If there is a truism that the Premier League is only as good as its last season, we're in for a treat in 2012/13. Never has there been a more dramatic denouement to a top-flight season than Sergio Aguero's 94th-minute, title-deciding goal against QPR. Only two minutes earlier, City were 2-1 down to 10-man Rangers and their dismayed fans, scarred by a history of disappointment, were leaving – another dream over. How wrong can you be?**

Man Utd
1992/93

Who could've guessed, 20 years ago, that this would become such a familiar sight?

1 Paul Parker
After his glittering Old Trafford career ended in 1996 he played for Derby County, Sheffield United, Fulham, Chelsea and Farnborough Town before uninspiring spells in charge of Chelmsford City and then Welling Utd. He now works as a fairly outspoken pundit writing for Eurosport.com, among other media outlets. He has blamed United's lack of midfield drive for their well-documented failures in 2011/12.

2 Brian McClair
Played 11 matches for his home-town team Motherwell but was soon back at United, after a tough spell as assistant manager to ex-Man Utd assistant manager Brian Kidd at Blackburn, failing to keep them in the EPL in 1998/99. He's occupied the reserve team manager, under-19s manager and shadow academy director positions at Old Trafford before being made youth academy director outright in 2006.

3 Eric Cantona
Both Beckham and Ronaldo went on to wear his number 7 shirt as Cantona retired to explore the field of acting: eventually securing the lead in 2009's *Looking For Eric* (if you can call playing yourself acting). Won Overseas Player of the Decade Award at the Premier League 10 Seasons Awards in 2003 and became Director of Football at New York Cosmos in 2011. Has said he'd like to return to United one day as "number 1".

4 Clayton Blackmore
Played for 15 more years after leaving United, ending up at Bangor City and Porthmadog, for whom he also managed, and finishing his playing career at 44 years of age at Neath Athletic in the Welsh Premier League. Has recently completed a charity trek, the 592-mile 2012 Big Red Bike Ride around Ireland, with Denis irwin, Brian McClair and David May to raise money for charity. "The scenery should be good," he said.

5 Andrei Kanchelskis
Played for Everton and Rangers, among others, when he departed Old Trafford and is currently the only player in history to have scored in each of the Glasgow, Merseyside and Manchester derbies. Expressed disappointment in the *Express* in December 2011 with the showing of Russian superstars – Andrei Arshavin in particular – in the Premier League and their inability to establish themselves, caring more, he thought, about money than about success.

6 Brian Kidd
A defector! Brian Kidd stood by the side of the greatest manager the Premier League has ever seen for seven years before going it alone. His travels took him from Blackburn to Leeds to Sheffield United to Portsmouth, and then to Manchester CIty, as the assistant to Roberto Mancini. Plays a pivotal role for them "noisy neighbours".

TOP 10
PREMIER LEAGUE WORST KITS

Foolish flecks, shameful stripes and all-round hideousness not becoming of a sporting arena

Chelsea
1994-96 Away

1 Orange monstrosity with feeble Dutch connotations that looks like one of Van Gogh's nightmares. Bad wallpaper.

Wolves
1992-93 Away

5 Looks like ol' Cyrille's been under the bonnet of an Opel Ascona pre-match here. Dirtiest, most pointless fleckage ever.

Coventry
1992-94 Home

6 An incoherent, bespattered marvel that could've only been approved in the 90s. A blueprint for tasteless kit design.

Norwich
1992-94 Home

7 Not dissimilar to the lacquered tablecloth at a cheap fish restaurant. Delia: "Where are ya?" Norwich fans: "In the toilets, getting changed."

Arsenal
1991-93 Away

2 Steve Morrow wasn't the most stylish footballer, but even he doesn't look truly comfortable in this awful Arsenal top. Ridiculous.

Everton
2010-11 Away

3 **Only Sicilians can hope to pull off pink football shirts and not have anyone poke fun at them. Effete nonsense.**

Man Utd
1995-96 Third

4 Blamed for a string of upsetting results and replaced by an all-white version after a contemptible drubbing at Southampton.

Aston Villa
1993-95 Away kit

8 The demented liquorice bar. Villa wore this lame Asics strip for two-and-a-half seasons and reached two League Cup finals.

Newcastle Utd
1997-88 Away

9 **Would've been better off following the away support's lead and playing with their shirts off. Adidas, how could you?**

Newcastle Utd
2009-10 Away

10 If you licked this shirt your tongue would probably go all neon and need to be scraped by a qualified physician.

TOP 10
PREMIER LEAGUE MAGICIANS

Men who can turn a match by producing something from nothing. Piff paff poof!

David Ginola
Newcastle Utd, Spurs, Aston Villa, Everton

1 Recruited at a time when Kevin Keegan was transforming the Toon, Ginola's smooth Gallic jinks and thunderous drives helped elevate Newcastle Utd to genuine title challengers and one of the most watchable football teams in the world. Perfectly equipped to launch this list, some Geordie fans labelled Ginola "David Copperfield" for his ability to produce rare magic. His extravagances were also deeply appreciated at White Hart Lane.

Steve McManaman
Liverpool

5 Despite being the curly-haired magician at the core of Liverpool's maligned Spice Boys era and taking an active part in 1996's "Dentist's Chair", McManaman's well-regarded *Times* columns suggest a much more thoughtful individual was at the heart of those ruminating runs in front of the Anfield faithful. He scored wondrous individual efforts and unlocked defences in order for Robbie Fowler to cash in. Remains the most decorated English footballer ever to have played overseas.

Ryan Giggs
Man Utd

6 Now in the twilight of his career at Old Trafford, let's not forget the young Ryan Giggs who terrified full-backs and helped transform a United side who hadn't won the league in over 25 years into perennial title-gatherers. Fergie has had many wonderful servants during his tenure at Old Trafford but none more inspirational, more imaginative, more enterprising and more faithful than Giggs. The Premier League's greatest ever player.

Georgi Kinkladze
Man City, Derby County

7 A cult hero at both Man City and Derby, Kinkladze was a supremely strong and squat Georgian with the perfect weight distribution and balance to be a strong and decisive dribbler at the highest level. Apparently, his father made him walk around their home on his knees to strengthen his legs, and this bizarre ritual literally stood him in good stead. He was spectacular on the ball, seeing gaps that others could not and brushing robust defenders aside. A special talent.

Juninho Paulista
Middlesbrough

2 One of the most sought-after creative midfielders in European football, no one was more surprised than Middlesbrough fans when Bryan Robson unveiled the Brazilian at the Riverside. He enjoyed three spells at the club he loved where his skills were devoured in much the same way Maradona's were at Napoli in the 1980s. When he wasn't wowing their dads on the terraces, Juninho would play football on the streets with the local kids. A gifted, transformative simpatico.

Gianfranco Zola
Chelsea

3 His artful back-heel goal against Norwich in 2002 prompted Claudio Ranieri to call him a "wizard", Alex Ferguson labelled him a "clever little so-and-so", he was named Football Writers' Player of the Year in 1997 and voted Chelsea's greatest ever player in 2003, so it's safe to say that the diminutive Italian left his own mark on the Premier League. Astounding skills and always approached the game with a smile on his face.

Matt Le Tissier
Southampton

4 A renowned one-club player, Guernsey-born Matt Le Tissier was the midfield heartbeat of Southampton, sporting the figure of a pie-eating supporter but the technique of a South American *malandro*. Nicknamed "Le God", he could produce moments of almost bizarre wizardry, scoring from elusive angles and distances and converting 47 of the 48 penalties he took for the club. In 2010, Xavi Hernandez, Spain's midfield talisman, described him as "out of the norm" and "sensational".

Cristiano Ronaldo
Man Utd

8 Bought from Sporting for £12.24m, in three short seasons at Old Trafford Ronaldo was moulded into the complete modern footballer. He has pace in abundance. He has more tricks than the Great Soprendo. He can strike the ball cleanly with both feet and dominates in the air. He can cross and assist, has vision and guile and is very capable from dead balls. In short, he's annoyingly good and more than holds his own in this exalted company.

Peter Beardsley
Everton, Newcastle Utd, Bolton Wanderers

9 The Geordie genius was the English forerunner to the likes of Zola, Kinkladze and Juninho. A wonderful second striker throughout his career, Beardsley could carve out chances in an instant or gently mould them from nothing. Or he could score with a grass-cutting thunderbolt from either foot. Dynamic, accurate, artful and unselfish, Gary Lineker once described Beardsley as "the best partner I could ever have". He probably wasn't the only footballer to think so.

Thierry Henry
Arsenal

10 One of the very few footballers who are beautiful to watch in motion. Much like Roger Federer on the tennis court and Ronnie O'Sullivan on the snooker table, when Thierry Henry was in galloping full flow on a freshly shaved football field, you felt no amount of tough-tackling defenders or canny sweepers could stop him. Transformed the fortunes of Arsène Wenger and was the only player ever to have won the FWA Footballer of the Year three times.

 When Roy Keane revealed the challenge which ended Alf-Inge Haaland's career was deliberate, his ban was increased from three to eight games.

Blackburn
1994/95

Between Walker, Dalglish, Shearer and a few million, Rovers turned the tables on the glamour sides...

1 Richard Witschge
Looking slightly isolated at the back of the group here, Dutch midfielder Richard Witschge had enjoyed successful periods at both Ajax and Barcelona before being loaned from Bordeaux in March 1995. He made only one appearance for the Rovers, before transferring permanently to Ajax for his second spell, then to Deportivo Alaves. He retired in 2004.

2 Jason Wilcox
A blustering left-winger, Wilcox played for England five times, his last game coming under Kevin Keegan against Argentina, and later for Leeds, Leicester and Blackpool before doing commentary for BBC Radio Lancashire. In 2011 he predicted that Wigan and Wolves would go down. Neither did. He has also written for the *Lancashire Telegraph*.

3 David Batty
After only playing five games in 1994/95, Batty refused a winners' medal. He started a fight with team-mate Graeme Le Saux during the Spartak Moscow Champions League game in 1995/96 and missed a crucial penalty against Argentina for England in the 1998 World Cup. He also starred in series three of Sky One's *The Match* to raise money for charity.

4 Henning Berg
Leaving Blackburn for Manchester United in 1997, Berg enjoyed a trophy-sprinkled three years at Old Trafford, and was a key member of the treble-winning class of 1999. Blackburn called again in 2000, and he helped promote Rovers before winding up his career at Rangers in 2004. Management beckoned, and a successful stint at Norwegian side Lyn was followed by a spell at Lillestrøm. He was fired in 2011.

5 Colin Hendry
Hendry moved to Rangers in 1998. Despite winning the domestic treble in his first season, he quickly moved on to Coventry, then Bolton, Preston North End and Blackpool. Retiring in 2003, Hendry managed Blackpool and Clyde to little glory. Retiring again in 2008, he then blew his fortune on gambling, and in 2010 was declared bankrupt.

6 Graeme Le Saux
Acquired by Chelsea for £5m in 1997, Le Saux helped the Blues win the League Cup in 1998 and the FA Cup in 2000. 2003 saw him move to Southampton before relegation in 2005 cued retirement. Punditry, and a first-round exit from ITV's *Dancing On Ice*, followed.

TOP 10
PREMIER LEAGUE BAD BOYS

What you gonna do when they come for you? We suggest moving – and/or an apology

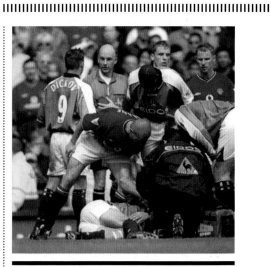

Roy Keane
Manchester United

1 Still unnerving as a pundit, Roy Keane was the archetypal midfield general at United. Lesser mortals would drain the last sinew from their being just so he didn't give them "the look". Notable spats were with Patrick Vieira, Mick McCarthy, the Old Trafford prawn-sandwich eaters and Alf-Inge Haaland (above), who, Keane admitted in his biography, he had deliberately hurt as revenge for a challenge that tore Keane's anterior cruciate ligament.

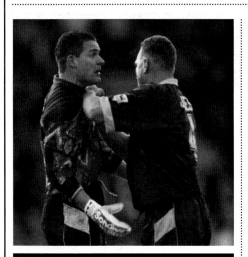

Vinnie Jones
Wimbledon

5 Cemented his bad-boy image by grabbing Paul Gascoigne's testicles to put him off his game during a match in 1987. Played for Leeds, Sheffield United and Chelsea before returning to Wimbledon to play 171 matches in the Premiership for the Crazy Gang. Presented the infamous *Soccer's Hard Men* video, which gave nefarious advice to budding toughs. It earned him a £20,000 fine and six-month ban. David Ginola once said: "Jones does not deserve to be considered a footballer."

Robbie Savage
Leicester, Birmingham, Blackburn, Derby

6 Once the record-holder of the most yellow cards (89) in the Premier League (before being usurped by Lee Bowyer and Kevin Davies), he was probably the most irritating footballer the Premier League has seen. All action, energy and sweeping blond locks, Savage had a unique ability to wind up his opponents and the crowd. Despite admitting to various illegal challenges during his career, he was only sent from the field of play twice.

Eric Cantona
Manchester United, Leeds

7 While inspiring Manchester United to their first title in more than 25 years, wearing the number 7 shirt of George Best and Bryan Robson, the pressure on King Eric would sometimes manifest itself in acts of petulance and violence. Away to Crystal Palace in 1995, after being sent off for kicking out at Richard Shaw, Cantona kung-fu kicked Palace fan Matthew Simmons – the most controversial moment in Premier League history resulting in a nine-month ban and £20,000 fine.

Joey Barton
Manchester City, Newcastle United, QPR

2 The outspoken Scouser has courted controversy throughout his 10-year career at three of the country's biggest clubs, being convicted twice for violent offences. In 2008, he was sentenced to six months in prison for affray and was given a four-month suspended sentence for assault occasioning ABH on former team-mate Ousmane Dabo. He has also punched Morten Gamst Pedersen in the chest during a game and received a 12-match ban on the last day of the 2011/12 season.

Lee Bowyer
Leeds, West Ham, Newcastle, Birmingham

3 First made the news in 1995, when he tested positive for cannabis during a random drug test and was dropped from the England under-18 squad. Was convicted of affray the year (1996) Howard Wilkinson signed him for Leeds; faced more affray and GBH charges, alongside Jonathan Woodgate, in 2000; and, in April 2005, fought with team-mate Kieron Dyer during Newcastle's Premiership match with Aston Villa (above).

Mario Balotelli
Manchester CIty

4 Eschewing the racism of Italian terraces and a debilitating relationship with José Mourinho at Inter, "Super Mario" brought Champions League and Serie A-winning experience – and his own brand of madness – to Manchester in 2010. Within days, he had been involved in a car accident, given thousands of pounds to homeless Mancunians and turned his garden into a quad-bike track. But it is his petulance on the pitch that may have signalled the end of his City career.

Kevin Davies
Bolton Wanderers, Blackburn, Southampton

8 Managers he has played for would describe him as a robust talisman, someone who can hold up the ball, bully defenders and bring more talented team-mates into play. Others would call him a fouler and rule-breaker, who's lucky to still be playing at the highest levels. Davies holds the record for most Premier League fouls conceded (782) and is in the top three when it comes to most yellow cards received (100). Consistently niggly.

El-Hadji Diouf
Liverpool, Bolton, Sunderland, Blackburn

9 El-Hadji Diouf joined Liverpool after the 2002 World Cup (he was elected for the tournament's all-star team), but gradually destroyed his reputation with a series of spitting incidents. He allegedly spat at a West Ham fan while warming up for Liverpool; he spat at Celtic fans during a televised UEFA Cup quarter-final; at Bolton, he was charged by police for spitting at an 11-year-old Middlesbrough fan; and in 2004 he gobbed in the face of Portsmouth's Arjan de Zeeuw. Tut tut, indeed.

Duncan Ferguson
Everton

10 A 6ft 4in powerhouse of a front man, Big Dunc was renowned for his overtly physical approach to the game and a hugely combative nature. This precipitated an on-the-field headbutt of John McStay in 1994, resulting in a three-month prison sentence, and eight red cards during his career in the top flight. In his defence, "Duncan Disorderly" scored more goals than any other Scottish player in the English Premier League.

TOP 10
NON-EU PREMIER LEAGUE IDOLS

Men from way beyond the river
who came and stole our hearts

Jay-Jay Okocha
Bolton Wanderers

1 So good, they named him twice, Augustine Azuka "Jay-Jay" Okocha played in midfield for the Trotters from 2002-06, making 124 appearances and scoring 14 times. Renowned for his big smile and even bigger stepovers, the Nigerian playmaker captured the hearts of those in the Premier League terraces with his multifarious trickery – and the fact he looked like he was doing it all just for fun.

Paulo Wanchope
Derby County, West Ham, Man City

5 Costa Rica's second-most prolific goalscorer made an immediate impact on the Premier League, beating four Manchester United defenders with apparent ease before slotting a debut goal for Derby County past man-mountain Peter Schmeichel. It was a goal since voted the greatest in the club's history by the fans and nicely summarises the relationship Wanchope enjoyed with Rams' followers. A sublime, animated Premier League legend.

Mark Viduka
Leeds, Middlesbrough, Newcastle United

6 An imposing slab of Australian kangaroo steak, Mark Anthony Viduka exhibited little in the way of grace and poise during his time in England's top flight, but lots in the way of power and intent. A centre-back's nightmare – or dream, depending on the calibre of opponent – Viduka was forceful, belligerent and productive in front of goal. He beats Harry Kewell and Tim Cahill on to the list as our singular antipodean.

Didier Drogba
Chelsea

7 Bowed out of his glorious Chelsea career by scoring decisive goals in their much sought-after 2011/12 Champions League and FA Cup victories, but has been a miraculous Premier League performer since his transfer to the Bridge from Marseille in 2004. Theatrical, spirited, overpowering, inspirational and annoying in equal measure, the Ivory Coast international scored 101 goals in 226 Premier League games for Chelsea, winning three titles in the process.

Dwight Yorke
Aston Villa, Man Utd, Blackburn, Birmingham

2 Nicknamed "The Smiling Assassin", for obvious reasons, Yorke formed a prolific partnership with Andy Cole at Manchester United – they scored 52 goals between them in the treble-winning 1999 season. He also enjoyed a fruitful social life. Once, in conversation with Cole, Yorke said: "These players today on £100,000 a week. If I earned that money I'd live like a £100,000-a-week player, with the best cars and birds!" "What do you mean, Yorkey?" replied Cole. "You already did."

Nwankwo Kanu
Arsenal, West Bromwich Albion, Portsmouth

3 **Seemingly awkward, ultimately rather graceful, Nwankwo "Long Lad" Kanu regaled fans in north London and on the south coast with his lazy, gangly locomotions and his sumptuous, unpredictable goals. The 6ft 4in striker won an Olympic gold medal with Nigeria in 1996, when they beat Argentina 3-2 in the final, and he holds the record for the most Premier League substitute appearances (105): as an impact player, he was second to none.**

Gus Poyet
Chelsea, Tottenham

4 The perma-beaming Uruguayan has recently transferred his ebullience and success on the pitch into football management, which is no surprise given his ability to ceaselessly gabble about the intricacies of the game. You just have to know his nickname, "The Radio", to know how he likes to talk. "I'd love my own radio show," he told *FourFourTwo*. "Although I think I'd need a six-hour slot, daily!" Another eccentric, endearing Premier League import.

Clint Dempsey
Fulham

8 **Beats fellow American Tim Howard on to this list by virtue of his persistent goalscoring in a mid-table Premier League side and the fact this deep-lying forward's most recent season was also his most prolific. Dempsey was fourth in the 2012 FWA Footballer of the Year list and became the first American to reach 50 goals in the Premier League, with a free-kick in Fulham's last home match of the season. Memorable stuff.**

Nolberto Solano
Newcastle United, West Ham

9 Peru's David Beckham, Nolberto Albino "Nobby" Solano Todco was the youngest of seven children born into a Lima *favela*, where they would kick tin cans into cardboard-box goals. Through football he transformed his life – and the lives of Geordie fans. "When I am driving into training in December, and it is dark and cold outside, I play loud salsa music in my car. It makes me happy. It makes me want to train. It makes me want to score great goals in a black-and-white shirt."

Park Ji-Sung
Manchester United

10 **The most decorated player in Asian history has been part of Sir Alex Ferguson's successful Manchester United midfield since 2005. Respected and utilised for his tremendous work ethic and ability to perform in big matches, "Three-lungs Park" is also the first Asian to have captained the Red Devils. A record-busting, milestone-breaching Korean phenomenon, with a bit still left in the tank.**

Arsenal 2003/04

This mob weren't just hard to beat, this mob were the Invincibles...

1 Patrick Vieira
The lynchpin at the heart of the Invincibles, Vieira won three titles with Arsenal and four FA Cups. After leaving the club in 2005 he joined Juventus, Inter Milan and then Manchester City. He retired from playing at the end of the 10/11 season and now works as the Football Development Executive at Manchester City, overseeing youth development and progressing the club's social responsibility programme.

2 Robert Pires
Returned as a 37-year-old to England in 2010, under Gérard Houllier at Aston Villa. With limited playing time, he only achieved minor success and was released by the club in May 2011. In January 2012, Indian side Howrah acquired his services to play in the inaugural Bengal Premier League Soccer competition.

3 Thierry Henry
Arsenal's all-time leading scorer with 228 goals, he was nominated for the FIFA World Player of the Year twice, and named both PFA Player of the Year twice and FWA Player of the Year three times. After eight years in north London he moved to Barcelona where he won the La Liga, Copa del Rey and Champions League treble in 2009. He retired from international football after the 2010 World Cup and now plays for New York Red Bulls in Major League Soccer. In 2012 he showed he's still not lost his touch, with an emotional loan spell back at Arsenal.

4 Dennis Bergkamp
Described by Thierry Henry as "a dream for a striker", Bergkamp would see things happening two steps ahead of everyone else, giving him the ability to play the right pass at the right weight, and always at the right time. A visionary footballer. Despite insisting he wasn't going to go into coaching, as of August 2011, Bergkamp has been Frank de Boer's assistant at Ajax.

5 Ashley Cole
Made 228 appearances for the Gunners but departed under a cloud, claiming in his autobiography that he had been "trembling with anger" when Arsenal only offered him £55,000 per week wages and was treated as a "scapegoat" concerning clandestine talks with their west-London rivals. He eventually joined Chelsea for £5m, with William Gallas going in the opposite direction. Cole is currently the most-capped black player ever for England and has won more FA Cups than any other player in history.

6 Gilberto Silva
Often called "the invisible wall" in Brazil, mild-mannered Gilberto is a patron of the Street League, a UK-based charity that organises football matches for homeless people and asylum seekers. He used to play the mandolin at his local pub in St Albans and has a giant anteater named after him at London Zoo.

TOP 10
PREMIER LEAGUE SUPER SAVERS

Can you believe Tim Howard,
Tim Flowers and Shaka Hislop
all slipped through our fingers?

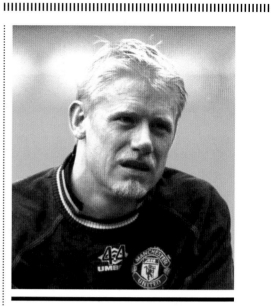

Peter Schmeichel

1 Voted the World's Best Goalkeeper in 1992 and 1993, at his peak Peter Boleslaw Schmeichel was 6ft 3in, 16st 7lb and wore specially crafted XXXL gloves. Holds the record for the greatest clean-sheets-to-games ratio in EPL history, with 42% – a benchmark that may never be topped. He was never on the losing side in the Manchester derby.

José Manuel Reina

5 An incredibly athletic, nimble stickman who is more than adept on the deck, Liverpool's "Pepe" Reina holds the record number of appearances by a Spanish player in the Premier League, with over 200 in his first five seasons, 108 of those 219 being clean sheets. Pepe won the Premier League Golden Glove award for clean sheets in his first three seasons. Vamos!

David Seaman

6 Perhaps the most recognisable Premier League goalkeeper ever with his booming joviality, ponytail phase and consistent national heroics, David Seaman played over 300 times in the Premier League for the Gunners, winning two Prem League and FA Cup doubles with the club. His positional sense, shot-stopping and presence were flawless.

David James

7 Took a while to wriggle free of the "Calamity James" tag he attained while keeping sticks for Liverpool, but by the time he arrived at Portsmouth he really made the move up in class, securing his status as a England's unquestionable no1, and one of the best shot-stoppers in the world. Holds the record for the most Premier League clean sheets, with a mightily impressive 173.

Petr Cech

2 Relatively unknown when he arrived at Stamford Bridge from Rennes for a cool £7m back in 2004, he was purchased as a rather pricey understudy to Carlo Cudicini but quickly usurped the Italian in the pecking order. Fractured his skull in a ghastly coming-together with Reading's Stephen Hunt but bravely returned to football only a few months later, sporting a rugby-style headguard.

Nigel Martyn

3 **British football's first £1m keeper when he moved from Bristol Rovers to Crystal Palace in 1989 and broke the transfer record again seven years later when he moved to Leeds. Kept goal for Everton during their greatest Prem season (2004/05), when they qualified for the Champions League, and was described by boss David Moyes as his "greatest ever signing".**

Edwin van der Sar

4 A member of Ajax's esteemed "Golden Generation", van der Sar's arrival at Craven Cottage was a huge coup for Jean Tigana. Moved to Man Utd four seasons later, winning the title in four of his six seasons. Not only one of the greatest goalkeepers the EPL has seen, but one of the greatest keepers ever, full stop. Won Best European Goalkeeper in 1995 (Ajax) and 2009 (Utd).

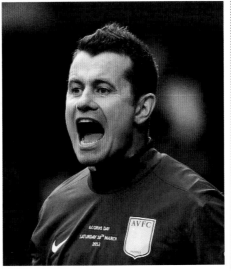

Brad Friedel

8 **Another stopper who initially signed for Liverpool but only realised his true potential once released from Anfield. In 2000 he moved to Blackburn, helping them regain Premier League status and going on to become one of the most dependable keepers in the game: current holder of the EPL record for most consecutive appearances with 304.**

Shay Given

9 Utterly revered at St James' Park, Shay Given was one of Kenny Dalglish's first signings in 1997, part of the FA Cup final runners-up teams of 1998 and 1999 and heavily involved in the club's memorable title challenge in 2001-02, playing every match. Only 34 games away from breaking Jimmy Lawrence's Toon appearance record, Given moved on to Man City in 2009.

Jussi Jaaskelainen

10 **Longest-serving foreign player in the EPL, wearing Bolton's no1 shirt from 1997 until 2012. His 15 years at the club saw the Trotters scale new heights, including securing a European spot for only the second time in their history in 2007. Had no desire to play for more "glamorous" clubs, a quality that elevates him above so many for this list.**

TOP10
PREMIER LEAGUE TWEETERS

Constant 140-character updates straight from football's frontal lobe. Scary...

Joey Barton
@Joey7Barton

1 Sample Tweet: "In times of universal deceit, telling the truth will be a revolutionary act. George Orwell"

Instigated a move from St James' Park using Twitter and has since endeared himself with random philosophical musings and attacks on all and sundry, including the Newcastle City board of directors, Neil Warnock, Alan Shearer, Ed Miliband and Gary Lineker.

Glen Johnson
@glen_johnson

5 Sample Tweet: "Well done lads great result. Congrats Stevie #MatchBall"

Defender on the football field and a bit defensive on Twitter too (not right-wing though!). After Paul Merson accused him of not being able to defend "for toffee", Johnson responded: "He was average at the best of times, the only reason he is on that show is coz he gambled all his money away. The clown!"

Emmanuel Frimpong
@FRIMPONG26AFc

6 Sample Tweet: "I'm dissapointed not to hav been picked for the euros I'm very gutted!"

Bit of a joker (see above), bit of a geezer and all-round tough-tackler, Arsenal's Ghanaian star has become renowned for taking no prisoners, his displays coining the verb "to be 'Frimponged'", which began trending on the site and has since found its way into footballing parlance.

Phil Neville
@fizzer18

7 Sample Tweet: "@GNev2 did u copy pacquio with ur tash?"

Worth a follow to witness the banter with his brother, Gary Neville, alone. After a strong performance against Spurs and Gareth Bale, Phil Neville was the third most tweeted-about subject in the world for a period of time. Celebratory Tweets included: "If Phil Neville was from Sparta, '300' would just be called '1'."

Jack Wilshere
@JackWilshere

2 Sample Tweet: "All spurs fans buzzing that they are ahead of us in the league (for once). It's a marathon, not a sprint!"

"I tell you what at the end of the season if spurs finish above arsenal I will give £3000 to charity and if arsenal finish above spurs every spurs fan that follows me must send me a pound each and I will give it to @Jack_Marshall_ charity! Do we have a deal!?" No stranger to a challenge, either on the pitch or off it.

Rio Ferdinand
@RioFerdy5

3 Sample Tweet: "Jonny Evans aka The Fartinator is a machine! Letting off bombs!"

Nothing escapes Rio's social media gaze, from his views on Whitney's back catalogue to what's in his fridge to banter exchanges with Frankie Boyle, Simon Cowell and Piers Morgan. Known for being gracious in defeat, he even has his Twitter handle stitched into his Nike boots.

Wayne Rooney
@WayneRooney

4 Sample Tweet: "Cant wait for game tonight. If everton win they go above liverpool. Come on everton"

Over 5m followers see Rooney tell Drogba to politely get back on his feet, wish his wife Coleen a happy birthday and share bland stories of narcolepsy with Rio Ferdinand. Oh, and he sometimes gets a bit angry: "I'll put u asleep within 10 seconds u little girl," he informed one Liverpudlian.

Nile Ranger
@NilePowerRanger

8 Sample Tweet: "Little Do They Know Its The Hate That Helps Create The Buzz."

Posted loads of pictures of his blinged-up Range Rover that has "Power Ranger" written all over it, the Nando's tattoo on his arm and, would you believe it, him brandishing two guns. Stay tuned and keep it real, OK Nile? "IM DA REALISSSTTT.... SAY NO MORE." Yikes.

Darren Bent
@DarrenBent

9 Sample Tweet: "1 of the nicest guys you'll ever meet and a top captain too. #Prayer4Petrov"

Bathes in Twitter hot water. In 2009, desperate for a move from White Hart Lane, he got down and busy on his laptop. "Do I wanna go Hull City? NO. Do I wanna go Stoke? NO. Do I wanna go Sunderland YES. So stop f******g around, Levy." It didn't go down well, but he did seal the move. The power of social media, eh?

Wojciech Szczesny
@13Szczesny13

10 Sample Tweet: "Started 2012 by beating @JackWilshere at table tennis with my left hand and then 21-3 with right hand!"

Quite the cheeky Tweety chappy, Poland and Arsenal's number one got in trouble after calling Aaron Ramsey a "rapist" on the site, and stopped his account on 22 January, saying: "Its just about time for me to grow up, delete twitter and focus on football!" We look forward to his return.

Chelsea
2004/05

Fuelled with Russian oil money, in 2004/05 José Mourinho added his Special ingredient to the mix...

1 Alexei Smertin
Russia's captain only played a bit-part role in 04/05, competing with Tiago Mendes, Lampard, Makelele, Geremi and Scott Parker for a central-midfield berth, and was loaned out the next year to Charlton. After a season at Dynamo Moscow and another at Fulham, he retired, and Arshavin took over the national armband. Smertin is now an elected politician in Russia's southern Altai region, which borders Mongolia, Kazakhstan and China, and has no train access. His aim is to create better lives for the 200,000 people living in the region. So there.

2 Claude Makelele
Currently works as assistant coach to Carlo Ancelotti at Paris Saint-Germain, the club he left Chelsea for in the summer of 2008, and which has recently seen a huge injection of cash from the Qatar Investment Authority.

3 Tiago Mendes
Atlético Madrid, Tiago's current club, represents the fifth country he has played in on his fine resumé. He spent just one title-winning season at Chelsea under Mourinho, then moved to Lyon, winning Ligue 1 twice, then to Juventus, and now to Spain's capital. Despite retaining the title in 2005/06, Mourinho admitted letting Tiago go after the first title success was "a big mistake".

4 Eidur Gudjohnsen
The greatest Icelandic footballer ever, Gudjohnsen was signed by Barcelona in 2006 to replace Henrik Larsson but, despite being a squad player in the treble success of 2009, he moved on soon after to Monaco, then Spurs, Stoke City, Fulham and AEK Athens, where he currently plies his trade in the Superleague Greece.

5 Mikael Forssell
A footballing journeyman, after the 2005 season and five loan spells during his seven-year stint at Chelsea, he joined Birmingham, scoring 13 in 65. He then played sporadically in the Bundesliga for Hannover 96 and appeared 15 times for Leeds in 2011/12. At the time of writing, Mikael is a free agent.

6 André Villas-Boas
Assistant coach to Mourinho at Porto and then Chelsea and Internazionale, Villas-Boas went out on his own in 2009/10, steering Académica away from trouble and introducing a pleasing new playing style to the team. FC Porto took note and appointed him on 2 June 2010. During his one-year spell in charge of the *Portistas*, he won the Portuguese Super Cup, the Primeira Liga, the UEFA Europa League and the Portuguese Cup. He wasn't so successful at Chelsea, who had compensated Porto to the tune of £13.3m for his services, and left his position after a paltry nine months.

TOP 10
PREMIER LEAGUE WORST SIGNINGS

They paid top dollar,
they got small change

Ali Dia
Southampton (trialist)

1 The Senegalese "sensation" once played for Southampton after dishonestly claiming he was the cousin of celebrated Liberia forward George Weah. Graeme Souness – with no time to check a CV decorated with only eight senior appearances at various small-time clubs – gave Dia the number 33 shirt against Leeds in November 1996, when he came on as a sub for Matt Le Tissier after 32 minutes. He was subbed off 53 minutes later.

Marco Boogers
Sparta Rotterdam to West Ham (£1m)

5 Harry Redknapp signed Boogers at the start of the 1995/96 season. Sent off after 90 seconds of his second substitute appearance against Manchester United (for a horror-challenge on Gary Neville), Boogers got depressed and did a disappearing act, a West Ham employee accidentally inducing *The Sun*'s back page: "Barmy Boogers Living In Caravan". A knee injury persisted and, after only 83 competitive minutes for the Hammers, he scuttled home.

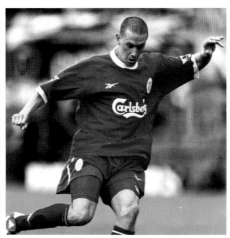

Sean Dundee
Karlsruher to Liverpool (£2m)

6 Liverpool have a host of embarrassing skeletons in the changing room, but none as impressive as Sean "Crocodile" Dundee. Looking for a striker to challenge Michael Owen and Robbie Fowler, Gérard Houllier went to recently relegated German side Karlsruher for a striker, allegedly as fast as Owen, who had scored just three times in the Bundesliga. He played five games in his only season at Liverpool, then left.

Eric Djemba-Djemba
Nantes to Manchester United (£3.5m)

7 In just five years, the Cameroonian went from winning the African Nations Cup in 2002, impressing at the World Cup in Japan and South Korea, and being touted as an eventual replacement for Roy Keane in the engine room of one of the world's biggest clubs, to below Steven Davis and Gavin McCann in Aston Villa's midfield pecking order. He finally went to Burnley on loan and then to Qatar SC. Perhaps Sir Alex Ferguson could be forgiven for not predicting that nosedive.

Winston Bogarde
Barcelona to Chelsea (free transfer)

2 A Champions League winner with Ajax and holder of two La Liga winners' medals from his time at the Camp Nou with Barcelona, Bogarde arrived at the Bridge in 1995. A free transfer appeared good business until his vast weekly wages of £42,000 were divulged and his intentions to run down his contract were realised. Over four years, Bogarde only made nine appearances for Chelsea in the Premier League, costing the Blues an eye-watering £970,667 a game!

Massimo Taibi
Venezia to Manchester United (£4.5m)

3 Taibi had big boots to fill when attempting to replace United legend Peter Schmeichel between the Old Trafford sticks, and he took little time in tarnishing his reputation. An error against Liverpool on his debut allowed Sami Hyppia to score; his gaffe against Southampton – letting Matt Le Tissier's fluffed shot dribble through his legs – led to him being dubbed the "Blind Venetian"; and he conceded five against Chelsea.

Bébé
Vitória de Guimarães to Man Utd (£7.4m)

4 Not one of Carlos Queiroz's greatest recommendations, the gangly Bébé was transferred from Vitória de Guimarães to Manchester United in August 2010. From the start, Bébé's lack of first-class ability was obvious. He was registered in United's 25-man Champions League squad and, to be fair, did score in his first Premier League start and his first Champions League outing, but his limitations were obvious. A recent loan spell at Besiktas has also been largely unfavourable.

Elena Marcelino
Mallorca to Newcastle United (£5.8m)

8 Even world-class players-turned-managers can be left red-faced when it comes to transfers. After Marcelino put on an imperious display in the 1999 Cup Winners' Cup final for Mallorca, Newcastle boss Ruud Gullit flushed £5.8m of the club's cash on the frail, buck-toothed defender. Marcelino hurt his groin during his club debut and a series of comical injuries followed, including a lengthy absence for a poorly finger.

Andriy Shevchenko
AC Milan to Chelsea (£30m)

9 By José Mourinho's own admission, Andriy Shevchenko's introduction into the Chelsea ranks, after their second successive title, was unnecessary and a bit of a frivolity by the club's owner, Roman Abramovich. "They are not arriving in a team that needs them to be champions," responded Mourinho. "They are arriving into a team who are already champions." It was the signing of the goal-shy Ukrainian that drove a bigger wedge between Blues coach and owner.

Stewart Downing
Aston Villa to Liverpool (£20m)

10 There are plenty of other duff signings we could have included on this list, but Stewart Downing makes the grade because he has failed to live up to his inflated price tag. He didn't provide an assist or score a goal in the Premier League for the *entire* 2011/12 season – and his profligacy on both counts helped to contribute to the sacking of a club legend, Kenny Dalglish, as manager. At least Alberto Aquilani was mostly injured.

Stat Zone

Everything from the longest-range goal to the fewest draws in a season, via the highest number of different clubs for a single player: the Stat Zone has it all

Alan Shearer became the first player to score 100 goals in the Premier League during the 1995/96 season

Scorelines

■ Biggest home win
9–0
Manchester United v
Ipswich (4 March 1995)

■ Biggest away win
1–8
Nottingham Forest v
Manchester United
(6 February 1999)

■ Highest-scoring game
7–4
Portsmouth v Reading
(29 September 2007)

■ Most frequent scoreline
1–0

The Premier League's highest-scoring match

Distances

■ Longest-range goal
93 metres (102 yards)
Tim Howard
Everton v Bolton Wanderers
(4 January 2012)

■ Longest-range free kick (direct)
88 metres (96 yards)
Paul Robinson
Tottenham Hotspur v
Watford
(17 March 2007)

■ Longest-range volley
42 metres (46 yards)
Matthew Taylor
Portsmouth v Everton
(9 December 2006)

■ Longest-range goal from open play
93 metres (102 yards)
Tim Howard
Everton v Bolton Wanderers
(4 January 2012)
(Deflections not considered)

Attendance

■ Highest attendance (single game)
76,398
Manchester United v
Blackburn Rovers
(Old Trafford, 31 March 2007)

■ Lowest attendance (single game)
3,039
Wimbledon v Everton
(at Selhurst Park, 26
January 1993)

Managers

■ Longest-serving manager
Sir Alex Ferguson
25 years
(Manchester United,
6 November 1986 to date)

■ Shortest-serving manager (excluding caretakers)
Les Reed
41 days (Charlton Athletic,
14 November 2006 to
24 December 2006)

■ Number of English managers who have won the Premier League
0

■ Number of non-English managers who have won the Premier League
6
(Alex Ferguson, Kenny
Dalglish, Arsène Wenger,
José Mourinho, Carlo
Ancelotti, Roberto Mancini)

PL Manager of the Year

Season	Manager	Club
1992/93	**Alex Ferguson**	Manchester United
1993/94	**Alex Ferguson**	**Manchester United**
1994/95	**Kenny Dalglish**	Blackburn Rovers
1995/96	**Alex Ferguson**	**Manchester United**
1996/97	**Alex Ferguson**	Manchester United
1997/98	**Arsène Wenger**	**Arsenal**
1998/99	**Alex Ferguson**	Manchester United
1999/2000	**Alex Ferguson**	**Manchester United**
2000/01	**George Burley**	Ipswich Town
2001/02	**Arsène Wenger**	**Arsenal**
2002/03	**Alex Ferguson**	Manchester United
2003/04	**Arsène Wenger**	**Arsenal**
2004/05	**José Mourinho**	Chelsea
2005/06	**José Mourinho**	**Chelsea**
2006/07	**Alex Ferguson**	Manchester United
2007/08	**Alex Ferguson**	**Manchester United**
2008/09	**Alex Ferguson**	Manchester United
2009/10	**Harry Redknapp**	**Tottenham Hotspur**
2010/11	**Alex Ferguson**	Manchester United
2011/12	**Alan Pardew**	**Newcastle United**

||||||||||||||||||||||||||||||||||||||||||||||||||||||||||||||||||||||||||||||||||||||||||||||||||||||||||||||||||||||||||||||

Match times and days

■ **Longest first-half additional time**
8 minutes 32 seconds
Blackburn Rovers v Birmingham City
(9 April 2011)

■ **Longest additional time**
12 minutes 26 seconds
Arsenal v Liverpool
(17 April 2011)

■ **Earliest kick-off**
11:15am BST
Manchester City v Everton
(2 October 2005)

■ **Earliest start to a season**
7 August 1999

■ **Latest finish to a season**
24 May 2009

Points

■ **Most points in a season**
95 Chelsea (2004/05)

■ **Fewest points in a season**
11 Derby County (2007/08)

■ **Most points in a season without winning the league (42 games)**
88 Manchester United (1994/95)

■ **Most points in a season without winning the league (38 games)**
89 Manchester United (2011/12)

■ **Fewest points in a season while winning the league**
75 Manchester United (1996/97)

■ **Most points in a season while being relegated (42 games)**
49 Crystal Palace (1992/93)

■ **Most points in a season while being relegated (38 games)**
42 West Ham United (2002/03)

■ **Fewest points in a season while surviving relegation**
34 West Bromwich Albion (2004/05)

Goalkeepers

■ **Goalscoring goalkeepers (excluding own goals)**
Peter Schmeichel
Everton 3-2 Aston Villa
(20 October 2001)
Brad Friedel
Charlton Athletic 3-2 Blackburn Rovers
(21 February 2004)
Paul Robinson
Tottenham Hotspur 3-1 Watford
(17 March 2007)
Tim Howard
Everton 1-2 Bolton Wanderers
(4 January 2012)

Edwin van der Sar kept 21 clean sheets in 2008/09

■ **Longest consecutive run without conceding a goal**
14 games (1,311 minutes)
Edwin van der Sar
(Manchester United, 2008/09)

■ **Most clean sheets in one season**
21 (joint record)
Petr Cech
(for Chelsea, 2004/05)
Edwin van der Sar
(for Manchester United, 2008/09)

■ **Most clean sheets in total**
173 David James

Titles

■ **Most titles**
12 Manchester United

■ **Most consecutive title wins**
3 Manchester United
Twice (1998/99, 1999/2000, 2000/01) and (2006/07, 2007/08, 2008/09)

Highest scoring games

Goals	Date	Home team	Result	Away team	Goal scorers
11	29 Sep 2007	**Portsmouth**	7 - 4	**Reading**	Benjani 7', 37', 70', Hreiðarsson 55', Kranjčar 75', Ingimarsson 81' (o.g.), Muntari 90' (pen) / Hunt 45', Kitson 48', Long 79', Campbell 90' (o.g.)
10	29 Dec 2007	**Tottenham Hotspur**	6 - 4	**Reading**	**Berbatov 7', 63', 73', 83', Malbranque 76', Defoe 79** / Cissé 16', Ingimarsson 53', Kitson 69', 74'
10	22 Nov 2009	**Tottenham Hotspur**	9 - 1	**Wigan Athletic**	Crouch 9', Defoe 51', 54', 58', 69', 87' Lennon 64', Bentley 88', Kranjčar 90', Scharner 57'
10	28 Aug 2011	**Manchester United**	8 - 2	**Arsenal**	**Welbeck 22', Young 28', 90+1', Rooney 41', 64', 82' (pen), Nani 67', Park 70', Walcott 45+3', Van Persie 74'**
9	9 Apr 1994	**Norwich City**	4 - 5	**Southampton**	Robins 37', Goss 49', Sutton 56', 64' / Ullathorne (o.g.) 44', Le Tissier 58', 63' (pen), 73', Monkou 90'
9	4 Mar 1995	**Manchester United**	9 - 0	**Ipswich Town**	Keane 15', Cole 19', 37', 53', 65', 87', Hughes 55', 59', Ince 72'
9	26 Aug 1997	**Blackburn Rovers**	7 - 2	**Sheffield Wednesday**	Gallacher 2', 7', Hyde (o.g.) 10', Wilcox 20', Sutton 24', 74', Bohinen 53', Carbone 8', 47'
9	25 Oct 1997	**Southampton**	6 - 3	**Manchester United**	**Berkovic 6', 63', Le Tissier 34', Østenstad 45', 85', 90', Beckham 41', May 56', Scholes 89'**
9	6 Feb 1999	**Nottingham Forest**	1 - 8	**Manchester United**	Rogers 6', Yorke 2', 67', Cole 7', 50', Solskjær 80, 88, 90, 90
9	12 Feb 2000	**West Ham United**	5 - 4	**Bradford City**	**Sinclair 35', Moncur 43', Di Canio (pen) 65', Cole 70', Lampard 83', Windass 30', Beagrie (pen) 44', Lawrence 47', 51'**
9	11 Mar 2000	**Tottenham Hotspur**	7 - 2	**Southampton**	Richards 28' (o.g.), Anderton 39', Armstrong 41', 64', Iversen 45', 78', 90', Tessem 26', El Khalej 33'
9	13 Nov 2004	**Tottenham Hotspur**	4 - 5	**Arsenal**	**Naybet 37', Defoe 61', King 74', Kanouté 88'** / Henry 45', Lauren 55' (pen), Vieira 60', Ljungberg 69', Pirès 81'
9	11 May 2008	**Middlesbrough**	8 - 1	**Manchester City**	Downing 16' (pen), 58' Alves 37', 60, 90', Johnson 70', Rochemback 80', Aliadière 85', Rochemback 80', Aliadière 85', Elano 87'

Goals

Most goals scored in a season
103 Chelsea (2009/10)

Fewest goals scored in a season
20 Derby County (2007/08)

Most goals conceded in a season (42 games)
100 Swindon Town (1993/94)

Most goals conceded in a season (38 games)
89 Derby County (2007/08)

Fewest goals conceded in a season
15 Chelsea (2004/05)

Best goal difference in a season
71 Chelsea (2009/10)

Worst goal difference in a season
-69 Derby County (2007/08)

Derby 2007/08 would've loved the firepower of Chelsea 2009/10

Highest percentage of season's goals scored in a single match
18.6% (8/43)
Middlesbrough
(8 - 1 v Manchester City 11 May 2008)

Most goals scored at home in a season
68 Chelsea (2009/10)

Most goals scored away in a season
47 Manchester United (2001/02)

Fewest goals scored at home in a season
10 Manchester City (2006/07)

Fewest goals scored away in a season
8 (joint record)
Middlesbrough (1995/96)
Southampton (1998/99)
Sheffield United (2006/07)
Derby County (2007/08)

Most goals conceded at home in a season (42 games)
45 Swindon Town (1993/94)

Most goals conceded
at home in a season (38 games)
43 (joint record)
Derby County (2007/08)
Wolverhampton Wanderers (2011/12)

Most goals conceded away in a season (42 games) 59 Ipswich Town (1994/95)

Most goals conceded away in a season (38 games)
55 Wigan Athletic (2009/10)

Fewest goals conceded at home in a season
4 Manchester United (1994/95)

Fewest goals conceded away in a season
9 Chelsea (2004/05)

Most clean sheets in a season
24 Chelsea (2004/05)

Fewest clean sheets in a season
3 (joint record)

Derby County (2007/08)
Birmingham City (2007/08)
Norwich City (2011/12)

Most games from the start of the season without a clean sheet
27 Blackburn Rovers (2011/12)

Fewest failures to score in a match in a season
0 (scored in every game) Arsenal (2001/02)

Most penalties conceded
47 (home)
93 (away)
Aston Villa 1992-2007

Most goals scored in total
1,541 Manchester United

Most goals conceded in total
1,020 Tottenham Hotspur

Biggest half-time lead in the Premier League
5 goals
Sheffield Wednesday 5-0 Bolton Wanderers

Multiple hat-tricks in the Premier League

Season	Player	Hat-tricks
1st	Alan Shearer	11
2nd	Robbie Fowler	9
3rd	Thierry Henry	8
	Michael Owen	
5th	Wayne Rooney	6
6th	Dimitar Berbatov	5
	Andrew Cole	
	Ruud van Nistelrooy	
	Ian Wright	
10th	Yakubu Aiyegbeni	4
	Kevin Campbell	
	Les Ferdinand	
	Jimmy Floyd Hasselbaink	
	Matthew Le Tissier	
	Teddy Sheringham	
	Chris Sutton	
	Carlos Tévez	
	Fernando Torres	
	Dwight Yorke	
	Emmanuel Adebayor	
20th	Nicolas Anelka	3
	Tony Cottee	
	Jermain Defoe	
	Didier Drogba	
	Dion Dublin	
	Robbie Keane	
	Frank Lampard	
	Robin van Persie	
	Ole Gunnar Solskjær	
	Demba Ba	
30th	Kevin Gallacher	2
	Steven Gerrard	
	Darren Huckerby	
	Steffen Iversen	
	Andrei Kanchelskis	
	Paul Kitson	
	Benjani Mwaruwari	
	Kevin Phillips	
	Fabrizio Ravanelli	
	Maxi Rodriguez	
	Paul Scholes	

Players in the Premier League who have scored two or more hat-tricks only listed in the table above.

(8 November 1997)
Burnley 1-6 Manchester City (0-5 at half-time)
(3 April 2010)

Largest goal deficit overcome to win 3
Leeds United 4-3 Derby County
(8 November 1997)
West Ham 3-4 Wimbledon
(9 September 1998)

Tottenham Hotspur 3-5 Manchester United
(29 September 2001)
Wolverhampton Wanderers 4-3 Leicester City (25 October 2003)

Largest goal deficit overcome to draw 4
Newcastle United 4-4 Arsenal
(5 February 2011)

III

Wins

■ **Most wins in a season (38 games)**
29 Chelsea
(2004/05, 2005/06)

■ **Fewest wins in a season (38 games)**
1 Derby County (2007/08)

■ **Most home wins in a season (19 games)**
18 (joint record)
Chelsea (2005/06)
Manchester United (2010/11)
Manchester City (2011/12)

■ **Fewest home wins in a season (19 games)**
1 (joint record)
Sunderland (2005/06)
Derby County (2007/08)

■ **Most away wins in a season (19 games)**
15 Chelsea (2004/05)

"We won the Fewest Away Losses In A Season award!"

■ **Fewest away wins in a season (19/21 games)**
0 (joint record)
Leeds United (1992/93)
Coventry City (1999/2000)
Wolves (2003/04)
Norwich City (2004/05)

Derby County (2007/08)
Hull City (2009/10)

■ **Most consecutive wins**
14 Arsenal
(between 10 February 2002 and 24 August 2002)

■ **Most consecutive games without a win (38 games)**
32 Derby County (2007/08)
(Unsurprisingly, Derby were relegated at the end of the 2007/08 season and have not played in the Premier League since. If they ever return to the top-flight this record could be extended)

■ **Most consecutive home wins**
20 Manchester City (between 5 March 2011 and 21 March 2012)

■ **Most consecutive away wins**
11 Chelsea
(between 5 April 2008 and 6 December 2008)

■ **Most wins in total**
500 Manchester United

Losses

■ **Most losses in a season (38 or 42 games)**
29 (joint record)
Ipswich Town (1994/95)
Sunderland (2005/06)
Derby County (2007/08)

■ **Fewest losses in a season (38 games)**
0 Arsenal (2003/04)

■ **Longest unbeaten run**
49 games Arsenal
(7 May, 2003 until 24 October, 2004)

■ **Most home losses in a season (19 games)**
14 Sunderland
(2002/03), (2005/06)

■ **Fewest home losses in a season (19 games)**
0 (joint record)
Manchester United
(1995/96, 1999/2000, 2010/11)
Arsenal (1998/99, 2003/04, 2007/08)
Chelsea (2004/05, 2005/06, 2006–07, 2007/08)
Liverpool (2008/09)
Manchester City (2011/12)

■ **Most consecutive losses in a season (38 games)**
15 Sunderland (2002/03)

■ **Most consecutive losses over more than one season (38 games)**
20 Sunderland
(2002/03, 2005/06)
(Lost their last 15 games of the 2002/03 season and were relegated. Followed this up by losing their first five games of the 2005/06 season, their next season in the Premier League.)

■ **Most away losses in a season (19 games)**
17 Burnley (2009/10)

■ **Fewest away losses in a season (19 games)**
0 Arsenal
(2001/02, 2003/04)

■ **Most consecutive away games undefeated**
27 Arsenal
(5 April 2003–25 Sep 2004)

■ **Most losses in total**
282 Everton

Premier League Golden Boot winners

Season	Player	Club	Goals	Games	Rate
1992/93	Teddy Sheringham	Tottenham Hotspur	22	41	0.54
1993/94	Andrew Cole	Newcastle United	34	40	0.85
1994/95	Alan Shearer	Blackburn Rovers 🏆	34	42	0.81
1995/96	Alan Shearer	Blackburn Rovers	31	35	0.89
1996/97	Alan Shearer	Newcastle United	25	31	0.81
1997/98	Chris Sutton	Blackburn Rovers	18	35	0.51
	Michael Owen	Liverpool	18	36	0.50
	Dion Dublin	Coventry City	18	36	0.50
1998/99	Dwight Yorke	Man Utd 🏆	18	33	0.55
	Michael Owen	Liverpool	18	30	0.60
	Jimmy Floyd Hasselbaink	Leeds United	18	36	0.50
1999/2000	Kevin Phillips ★	Sunderland	30	36	0.83
2000/01	Jimmy Floyd Hasselbaink	Chelsea	23	35	0.66
2001/02	Thierry Henry 🏆	Arsenal 🏆	24	33	0.73
2002/03	Ruud van Nistelrooy	Man Utd 🏆	25	34	0.74
2003/04	Thierry Henry ★	Arsenal 🏆	30	37	0.81
2004/05	Thierry Henry ★	Arsenal	25	32	0.78
2005/06	Thierry Henry	Arsenal	27	32	0.84
2006/07	Didier Drogba	Chelsea	20	36	0.56
2007/08	Cristiano Ronaldo ★	Man Utd 🏆	31	34	0.91
2008/09	Nicolas Anelka	Chelsea	19	36	0.53
2009/10	Didier Drogba	Chelsea 🏆	29	32	0.91
2010/11	Carlos Tévez	Manchester City	20	31	0.65
	Dimitar Berbatov	Man Utd 🏆	20	32	0.63
2011/12	Robin van Persie	Arsenal	30	38	0.79

■ In a 38-game season the honours are shared between Shearer and Ronaldo with 31 goals in 35 and 34 games respectively.
■ Thierry Henry has won the Golden Boot the most times (4) and along with Alan Shearer managed to retain it for three seasons in a row.
■ The 🏆 denotes Championship winners and the ★ means that player also won the European Golden Shoe that year.

Biggest winning margin

Margin	Date	Home team	Result	Away team	Goal scorers
9	4 Mar 1995	**Manchester United**	9 - 0	**Ipswich Town**	Keane 15', Cole 19', 37', 53', 65', 87', Hughes 55', 59', Ince 72'
8	19 Sep 1999	**Newcastle United**	8 - 0	**Sheffield Wednesday**	Hughes 11', Shearer 30', 33' (pen), 42', 81', 84' (pen), Dyer 48', Speed 78'
8	22 Nov 2009	**Tottenham Hotspur**	9 - 1	**Wigan Athletic**	Crouch 9', Defoe 51', 54', 58', 69', 87', Lennon 64', Scharner 57'
8	9 May 2010	**Chelsea**	8 - 0	**Wigan Athletic**	Anelka 6', 56', Lampard 32' (pen), Kalou 54', Drogba 63', 68' (pen), 80', Cole 90'
7	6 Feb 1999	**Nottingham Forest**	1 - 8	**Manchester United**	Rogers 6', Yorke 2', 67', Cole 7', 50', Solskjær 80', 88', 90', 90'
7	18 Nov 1995	**Blackburn Rovers**	7 - 0	**Nottingham Forest**	Shearer 20', 57', 68', Bohinen 28', 76', Newell 82', Le Saux 89'
7	25 Oct 1997	**Manchester United**	7 - 0	**Barnsley**	Cole 17', 19', 45', Giggs 43', 56', Scholes 59', Poborský 80'
7	11 May 2005	**Arsenal**	7 - 0	**Everton**	Van Persie 8', Pires 12', 50', Vieira 37', Edu 70' (pen), Bergkamp 77', Flamini 85'
7	14 Jan 2006	**Arsenal**	7 - 0	**Middlesbrough**	Henry 20', 30', 68', Senderos 22', Pires 45', Silva 59', Hleb 84'
7	11 May 2008	**Middlesbrough**	8 - 1	**Manchester City**	Downing 16' (pen), 58' Alves 37', 60', 90', Johnson 70', Rochemback 80', Aliadière 85', Elano 87'
7	25 Apr 2010	**Chelsea**	7 - 0	**Stoke City**	Kalou 24', 31', 68', Lampard 44' (pen), 81', Sturridge 87', Malouda 89'

Draws

Most draws in a season (42 games)
18 (joint record)
Manchester City (1993/94)
Sheffield United (1993/94)
Southampton (1994/95)

Most draws in a season (38 games)
17 joint record
Newcastle United (2003/04)
Aston Villa (2006/07, 2011/12)

Most consecutive draws in a season
(38 or 42 games)
7 (joint record)
Norwich City (1993/94)
Southampton (1994/95)
Manchester City (2009/10)

Fewest draws in a season (38 games)
3 Chelsea (1997/98)

Most home draws in a season (19 games)
10 (joint record)
Sheffield Wednesday (1996/97)
Leicester City (1997/98), (2003/04)

Fewest home draws in a season (19 games)
None
Manchester City (2008/09)

Most away draws in a season (19 games)
12 Newcastle United (2003/04)

Fewest away draws in a season (19 games)
19 times

Most draws in total
240 Aston Villa

Promotion and change in position

Best season for promoted clubs (All three promoted sides avoided relegation)
2001/02
Fulham, Blackburn Rovers and Bolton Wanderers
(Incidentally, another record: not one of these 3 promoted clubs was relegated for a decade, until last season in fact. Fulham are the only team who can continue on their run, as Blackburn Rovers and Bolton Wanderers were both relegated in 2011-12).
2011/12
Queens Park Rangers, Norwich City, Swansea City

Worst season for promoted clubs (All three promoted sides were relegated)
1997-98
Bolton Wanderers, Barnsley, Crystal Palace

Lowest finish by the previous season's champions
7th Blackburn Rovers (1995/96)
Leeds United were technically defending champions in 1992/93, finishing 17th, but they were technically the Division One holders rather than the Premier League holders due to the League's reorganisation.

Highest finish by a promoted club
3rd (joint record)
Newcastle United (1993/94)
Nottingham Forest (1994/95)

Biggest rise in finishing position
13 places Everton
(17th in 2003/04; 4th in 2004/05)

Biggest fall in finishing position
13 places (joint record)
Blackburn Rovers
(6th in 1997/98, 19th in 1998/99)
Ipswich Town
(5th in 2000/01, 18th in 2001/02)

Players

Most Premier League appearances
598 Ryan Giggs
(Manchester United, 1992 to 13 May 2012)

Most Premier League appearances at one club
598 Ryan Giggs
(Manchester United, 1992 to 13 May 2012)

Oldest player
John Burridge
43 years and 162 days
(for Manchester City v QPR, 14 May 1995)

Youngest player
Matthew Briggs
16 years and 65 days
(for Fulham v Middlesbrough 13 May 2007)

Most consecutive Premier League appearances
314 Brad Friedel

Most seasons appeared in
20 Ryan Giggs
(only player to have appeared in every Premier League season)

Most seasons scored in
20 Ryan Giggs
(only player to have scored in every Premier League season)

Golden gloves

Season	Player	Club	Clean sheets
2004/05	**Petr Cech**	Chelsea	21
2005/06	**Pepe Reina**	Liverpool	20
2006/07	**Pepe Reina**	Liverpool	19
2007/08	**Pepe Reina**	Liverpool	18
2008/09	**Edwin van der Sar**	Man United	21
2009/10	**Petr Cech**	Chelsea	17*
2010/11	**Joe Hart**	Man City	18
2011/12	**Joe Hart**	Man City	17

■ *Pepe Reina also secured 17 clean sheets but played in less games.

II

Individual

■ Most Premier League winner's medals
12 Ryan Giggs
(Manchester United – 1993, 1994, 1996, 1997, 1999, 2000, 2001, 2003, 2007, 2008, 2009, 2011)

■ First Premier League goal
Brian Deane
(for Sheffield United v Manchester United, 15 August 1992)

■ Most Premier League goals
260 Alan Shearer

■ Most Premier League seasons scored in
20 seasons Ryan Giggs

■ Most goals in a season (42 games)
34 (joint record)
Andrew Cole
(Newcastle United, 1993/94)
Alan Shearer
(Blackburn Rovers, 1994/95)

■ Most goals in a season (38 games)
31 (joint record)
Alan Shearer
(Blackburn Rovers, 1995/96)
Cristiano Ronaldo
(Manchester United, 2007/08)

■ Most goals in a debut season (38 games)
30 Kevin Phillips
(Sunderland, 1999/00)

■ Most goals in a game
5 (joint record)
Andrew Cole
(for Manchester United v Ipswich Town, 4 March 1995)
Alan Shearer
(for Newcastle United v Sheffield Wednesday, 19 September 1999)
Jermain Defoe
(for Tottenham Hotspur v Wigan Athletic, 22 November 2009)
Dimitar Berbatov
(for Manchester United v Blackburn Rovers, 27 November 2010)

■ Most goals in one half
5 Jermain Defoe
(for Tottenham Hotspur v Wigan Athletic, 22 November 2009)

■ Youngest goalscorer
James Vaughan
16 years and 271 days
(for Everton v Crystal Palace, 10 April 2005)

■ Oldest goalscorer
Teddy Sheringham
40 years and 268 days
(for West Ham United v Portsmouth, 26 December 2006)

■ Fastest goal
9.9 seconds Ledley King
(for Tottenham Hotspur v Bradford City, 9 December 2000)

■ Most goals scored by a substitute in a game
4 Ole Gunnar Solskjaer
(for Manchester United v Nottingham Forest, 6 February 1999)

■ Most consecutive league matches scored in
10 Ruud van Nistelrooy
(for Manchester United, 22 March 2003 to 23 August 2003)

■ Most consecutive away league matches scored in
9 Robin van Persie
(for Arsenal, 1 January 2011 to 22 May 2011)

■ Most consecutive seasons to score 10 or more goals
9 (2003-2012)
Frank Lampard
(for Chelsea)

■ Fastest Premier League hat-trick
4 minutes 33 seconds

Ledley King scored the fastest EPL goal ever after 9.9 seconds against Braford City in 2000

Premier League players with 100 goals or more

#	Player	Clubs	Goals
1	Alan Shearer	Blackburn Rovers, Newcastle United	260
2	Andrew Cole	Newcastle United, Manchester United, Blackburn Rovers, Fulham, Manchester City, Portsmouth	187
3	Thierry Henry	Arsenal	176
4	Robbie Fowler	Liverpool, Leeds United, Manchester City	163
5	Frank Lampard	West Ham United, Chelsea	150
6	Les Ferdinand	Queens Park Rangers, Newcastle United, Tottenham Hotspur, West Ham United, Leicester City, Bolton Wanderers	149
	Michael Owen	Liverpool, Newcastle United, Manchester United	149
8	Teddy Sheringham	Nottingham Forest, Tottenham Hotspur, Manchester United, Portsmouth, West Ham United	147
9	Wayne Rooney	Everton, Manchester United	144
10	Jimmy Floyd Hasselbaink	Leeds United, Chelsea, Middlesbrough, Charlton Athletic	127
11	Robbie Keane	Coventry City, Leeds United, Tottenham Hotspur, Liverpool, West Ham United, Aston Villa,	126
12	Nicolas Anelka	Arsenal, Liverpool, Manchester City, Bolton Wanderers, Chelsea	123
	Dwight Yorke	Aston Villa, Manchester United, Blackburn Rovers, Birmingham City, Sunderland	123
14	Ian Wright	Arsenal, West Ham United	113
15	Dion Dublin	Manchester United, Coventry City, Aston Villa	111
	Emile Heskey	Leicester City, Liverpool, Birmingham City, Wigan Athletic, Aston Villa	111
17	Jermain Defoe	West Ham United, Portsmouth, Tottenham Hotspur	110
18	Ryan Giggs	Manchester United	107
19	Paul Scholes	Manchester United	105
20	Matthew Le Tissier	Southampton	102
21	Darren Bent	Ipswich Town, Charlton Athletic, Tottenham Hotspur, Sunderland, Aston Villa	100
	Didier Drogba	Chelsea	100

■ Alan Shearer became the first player to score 100 goals in the Premier League during the 1995/96 season. He is also the only player to score 100 goals each for two different clubs: Blackburn Rovers and then Newcastle Utd.

Robbie Fowler
(for Liverpool v Arsenal, 28 August 1994)

■ Highest number of different clubs to

**score for
6 (joint record)**
Andrew Cole
(for Newcastle United, Manchester United, Blackburn Rovers, Fulham, Manchester City, Portsmouth)
Les Ferdinand
(for Q.P.R, Newcastle United, Tottenham Hotspur, West Ham United, Leicester City, Bolton Wanderers)
Marcus Bent
(for Charlton Athletic, Everton, Ipswich Town, Leicester City, Crystal Palace, Wigan Athletic)
Nick Barmby
(for Liverpool, Everton, Leeds United, Middlesbrough, Tottenham Hotspur, Hull City)

Craig Bellamy
(for Liverpool, Manchester City, Newcastle United, West Ham United, Coventry City, Blackburn Rovers)
Peter Crouch
(for Aston Villa, Southampton, Liverpool, Portsmouth, Tottenham Hotspur, Stoke City)
Robbie Keane
(for Aston Villa, Coventry City, Liverpool, Tottenham Hotspur, Leeds United, West Ham United)

■ Most Premier League assists
126 Ryan Giggs

■ Most Premier League own goals
10 Richard Dunne

All-Time Premier League Dream Team 1992/2012

Forward
Alan Shearer
Newcastle

The most consistent
scorer of goals the
EPL has ever seen

Forward
Thierry Henry
Arsenal

Glided around
Highbury like a swan
through zero gravity

Midfielder
Cristiano Ronaldo
Man Utd

Can do everything.
The complete modern
footballing package

Midfielder
Ryan Giggs
Man Utd

Plays defenders for
fun and killer balls
for breakfast

Midfielder
Paul Scholes
Man Utd

Most gifted English
midfielder of his
generation, no doubt

Midfielder
Steven Gerrard
Liverpool

The complete box-to-
boxer, his engine can
inspire others

Defender
Tony Adams
Arsenal

An excellent leader
of a line: played every
game with true spirit

Defender
Nemanja Vidic
Man Utd

So tough, so intense,
so uncompromising.
A great competitor

Defender
Ashley Cole
Arsenal & Chelsea

Quite simply the best
left-back England has
ever produced

Goalkeeper
Peter Schmeichel
Man Utd

Commanded his
area like an albino
bear in a cage

Defender
Gary Neville
Man Utd

The most dependable
defender Man Utd
have ever had

■ This team was voted for by the public at the recent EPL 20 Seasons Awards. The expert panel preferred Rio Ferdinand to Nemanja Vidic and Roy Keane to Steven Gerrard.

Firsts & Lasts

Some noteworthy benchmarks and bullet points from 20 breakthrough years of the world's most exciting league

1992/93

■ **The first season of the Premier League begins!**

■ The first Premier League title goes to Man Utd: the club's first title for 26 years

■ **Blackburn, in the top division for the first time in almost 30 years, finished in fourth place**

■ Ryan Giggs becomes the first player ever to win the Young Player of the Year award twice

■ **The newly formed League Managers Association makes its own award for the first time, an acknowledgement which recognises "the manager who made best use of the resources available to him"**

1993/94

■ Sheffield Utd fail to win any of their first 17 games, but finish a creditable 13th. It takes Swindon Town 16 games to register their first win but they only manage four more in the entire season, becoming the first top-division team in 30 years to concede 100 goals

■ **Alex Ferguson becomes**

Chris Sutton helped Blackburn qualify for the Champions League in 1994/95 for the first time in their history

the first recipient of the FA Premier League Manager of the Year award

■ Arsenal's victory, 1-0 over Parma, in the Cup Winners' Cup brings the club their first European trophy since 1970

■ **Chelsea qualify for Europe for the first time in over 20 years and Newcastle for the first time since the 1970s – and Norwich City for the first time in their entire history**

■ Tim Flowers becomes Britain's first £2m goalkeeper when he transfers from Southampton to Blackburn

1994/95

■ Blackburn win the title for the first time since 1914

■ **Blackburn Rovers qualify for the Champions League for the first time in their history**

■ Nottingham Forest finish third in their first season back in the Premiership

■ **Everton won their first major trophy for eight years, triumphing over Man Utd in the FA Cup, and qualifying for their first European campaign of the post-Heysel era**

■ Newcastle won their first six games

■ **England's first £5m transfer is completed when Chris Sutton swaps Carrow Road for Ewood Park**

1995/96

■ Despite being knocked out of the UEFA cup in the first round to Rotor Volgograd,

Manchester United become the first team to complete a second league championship and FA Cup double when Eric Cantona gives them a 1-0 win over Liverpool in the FA Cup final.

■ **Man City lost their first 12 games and, despite getting a draw with Liverpool on the final day of the season, were relegated nonetheless**

■ Middlesbrough moved from Ayresome Park to the Riverside Stadium: the first new stadium in top division football in 72 years

1996/97

■ **Ruud Gullit's Chelsea won the FA Cup with a 2-0 victory over Middlesbrough, ending the club's 26-year trophy drought and becoming the first foreign manager to win a major English trophy.**

■ Leicester also beat Middlesbrough in the Coca-Cola Cup to secure the underestimated Foxes their first trophy in 33 years.

■ **Man Utd reached the Champions League semi-finals for the first time since 1969, losing both legs 1-0 to the eventual winners, Borussia Dortmund**

1997/98

■ Barnsley compete in the English top flight for the first time in their 102-year history. They fail to avoid relegation but do manage to knock Manchester United out of the FA Cup in the fifth round

■ **In Arsene Wenger's first full season of Premier League management, Arsenal lifted their first league title since 1991 and went on to complete a domestic double after an incredible run of form in the last three months of the season. Arsenal become the first team to match Manchester United's record of two "doubles", Arsenal's last double was in 1971**

- Leicester's first and last foray into Europe since the 1960s was short-lived, after defeat to Atlético Madrid in the UEFA Cup first round

- **Newcastle Utd reached the FA Cup final for the first time in 24 years, losing the final 2-0 to Arsenal**

- All the teams who qualified for the UEFA Cup – Aston Villa, Blackburn, Leeds Utd and Liverpool – are knocked out in the first round

1998/99

- **First time in Liverpool's history that two managers are put in charge of the first team, when Gérard Houllier is appointed to work alongside Roy Evans**

- First time an English team had completed the treble. Man Utd won the league by one point from Arsenal, beat Newcastle 2-0 in the FA Cup Final and Bayern Munich 2-1 in a their first European Cup final in 31 years. (At the Nou Camp, ref Pierluigi Collina signalled for three minutes' stoppage time, Teddy Sheringham equalised in the first minute of it and Ole Gunnar Solskjaer scored the winner with the last kick of the game)

1998/99
Dwight Yorke was the first Man Utd player to receive the Golden Boot award

- **First time a Man Utd player received the Golden Boot award. Dwight Yorke scored 18 goals in 33 games and shared the honour with Michael Owen of Liverpool and Jimmy Floyd Hasselbaink of Leeds Utd**

- Harry Redknapp guides West Ham to fifth place in the Premiership, meaning the Hammers will play in European competition for the first time in nearly 20 years

- **Watford seal promotion to the Premier League becoming the first team**

since Notts County in 1991 to reach English football's highest echelon with two successive promotions

- An 18-year-old Steven Gerrard makes his first appearance as a subsititute for Liverpool against Blackburn in November and John Terry also makes his first appearance at 17 for Chelsea, coming on in the final minutes of a League Cup win against Aston Villa

1999/00

- **Four defeats in his first five Premier League fixtures convinced Ruud Gullit to wave goodbye to Newcastle Utd, opening the door neatly for 66-year-old Bobby Robson**

- Aston Villa reached the FA Cup Final for the first time in 43 years

- **Bradford City play top-flight football for the first time since 1922, eventually securing**

Premiership survival on the last day of the season by beating Liverpool 1-0, the Reds surrendering the all-important Champions League spot

- By his standards, Matt Le Tissier's six-goal season haul was extremely modest, but he did become the first midfielder in Premiership history to reach the 100-goal benchmark

- **Because of commitments in the FIFA Club World Cup, Manchester Utd pull out of the FA Cup and for the first time in its history a random team, Darlington FC, is chosen to replace them in a random draw of "lucky losers". Darlington lose 2-1 to Aston Villa in the third round. In a one-off experiment, the first round was played in late October rather than mid-November and the third round was played in the second week of December rather than its traditional spot at the start of the New Year. It was the last and only time this schedule was implemented**

Gérard Houllier and Roy Evans: the first ever management duo at Liverpool

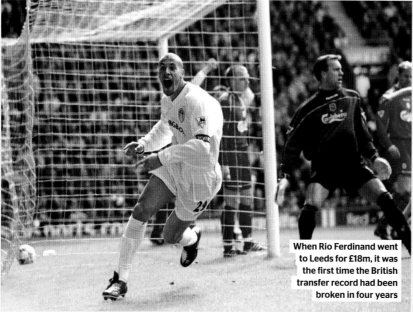

When Rio Ferdinand went to Leeds for £18m, it was the first time the British transfer record had been broken in four years

2000/01

■ For the first time since the Premier League was formed, all of the promoted teams had been in the Premiership before

■ Sir Alex Ferguson, fresh from a knighthood in June 1999, becomes the first English manager to win three successive English titles. However, Utd are not the first team to do it. Huddersfield Town, Arsenal and Liverpool had all managed the feat before, but with managerial changes in between

■ George Burley's Ipswich Town, among the favourite for the drop, defy all the odds to finish fifth and achieve European qualification for the first time in almost 20 years

■ **The English transfer record is broken for the first time in four years when Leeds Utd pay £18m to West Ham for Rio Ferdinand**

■ The FA Cup Final is played at Cardiff's Millennium Stadium for the first time while Wembley is being redeveloped and David O'Leary takes Leeds Utd to their first European Cup semi-

final since 1975. (Their failure to re-qualify for it the next year instigated the club's financial demise)

■ **After a dismal Euro 2000 campaign under Kevin Keegan, Sven-Göran Eriksson is appointed as the first foreign coach to take charge of the English national team. He wins his first match 3-0 against Spain and his first five matches on the trot**

2001/02

■ Man Utd break their club transfer record twice in quick succession, signing two world-class players: the first was prolific Dutch striker Ruud van Nistelrooy, the second was silky Argentine midfielder Juan Sebastian Véron

■ **Fulham become the first team to have played in all four divisons of the English league since the Premiership was created**

■ First season sponsored by Barclaycard, replacing the previous sponsor, Carling

■ **For the first time in the history of the Premiership all of the promoted clubs remain in the top division**

becomes the first foreign player to win the Golden Boot outright (he shared it with Dwight Yorke in 1998-99)

2002/03

■ **A 16-year-old makes his first appearance at Everton, scoring a masterly winning goal in a 2-1 victory against Arsenal. Wayne Rooney also gets his first Premiership straight red card two months later on Boxing Day, for an impulsive challenge on Birmingham City's Steve Vickers at St Andrew's**

■ West Brom beat Fulham 1-0 on 31 August 2002 to record their first top-flight victory since March of 1986 and Birmingham City thrash Villa 3-0 on 16 September in the first Second City Derby in the league for 15 years and in the top-flight for 17 years

■ **First time since the 1991-92 season that Man Utd have failed to beat Man City in either derby game**

■ Arsenal retain the FA Cup, the first side to do so in 21 years

2003/04

■ **Arsenal go through the whole season without**

■ After winning their first three games, Sam Allardyce jokingly crows that his overachieving Bolton Wanderers side can indeed go on and win the Premier League title for the first time. They finish 16th, four points from relegation

■ **Manchester United endure a trophyless season for the first time since 1998**

■ Jimmy-Floyd Hasselbaink

losing, the first team to accomplish this in a 38-game league season

■ Henry becomes the first player to win back-to-back PFA Player of the Year awards

■ **First time that a whole team is outscored by single players in the Premier League: Ruud van Nisterooy (25), Thierry Henry (24) and James Beattie (23) all scoring more than Sunderland (21)**

■ Middlesbrough win their first major trophy, beating Bolton Wanderers 2-1 in the League Cup final. Steve McClaren also becomes the first English manager to win a trophy since Brian Little guided Aston Villa to the same trophy in 1996. And Middlesbrough qualify for Europe for the first time

■ **Despite their highest league finish in 50 years and reaching the semis of the Champions League for the first time, Claudio Ranieri is given the chop by Roman Abramovich and replaced with Jose Mourinho**

■ Millwall play their first ever major cup final, losing 3-0 in the FA Cup to a coasting Man Utd. Utd's Champions League commitments mean Millwall go into the UEFA Cup draw for

Fulham: the first team to play in all four English divisions since the Premier League was initiated

2004/05

José Mourinho led Chelsea to their first Premier League title and first top-flight title in 50 years

2004-05, their first ever foray into Europe

2004/05

■ **Chelsea win the Premier League for the first time and their first top-flight title in 50 years on 30 April 2005**

■ First season to feature the rebranded Football League: The First Division, Second Division and Third Division were renamed the Football League Championship, Football League One and Football League Two respectively. Coca-Cola replaced the Nationwide Building Society as the title sponsor

■ **First time an entire squad of foreign players is selected in the Premier League when Arsenal play Crystal Palace in January**

■ For the first time since the Premier League began, none of the relegation spots have been mathematically decided until the final day of the season

■ **West Bromwich Albion become the first club in Premiership history to avoid relegation after being bottom of the table on Christmas Day**

■ Arsenal win the FA Cup, the first time it is decided on penalties, against Man Utd

2005/06

■ **Manchester United become the first team to score 1,000 Premier League goals**

■ Middlesbrough's 3-0 win over Chelsea on 11 February

2006 was the first time José Mourinho's Chelsea had lost by more than a single goal

■ **Blackburn completed a League double over Manchester United for the first time in 75 years**

■ FC United of Manchester play their first competitive game in the North West Counties Football League Division Two, after being formed by fans disgruntled by the direction of Man Utd under the ownership of the Glazer family

■ **Wigan Athletic play their first ever season of top-flight English football and comfortably retain their Premier League status**

■ Park Ji-Sung becomes Man Utd's first ever Asian player when he is transferred for £4m from PSV Eindhoven

■ **Johnny Haynes, who was Britain's first £100-per week player, dies at 71 at the wheel of his car in Edinburgh**

■ Manchester United become the first team to beat Chelsea in 41 Premier League games (on 6 November 2005), with a 1-0 victory at Old Trafford

■ **Despite finishing a disappointing 14th in the Premier League, Middlesbrough reach their first European Final, losing 4-0 to Sevilla**

2006/07

■ Arsenal's first game in the 60,000-seater Emirates stadium is a testimonial for brilliant Dutchman, Dennis Bergkamp, with the Gunners beating Ajax 2-1. Their first

competitive game on 19 August is a 1-1 draw with Villa

■ **Fulham were the first visitors to the all-new 76-000-seater Old Trafford, losing 5-12 in front of a record 75, 511-strong crowd**

■ Reading were participating in their first season in the top-flight in their 135-year history. They moved into the new Madejski stadium, completing a brilliant 3-2 comeback, from 0-2 down, in their first game against Middlesbrough. They went on to finish eighth

■ **Spurs goalkeeper Paul Robinson scores an 83-yard free-kick, which bounces over Watford goalkeeper Ben Foster, becoming the third goalkeeper to score in the Premier League, but the first keeper to score for the winning team in a Premiership match**

■ Cristiano Ronaldo becomes the first player to win the PFA Young Player of the Year and the PFA Player's Player of the Year awards in the same year since Andy Gray in 1977

■ **Under Martin O'Neill, Aston Villa go unbeaten in their first nine and last nine matches, finishing a creditable 11th**

2007/08

■ Derby County become the first team in Premier League history to be relegated in March

■ **During Wigan's 5–3 home win over Blackburn on 15 December 2007 Roque Santa Cruz (Blackburn) and Marcus Bent (Wigan) both scored hat-tricks. It represented the first time in Premier League history that players on opposing teams both scored hat-tricks during the same fixture**

■ The first time that the English league had topped the UEFA rankings since the events at the Heysel Stadium in 1985

■ **Arsenal's Emmanuel Adebayor scores a hat-trick at home and away against Derby County becoming the**

first player to score a hat-trick against the same team twice in the same season

■ Cristiano Ronaldo becomes the first person in 12 years (since Alan Shearer's 31-goal haul for Blackburn) to score 30 goals in a Premier League season

2008/09

■ **Hull's 1-2 victory over Arsenal at the Emirates Stadium is their first ever win over the Gunners in English football**

■ Paul Ince became the first black British manager ever in the Premier League

■ **First time since the 2005–06 season that more than one promoted club maintained their Premier League status**

■ When Ashley Young won the Player of the Month for December, the Villa winger became the first player to win the award three times in a calendar year

■ **Liverpool's 4-1 victory at Old Trafford was the first time Man Utd had conceded four goals at home since 1992**

■ For the first time clubs

Gianfranco Zola was the first non-British manager of West Ham Utd

were allowed to name seven substitutes on the bench instead of five

■ **Former Chelsea striker Gianfranco Zola becomes West Ham United's first non-British manager**

■ Roy Hodgson's Fulham qualify for Europe for the first time in the club's history

2009/10

■ **Chelsea win their first**

league and FA Cup double, scoring a record 103 goals (2.79 per game) and becoming the first Premier League club to reach three figures in Carlo Ancelotti's first season at the club

■ In February 2010 Portsmouth become the first Premier League club to go into administration, had nine points deducted as punishment, and became the first team to be relegated on 10 April 2010

■ **Liverpool finish outside the top four for the first time since 2004/05**

■ Newcastle suffer their first relegation from the Premier League since promotion in 1993

■ **Burnley return to the top-flight for the first time in 33 years**

■ Wigan become the first team to lose two matches by eight goals in a Premier League season

■ **Harry Redknapp becomes the first non-title-winning manager since George Burley in 2000/01 to win Manager of the Season after guiding Spurs to Champions League qualification**

■ The 31 January 2010 clash between Arsenal and Man Utd is the first sporting event anywhere in the world to be broadcast entirely in 3D

2010/11

■ **First time since 1983/84 that all four West Midlands clubs – Birmingham City, West Brom, Aston Villa and Wolves – are in the top-flight division at the same time. And also the first time that the Black Country derby was contested in the Premier League**

■ First time the Golden Boot is shared since 1998/99, with Dimitar Berbatov of Man Utd and Carlos Tevez of Man City both registering 20 goals

■ **Blackpool win their first top-division game since 1971 4-0 against Wigan at the DW Stadium**

■ On 31 October 2010, Kevin Nolan becomes the first player to score a hat-trick in the Tyne-Wear derby since Peter Beardsley in 1984/85

■ **When Blackburn are taken over by the Rao family for £23m they become the first Indian family to run a Premier League club**

Cristiano Ronaldo: first to win Young Player and Players' Player Awards in the same season since Andy Gray in 1977

2011/12

Man Utd conceded six goals at Old Trafford (against Manchester City) for the first time ever in the Premier League and the first time since 1930

■ On 5 February 2011 Arsenal go 4-0 up against Newcastle after only 26 minutes and then become the first Premier League side to relinquish a four-nil lead

■ **Dirk Kuyt becomes the first Liverpool player to score a hat-trick against Man Utd since Peter Beardsley in September 1990. Liverpool win 4-1**

■ A lone Yaya Toure strike secures Man City their first FA Cup final spot for 30 years and Stoke City run riot against Bolton, winning 5-0 in the other semi to secure the first final in their history

2011/12

■ **Man City win their first title since 1968 and their first ever Premier League crown**

■ First time that the Premier League title is decided on goal difference – and the first time a previously relegated club in the Premier League had won the title

■ **Swansea City become the first Welsh club to play in the Premier League and QPR appeared in the top flight for the first time in 15 years**

■ The first time that the club finishing fourth in the Premier League had not qualified for the Champions League since the fourth qualifying spot was introduced in 2001/02

■ **On 23 October 2011, Man Utd concede six goals for the first time at Old Trafford since 1930, and suffer their worst loss at home since 1955, after losing 6-1 to rivals Man City**

■ Clint Dempsey becomes the first American player to score a hat-trick in the EPL in the 5-2 win over Newcastle United in January, and also the first American to reach 50 goals in the Premier League, scoring a free kick against Sunderland in the last home game of the season

TOP5 GAMES

Five of the most electrifying Premier League clashes ever

Liverpool 4-3 Newcastle Utd
(1995/96)

1 Newcastle travelled to Anfield three points behind Man Utd, needing victory to keep the title chase alive. Les Ferdinand and David Ginola responded to a Robbie Fowler opener, then the Liverpool striker levelled before Faustino Asprilla restored the lead. Enter Stanley Victor Collymore, first to bundle in an equaliser and, with seconds left, smash in a near-post drive to make it 4-3 and virtually end the Toon's title aspirations.

Man City 3-2 QPR
(2011/12)

2 To win their first league title since 1968, all City had to do was beat relegation fodder QPR at home, and Manchester United (playing simultaneously at Sunderland) would relinquish their title on goal difference. Things didn't go quite to plan, and after 90 minutes United looked like they were champions again, thanks to a stoic performance by a 10-man QPR and a Rooney goal at Sunderland. Two goals in an incomparable injury time, from Dzeko and Aguero, saved Manchester City's blushes.

Liverpool 4-4 Arsenal
(2008/09)

3 In what must rank as one of the greatest individual performances in EPL history, Andrei Arshavin took Liverpool to the sword with only the guile of Fernando Torres and Yossi Benayoun saving Liverpool serious embarrassment. A crashing opening goal from the Russian lit the fuse, and the three continued to trade goals throughout the game until, when it looked like Arsenal would win the day, Benayoun scored an equaliser in injury time.

Man Utd 4-3 Man City
(2009/10)

4 A game that typifies the spirit of the Manchester derby. Wayne Rooney opened the scoring, before Gareth Barry levelled things on half time. After the break Darren Fletcher headed United into the lead, but a thunderous strike from Craig Bellamy levelled once again. Ten minutes from time, Fletcher thought he'd won man of the match with another goal, which was promptly nullified by Bellamy – then, six minutes into injury time, Owen struck to secure the home side full spoils.

Newcastle Utd 5-0 Man Utd
(1996/97)

5 Nothing could make up for the disastrous title capitulation of the previous season but a 5-0 stomping did restore a modicum of pride to St James' Park, and to the footballing philosophies of Kevin Keegan. A Darren Peacock header made it 1-0, a Ginola curler two, Sir Les popped up for the third, Alan Shearer slammed in a fourth before an exquisite Philippe Albert chip over Peter Schmeichel finished off the rout.

In 2008, the Champions League final was contested by two Premier League teams for the first time, Man Utd beating Chelsea on penalties.